WIND

ALOFT

WIND

By
MARIN-MARIE
Painter to the
French Ministry
of Marine

LONDO

READERS UNION

ALOFT

*Being the narrative
of his single-handed
crossing of the Atlantic
under sail in the
'Winnibelle'*

MCMXLVII

~~~~~PETER DAVIES

This volume is produced in Great Britain in 1947 *in complete conformity with the authorized economy standards. First published in* 1945 *by Peter Davies Ltd., it has been set in Plantin* 11 *on* 12 *point and reprinted at the University Press, Glasgow, by Robert MacLehose & Co., Limited. It is one of the books produced for sale to its members only by Readers Union Ltd., of* 38 *William IV Street, London, and of Letchworth, Hertfordshire. Particulars of Readers Union are obtainable from either of these addresses*

PUBLISHERS' NOTE

ALTHOUGH M. Marin-Marie's original French MS. of this book was in the hands of Messrs. Peter Davies Ltd. as long ago as the summer of 1939, *wartime difficulties of one sort and another inevitably postponed publication of the English version, entitled* WIND ALOFT, WIND ALOW, *until after the war. Even so the author had no opportunity of revising the translation or of seeing the book through the Press: indeed it was only through the fortunate chance of an advance proof copy finding its way into the hands of his brother, lately commanding the French Naval Air Service in Great Britain, that it was learned with no small relief of the safety and well-being of the author and his family.* WIND ALOFT, WIND ALOW *contained, in addition to the narrative here printed, Marin-Marie's account of his second single-handed crossing of the Atlantic, under motor-power in the "Arielle".*

'Marin-Marie', as connoisseurs of marine painting have long been aware, is the professional signature of M. M-M. Durand de St. Front, several of whose admirable sea-pieces are reproduced in this volume. He here makes his bow as an author under the same nom de plume; *for, when the original edition was issued, it was the first appearance in any language of the story of his remarkable exploits in the sphere of seamanship.*

CONTENTS

vii

ILLUSTRATIONS

CHAPTER I

ATAVISM

I⊤ struck me, not for the first time, that yachting caps had got bigger and bigger in recent years.

When I said as much to a hatter of my acquaintance, he politely assured me that it was a matter which concerned Fashion alone, and was none of my business. Fashion, however, may take it from me that one of these days it is going to be necessary for these martial head-dresses to carry a bit of ballast, if the wearers want to keep them on—I won't say at sea, for that would be too ambitious —but merely when rounding draughty street corners.

Nothing is better calculated to bring home the tyrannies of Fashion than a glance at the pages of an old photograph album.

Before settling down to write, a little while ago, I thought I would rummage through a collection of portraits of my forbears, in the hopes that I should there find an easy clue, in the form of some compelling hereditary strain, to the odd taste I have for sailing into trouble and sometimes getting more than I bargained for.

But alas, in those faded photographs I myself might already be taken for one of my own ancestors. A snapshot dated 1920 shows me wearing a deplorable little round hat, practically rimless, the sort of thing you see in caricatures of Dutch sailors. I remember now that I borrowed it from my father, who had bought it in Hamburg, and I thought it superb. . . .

But where complications set in, is when I get back to the second generation.

It is obvious, on reflection, that if my grandfather had followed the sea as a calling, he would have worn a top-hat, like all skippers belonging to good lines. But he was in fact an ex-prefect of the Second Empire, and whenever he went for a sail in his boat, he would have thought himself improperly dressed unless he had had on a big straw hat of the sort that gleaners wear in our part of the

world, turned down in front and up behind. After all, yachting only
dates from the days when sea bathing, I had almost said bathing-
costumes, came into fashion. My grandfather hated the word
yacht, which he found impossible to pronounce; and he had the
lowest opinion of the habits of seamen: to him they were people
who chewed tobacco, spat through their teeth and brought home
parrots and coloured women from their voyages. In fact, the only
less reputable avocation was that of artist, which in his view was
confined to long-haired eccentrics who ate their own still-lives and
took pleasure in mystifying honest folk.

Yet what does his grandson do but become sailor and painter
too? It was well for grandfather that he did not live to taste such
shame, and well for me too, by the same token.

I see him still, going on board his boat. Apart from the famous
hat, he used to wear a beautiful grey frock-coat and elastic-sided
shoes; thus arrayed, he would make a kind of royal progress down
the big slipway, smiling condescendingly to right and left, and
offering scrofoloso pills to all the little ragamuffins who were then
my chosen companions, as indeed they are today, except that they
have grown bigger.

Scrofoloso was a homeopathic remedy which of course we all
laughed at.

Having reached the water's edge, where his boat awaited him,
he would give it a cautious prod with his twisted walking-stick;
then, placing a hand on the broad back of the man who held her
alongside, and somehow contriving to avoid falling over backwards, he would boldly step on board, and make straight for the
stern-sheets. On his safe arrival there, he pulled up his coat-tails,
sat down, or rather subsided into a comfortable position, and forth-
with demanded his fishing lines.

He adored fishing, but would have no truck with the handling
of boats, and distrusted on principle all those which gave under
foot, a category which included every variety of rowing-boat, as
well as anything which heeled over when sailing. He had given my
father the task of finding him an absolutely stable vessel, and my
father, to avoid all future complications, had deliberately picked
out for him the heaviest and most pot-bellied hearse that could be
found on the coast anywhere from Carteret to Fréhel. We nick-

named her in derision La Bourdine. 'Crops the sea like a cow,' the fishermen used to say of her, with broad grins. I am forced to admit that in her, and in nothing better, I had my nautical baptism.

'Jules,' my grandfather used to say to his son-in-law, as though to turn the steel in the wound, 'I admire your own boat, but the actual one you chose for me is the finest craft you ever had the buying of.'

He invariably got away with the wind aft, and it was the greatest fun in the world, when the time came to turn back, to hear him grumbling about the beat home, the more so as the Bourdine scarcely shone to windward.

'Go straight in,' he would command. 'All these zig-zags are pointless. We're going to be late for lunch again. . . .'

The reader will by now have realised why I had to give up my search for that atavistic strain which would have been so convenient, and will also understand how the question of hats came up.

Even as recently as when my father took to 'messing about in boats,' the game had hardly begun to acquire the standing of an organised sport. Neither the Union des Yachts Francais, which was founded in 1892, nor the Yacht Club de France, with which the former became merged, as yet existed. By the world at large it was regarded as an odd and not particularly commendable form of amusement, confined to an eccentric few.

At the time, namely about 1885, he was in process of taking his degree in law at Caen, and kept not far from there, more or less clandestinely, at Ouistreham, a small clincher-built cutter called the Henriette, with the complicity of an old caulker named Virgile, who acted as hand.

The Dean of the Faculty at Caen very quickly got wind of these goings on. 'It has come to my notice', he one day observed to my father during an examination, 'that you study the course of the Orne a good deal more closely than the course of the Law.'

Virgile was not the only poetical element in the Henriette's crew. One Millet, a real live poet in his own right, frequently joined the party. He was the possessor of a romantic profile, and had soft, dreamy eyes, the effect of which was unfortunately marred by pince-nez which had a habit of falling off. Millet was always banging his head on the beams of the cabin, which was indeed so low that if you stood upright you rose through the skylight from the waist upwards. He must have cut a truly remarkable figure on the day when the boat capsized in the middle of Le Havre bay, and he found himself marooned astride the keel, while my father swam ashore. . . . His spectacles had disappeared and he was as blind as a bat in consequence, but his lyrical ardour enabled him to contemplate the surroundings with equanimity, to judge by a certain copy of verses which still survives, and in which he visualises a voyage not merely to Port-en-Bessin but all the way to Lisbon. . . .

As a mere matter of detail, in order to realise this delightful dream it would have been necessary to find a substitute for the Henriette, for the derelict hull of the little craft was cut in two like a carrot the very next night by the tug Ursus, returning from a job at sea.

Since those days amateur cruising has made great strides. The sailing men you meet nowadays are all knowledgeable and practical people, as trim as theodolites. There is no room for a poet—the genuine professional article—in a modern ocean racer's crew. . . .

I know the names of the many boats my father owned subsequently, thanks to the cap bands round the walls of his study: the Marie-Georgette, Gwendoline, Miss Jane and others. The last-named was a sizeable cutter, of Jersey pilot type, copper bottomed, but bought second-hand and already ripe. My father has often told me that when he slackened away the shroud lanyards, her mast came ashore by itself, in two pieces, on the quay-side.

But it was mainly on board the Havre pilot boats that he got his real experience. And it was a rough school. He sailed chiefly with a certain Gustave Vasse, who was skipper of No. E 11. They used to meet the great windjammers, and certain steam vessels which still at that date spread a few sails, as far afield as the entrance to the English Channel, i.e. off the Scillies. It was a fine calling, full of unforeseen happenings and hard knocks, and the competition bred fast, seaworthy vessels of a class like the Jolie Brise.

A thing which shows to what an extent yacht-building was then in its infancy, was the difficulty my father found in getting a boat built to his own specification.

He had picked upon Cancale, whose builders then had the reputation of being able to turn out even better vessels than the Havre pilot boats. But at Cancale they knew nothing of either cutters or ketches. For them there was only the bisquine and the 'triple-sail', to the absolute exclusion of all other designs. Nowadays it is the other way round, and only a few rare bisquines remain, the pride of the famous Cancale regattas.

The yard selected by my father had furthermore to get hold of mahogany for the sky-lights and cabin accommodation; make the castings in bronze; galvanise the ironwork; use paint instead of tar, and manilla instead of hemp ropes. All this gave rise to much palaver with the builder himself, and the master shipwright and rigger, who were all put out of their usual stride. The sails had to be made in Guernsey, and were of cotton, a sensational innovation.

The first boat built under these conditions was the Harcouët, a 38-foot cutter, with an immense pole mast and a boom to make you shudder. She was, nevertheless, an excellent vessel, with nothing against her that I ever heard except for those exaggerated spars.

The René-Marie was the second. Much larger, and ketch rigged, she was from every point of view a remarkable boat. Built in 1893, she is still afloat, after a long run of service as a pilot vessel to the port of St Nazaire. In her, my father attended the Naval Review at Portsmouth on the occasion of Queen Victoria's diamond jubilee. She was one of the only three French yachts present. Although I never knew her, any more than her predecessors, I believe I could recognise her at a glance if I saw her, even as a wreck.

On the other hand, the last two boats owned by my father, the Holiday I and Holiday II, one of which was built at St Servan in 1907 and the other at St Nazaire in 1908, I have handled myself. The former still survives in the Chausey Isles, and acquits herself more than honourably in the small regattas of the district. The other conformed very nearly to the present-day formula for ocean racing, and by R.O.R.C. rules would have had an excellent rating. She was a very fast vessel to windward, and phenomenally easy to handle. 'The only thing she can't do is talk', they used to say of her in Granville. And indeed she worked well under mainsail or trysail alone, and sometimes under nothing but a jib.

In this boat and in others I early sailed the Channel waters, especially round and about the Channel Islands between Cherbourg, St Malo and Chausey, which was my father's home port and in due course became my own. It was there that I first picked up the rudiments of sailing and seamanship with, as a natural consequence, a horror of all that is against the rules of the art, such as shouting on board, whistling, unnecessary movement, sartorial peculiarities, striking attitudes, badly set up rigging, high heeled shoes on deck, and the rest of it, not to mention the highly objectionable word rabbit, never to be uttered on any true Norman ship, heaven knows why!

CHAPTER II
SURROUNDINGS

THE Chausey Isles form an exceedingly compact group of islets and reefs, about seventeen miles in circumference, situated due south of the Channel Islands and equidistant from the Cotentin and the coast of Brittany. Among the few prominent objects they exhibit are a pyramid and a tower, which serve, when in line, to indicate the division between Norman and Breton waters. The division has little meaning except for the oyster-fishery police, an entirely superfluous body nowadays, be it said in passing.

Unlike the other so-called Anglo-Norman islands, which fly the British flag, Chausey has always remained a French possession. It is private property, though few people are aware of it, for neither tax nor toll is levied on arriving tourists, as is done at Sark.

The French coast curves round Chausey in a wide semi-circle, unfolding a panorama more than 120 miles wide, from Coutance to Cap Fréhel. Mont St Michel stands out very distinctly; Mont Dol, the rock of Cancale, and the Isle of Sezembre, at the entrance to St Malo, are also conspicuous. To the North, a long silhouette, blue in the distance, lies the isle of Jersey.

On clear nights the horizon scintillates in every direction. It is easy to distinguish the casinos of Parame and Dinard, the promenade of Plat Gousset at Granville, and the town of St Helier. The coastal navigating lights, mostly very powerful in those hazardous waters, flash and fade with mechanical regularity. They vary from livid white (electric) to golden yellow (petrol gas), or reddish yellow (oil gas). To the North-East, Carteret, Senequet, le Pignon, Cap Lihou; to the South, the Pierre de Herpin, the Jardin (St Malo), the Cap; Westward, the buoys N.W. and S.W. of the Minquiers, as well as those of the Sauvages; and then, far in the North, the Corbière, the Greve d'Azette, the Demie des Pas, the Ardentes, and the Bouée des Caux, which the Jersey people call the Cow-Buoy, on account of its sound apparatus which lows night and day.

Once or twice a year, a particularly favourable ceiling of cloud reflects the brief, imperious gleam of lights normally beyond range, such as Roche-Douvres, the Hague and even Barfleur: points familiar to navigators the world over, ranking with the Longships, Start Point, and Dungeness.

It would be hard to find waters more rockbound, or swept by stronger currents, than those of the Norman Archipelago. Two or three years ago I boarded, with the pilot, an English cargo vessel, which had come straight from Indo-China with a load of coal for Granville. The Captain, who had not seen his home port, London, for two and a half years, confided to me that ever since leaving the Persian Gulf he had been worried by the thought of this landfall, and had spent hours over his chart, which was a poor one in any case, but in which this particular bit of the French coast looked an inextricable labyrinth; 'and yet', he added, 'in the last few years I have negotiated Kamstchatka, Sakhaline, and the Phillipines, which are none of them exactly child's play either.'

In the Cowes to Dinard cruising races, entrants are obliged to give this group a wide berth and pass to the West, by the Minquiers, in case any of them should come to grief in attempting a short cut. The Raz Blanchard, between Alderney and the Cotentin, is also put out of bounds, purely as a safety measure. I disagree with this rule, not for the sake of any advantage my own knowledge of these waters might give me, for, as the saying is, in fog or rain there is no pilot, only compass, log, lead, and chart, but solely because the competitors are denied all chance of proving their worth in this kind of work, which should be an essential feature of races. If, nowadays, ocean racing is only to be allowed in open water and fair weather, we may as well put the vessels in charge of boys of five.[1]

---

[1] This is only a personal opinion. Certain experts in the matter of ocean racing, such as the late Major Heckstall-Smith, think differently; the formidable tide-rip which runs in the Raz Blanchard, according to him, would have the effect of holding up all the vessels in the race level with Cherbourg if they struck a foul tide there, which would mean a sort of double starting point in the middle of the race; in fact it has happened, more than once, that all competitors have found themselves bunched together there, and held up by the Raz, after crossing the channel. I think myself, however, that the shrewder competitors could have gone outside the Isles and got

Formerly, several of the principal islets were inhabited; this was in the days when the granite quarries, which have yielded countless thousands of tons, were being worked for the quays of Cherbourg, the fortifications of Jersey, and those of Vauban at St Malo; and before that, for building the cathedral of Mont-St-Michel. Now, only the big island, measuring a mile and a half in length, possesses any buildings, amongst which are the lighthouse, a coast-guard station, a church, two small hotels, a farm, and a few fishermen's houses, not forgetting my father's house, of whitewashed granite.

At spring tides the sea washes the foot of this building, and covers the flagstones of the shed where the dinghies are laid-up in winter. For it is at Chausey that the greatest difference in the whole world occurs between high and low tide level, the Bay of Fundy, in Canada, alone excepted.

During the summer season, Chausey Sound is literally crammed with boats, and holiday-makers and anglers invade the islands.

The father of Gerbault, the single-hander, used often to come to Chausey. At one time he kept a small dinghy there called the Mavourneen, which Alain later gave to a fisherman by the name of Vidament, and which was still afloat only the other day. Gerbault came from Dinard on the St Louis, a cutter belonging to Messrs Poussin, de Causans and others whose names I have forgotten. The St Louis today still sails the seas with her immense bowsprit and her impudent bow sticking out in front like a ram. Really, boats have a hard life with us.

I have seen Alain Gerbault but twice since those days, once at Havre on his return from the famous voyage, when I invited him aboard a schooner in which I was just about to leave for the Plymouth-Santander race; and the last time at Cowes, where he was busy choosing a log for his new boat in Pascall Atkey's shop. It was the very day when the old Firecrest was taken in tow from Havre to Brest in charge of the Admiralty and sank suddenly in the very middle of the channel. I had just heard myself, but realised at once

ahead. In any case the local conditions are well enough known, and charts are sufficiently clear for the navigator of each vessel to use his head a little and to make the best of a bad job. I do not say that it is an easy course, but it is one which, like every other, has its own individual problems. Nobody is forced to take the Raz route.

that Gerbault had not, and I preferred to let someone else break the news to him.

Chausey was also the sailing headquarters of Doxie Moulton, an American acclimatised at Dinard, who had settled there. Moulton had acquired some notoriety by going out only in bad weather, for fun. He was looked at askance by all the local coastguards who, unable to discover any reason for such fantastic behaviour, suspected him of smuggling.

His two best boats were Korai I and Korai II, both still afloat. It was on board the Korai II that he lost his life off the Minquiers in a sudden snow squall, as a result of a wager he had won. The story was that he celebrated his victory at Tremel's in St Helier with much champagne: that on top of that he put to sea, according to his wont, in appalling weather, was petrified by the cold as he stood at the helm, fell overboard, and sank like a stone. That, at least, was the tale told by his hand, who got back somehow or other to Dinard, half crazed with fear.

The Korai II had many subsequent owners, and was eventually re-named Penboch, by whom I know not. As Penboch she passed into the ownership of one of the cleverest ocean-racing skippers of my acquaintance, Robert Somerset. He handled the Penboch with outstanding success from the very first Channel Race in 1928, which he won against larger and more modern competitors; and two years later, in the hands of Dr Brownlow Smith, she took a very honourable third place. Which just goes to show that one should never make fun of old boats.

My father had much the same reputation as Moulton with the customs authorities, with as little justification, I need hardly say. But as he was rather impatient, there were regrettable incidents. In one of the attics at home the debris of three or four chairs can still be found, which he hurled through the air one day at a coastguard petty officer and two superintendents, when he had asked them to leave the house and they did not move fast enough to please him.

In consequence it is not surprising that in the eyes of the sons, nephews, friends and successors of the three brave victims of duty, I am myself to this day a marked man.

Nor is it any more surprising that I had boats of my own from the very first moment I was able to handle them. It was, in fact, the first use I made of the first money I ever had of my own.

The moment came when the good examples I had assimilated bore full fruit: in other words, the time when my father began to think I had gone beyond the limit (his limit, of course). After five years of toiling at the Law and quill-driving in Chambers, I suddenly threw in my hand and exchanged the office for the forecastle, where the air agreed with me infinitely better. It is only fair to add that the author of my being was sufficiently sporting not to reproach me with things he had done himself in his own time. As one says in racing parlance, 'I took his wind.'

CHAPTER III

CIRCUMSTANCES

Here are the infinitely banal circumstances of the drama which decided my career. I had been called to the Bar, and got the job of secretary to a politician who was later to shine as a Minister of State. This was in 1921. By him I was entrusted with some research work in the Reading Room at the British Museum, and accordingly went to live in London where, by virtue of my vastly important labours, the club house of the Institut de France in Kensington threw open its doors to me. I was not the only one to profit by this hospitality, and the director, Monsieur Cru, had his hands full in his efforts to preserve the eminent respectability of the house. He did his best to make us come down to breakfast in time, dress for dinner and in general keep us in order.

The learned professors who frequented the club soon lost much of their gravity in this environment. It was a good place. Unfortunately M. Cru saw me go out armed with drawing materials, and was not long in learning that I resorted chiefly to the Port of London, a fact which was impressed upon him all the more one day when he received a discreet report from the police, pointing out that I had been caught astride the parapet of the Tower Bridge, or on the wrong side of the railings of some prohibited wharf area.

I was equally often to be found in Chelsea, where I met a number of marine painters, some of whom have since made their names.

One of my vividest recollections of those days is of wandering over the house in search of some unoccupied space, well enough lighted, in which to finish a canvas, and settling in a large room where the furniture was all in dust covers. One afternoon soon afterwards, when I was lost in my work, the door opened and who should come in but our Prime Minister, M. Poincaré, followed by all his suite and a whole regiment of porters, with M. Cru bringing up the rear. As I do not read the papers I was unaware of M. Poincaré's presence in England. Too late, hedged in by my brushes, in shirt sleeves, and rather unshaven, I realised that I had made a studio of one of the rooms destined for our Premier. The great man tried to spare my blushes by pretending to be interested in my canvas, a view of the north front of St James's Palace, shewing the changing of the Guard. 'From that window', he said to me, pointing to it, 'I used to look out when I came here first, many years ago.' I lost no time, as may be imagined, in collecting my things and making myself scarce. The good M. Cru, however, humiliated by this episode, called me to his office and told me he had seen quite enough of me. I improved on the opportunity by writing to my employer, sending him my work and offering my resignation, which was promptly accepted.

I very nearly took a job with an eccentric old man who had advertised in the *Daily Mail* for a secretary speaking fluent French and able to drive a car, but at the last moment, when he seemed on the point of selecting me from a numerous field of candidates, I suddenly decided to return to my ships in the Port of London. They exercised for me an irresistible fascination, particularly the big sailing ships.

Already there were only three left which flew the British flag; the William Mitchell, the Monkbarns and the Garthpool, the two first being full-rigged ships, and the last a four-masted barque. I knew in my bones that it would not be long before they were sold to the miserable iron-dealers, and broken up as scrap; their rust-coated stanchions and plates re-cast, passed through the blast-furnace and transformed into lengths of rail, rustless table-knives or steel studs for safety crossings. It was high time to get busy if I was to see them sail again.

That is what I did, and I certainly do not regret it now.

I have known those three vessels; and I also knew the Vinnen boats of Hamburg, and all that remained of the Laesz fleet, the so-called 'P' Boats; Pamir, Penang, Posen, Padua, Pommern, Priwal, etc., with their steel masts that soared 180 feet above the water line. I have known those of which Alan Villiers writes in his remarkable books; the big Finns of the Grain Race, which Leif Erikson used to keep going by patching one up with the bits and pieces left over from the wreckage of another, and never spending a farthing on insurance. What was the use? Ah, but he was a character, was old Erikson, with his otter-skin cap pulled down over his ears.

I also knew Potez, when he ruined himself fifteen years ago trying to collect at Havre what remained of the Nantes and Dunkirk fleets to ship lumber from the Antilles; the Marguerite Molinos, Trielen, General de Sonis, Bonchamp, Bonne Veine, Jeanne d'Arc and Bossuet. I was present when the Bossuet was wrecked under the cliffs of Blanc Nez in 1933; and present also when the Sonis was knocked down at auction for 24,000 francs (about £200). The instruments on board alone (chronometer, compass, etc.) were worth double. She was the last of all of them, and I possess her teakwood wheel which weighs as much as a man, as well as a shark's tail which once adorned the bowsprit of the Avenir, a large four-masted barque which the Belgian government sold to Erikson.

I still, sometimes, meet those incredible shipowners of Dunkirk, Messrs Antonin and Alexander Bordes, who live today wrapped in memories of departed splendour. No firm of owners in the world had a greater reputation; they maintained in 1914 a fleet of forty-six full rigged ships totalling 118,780 tons burthen. It was this company of A. D. Bordes that built on the Clyde the France, the first ship ever rigged as a five-masted barque and the largest sailing vessel of the period. Captain von Luckner, the celebrated German raider, who carried out his operations in a large full-rigged 'Q' ship with auxiliary power, the old British Pass of Balmaha (renamed See-Adler), confesses that his seaman's heart had never been so touched as the day he had to send the Antonin (one of the Bordes boats) to the bottom. 'She is the loveliest ship I have ever seen afloat', he said to the Captain, 'it breaks my heart to do it.'

Merely to have seen what remained of those vessels, as anyone could, after the War, at Antwerp or in the Martiniere Canal near Nantes, weeping rust, still proud in their last berths, is at least better than to have only known them from photographs. But to have seen, be it only once, the great following wave surging under their sterns, and their vast pyramids of canvas; to have known their crews of nineteen year old boys, and their captains of twenty-four; to have walked as easily along their yards as one walks a gangplank, so broad were they; to have watched the weather and noticed every slightest change of air instead of scorning it, as one does nowadays; to have kept one's nose to windward and one's eye on the topsails, as one stood at the wheel in a freshening breeze; to have been well walloped by the old hands for whistling on board, which was simply not done, whether from superstition or for a good reason makes no difference; to have brought up at last in harbour, after months at sea, feeling queer and positively foolish, not knowing what to do with one's feet; all this was a luxury one just had time to invest in yesterday, before the market closed for ever.

The era of sail passed like a breath, like a ripple on the water, though most people imagine that it started in the womb of time and still goes on, in a sense. Yes, I know, the Phoenicians, etc., etc. . . . Not a bit of it. In those days the idea of going to windward under sail was as chimerical as the idea of pigs flying. And indeed why should they have bothered their heads with the problem when it was so easy to sign on twenty pairs of oars at the price quoted then for elbow grease? To say even that a galleon or a ship of the line of Louis XIV was at all weatherly would be an exaggeration. It is not so long ago since sailing vessels, what I call sailing vessels, began to plough in their hundreds every sea on the globe. Hardly had they time to spread their great wings before the reign of steam began, and men bethought them of driving ships with mighty strokes of the paddle-wheel and screw.

Nowadays, in all the great highways of ocean traffic, you may search the horizon in vain for a glimpse of sail. Smoke is all you will see. One, three, ten, fifty blobs of smoke; the page has been turned (square-rigged sailors would say 'capsized') once and for all.

CHAPTER IV

SOUL

IT will be clear from what I have written that I have not always sailed on my own account; nor invariably for pure pleasure.

I might have had considerable difficulty in getting a seaman's berth if my parents had not, in effect, paid for my apprenticeship. One result of serving this apprenticeship was that I automatically came to share the average professional opinion of the seafaring whims of certain amateur heroes of the sailing world. Perhaps it is less a question of a definite opinion than a sort of half humorous indifference.

'Solitary' sailors were then really hardly spoken of. With the public they were not yet in vogue. In 1923, when I held my first exhibition of off-shore subjects at the Devambez, amongst a fairly diverse group, which included Foujita, Louis Dauphin, Utrillo, and Maurice de Lambert as well as myself, Gerbault had not yet made his famous transatlantic passage. On the other hand, amongst seamen, as I have just said, his sort of performance aroused neither envy nor curiosity, and the term 'solitary' was hardly ever used. We were content to say of those who got into or out of trouble alone in their dinghies, or who had a habit of pulling away from the side by themselves for any reason, that they rowed 'en cochon'. This expression, and many more that I would hesitate to mention, has long given way to the more elegant word used to-day. Even so, I still find in it something rather beside the point and slightly laughable, doubtless because it starts a train of thought, and one which is of secondary interest beside the basic fact of sailing unaided over distances more or less great.

It may be that solitude, which is a burden to some and agreeable to others, according to temperament, is inseparable from the general picture, but in any case it is not the kernel of the matter. It is a pity that the expression 'single-handed' has no equivalent in French: its specifically nautical meaning of 'handled by one person', 'one pair of hands all told' defines the performance exactly, and in so doing emphasises whatever merit there may be in it.

If we ask ourselves to what extent those who use the sea daily find any virtue in the game, it will soon be apparent that for them, the single-handed sailor is of a species neither as precious, nor as rare, as books would lead us to believe. Almost any day, if you take the trouble, you may come across men alone in boats far out at sea off our coasts, out of sight of land; old shellbacks (and there are young ones as well) who go out line fishing from morning till night, all alone (quite like grown-ups) without seeing anything particularly sensational in it. They smoke their pipes, take a drink, talk all alone to themselves, in short, they are a sort of sea-hermit.

If one hardly notices them, if one knows little of their lives, it is because every morning, long before dawn, their 'old women' have cleared them for action, and pushed them out of the house, without either interview, waving handkerchiefs or fanfare of trumpets. 'Off with you, now. Here's your bag.' In the 'bag' are a couple of slices of bread and butter, one or two onions, and a litre or so of cider. That is for the whole day. He makes for the first lighted bar, for the sole purpose of 'knocking one back' with a coffee, and then gropes his way aboard in the shadow of the quayside; to see him move so slowly you might think him half-paralysed. It is true he is not particularly fit: physical jerks are hardly in his line, nor is he addicted to dieting or massage.

You come across him at sea, huddled over the tiller, apparently indifferent to all that might well happen, and when given a hail, hardly bothering to lift a numbed arm; but he has eyes like needles, which rake the sea in every direction, never letting him be caught out. If a squall comes he changes jibs and takes in a reef without worrying, mutters an oath for form's sake by all the thousand names of God, puts on oilskins and sea-boots—and that's all. . . .

It is dark by the time he comes ashore. He hands over the 'bag' and the empties to his waiting wife, pays another short visit to the bar, and so to bed. From all of which we are forced to conclude that 'single-handed sailing' is not a matter of colossal physical strength. If you want to be considered an idiot, go and tell one of these old shellbacks, as I have seen happen more than once, that his is a great game; that he braves a furious element; that he is only removed from death by the thickness of a plank, etc. . . . and other absurdities. (The thickness of a plank, by the way, is not sensational when one compares it with a liner's plate.)

It may be objected that there is a vast difference between our fisherman and the 'real sailing man', the man who makes long ocean passages and doesn't go home every night.

Remember, however, that the fact of coming home does not prevent him going far enough off shore to be exposed sometimes to the full force of a north-westerly gale. Otherwise there wouldn't be so many widows in the vicinity of the Mariners' Pension office at the end of the month. Reflect, too, how many sea-miles his little ocean wanderings, without hurry, add up to in the course of a year's work. As to the coast always being handy, the significance of that is simply that he has to carry out every day the most delicate of all sailing operations, namely getting in and out of harbour, without hitting anything, even when unable to see a yard in rain and darkness. And one must take into account the sort of seat-wetting boats these fishermen sail, seldom decked, and rigged anyhow. To compare them with those of the so-called adventure-loving yachtsman, with mine for example, is to put an old ship's boat up against a modern lifeboat. And that's no exaggeration.

In spite of it all, accidents are not as frequent as one might expect. Now and again one of them falls overboard: then it is 'lost at sea', and a couple of lines in small type. Roger Quesnel told me he swam about for two hours once while his boat held very prettily on her course, and that it was by the merest chance that a friend of his was near enough to hear his shouts at last, and hoist him inboard like a fish, just in time. There are others, whose vessels capsize or sink, and then, far out or near the shore, it is the same story. Father Jaslin was lost in this way, two cables off the Granville pierhead, in a perfectly smooth sea, to make it all the worse.

From this one can well imagine that the majority of professional seamen are not too keen on reading stories of 'single-handed' sailing. Nor can one expect them to be great story-tellers themselves; their noses are much too near the grindstone, and I have never heard such men enlarging on the call of adventure, or on the charm of the wide open spaces and distant isles. . . .

I give this point of view for what it is worth, and only remark that most people ignore it. Those who could best give expression to it generally have a splash of salt-water in the inkwell, that is to say, they either distrust writing or don't know how. This leaves a clear field to the others, who get intoxicated with self-importance and the magnitude of their own performances, good, bad, or in-different, and are much too apt to make sarcastic remarks about poor devils who earn their living on filthy steamboats—which, of course, makes the latter rank outsiders—and to make themselves out the only true sailors. For myself, I can only see something ridiculous in inviting a professional seaman to go sailing for the fun of the thing.

I am well aware that the average fo'c'sle hand would find it difficult to make a long passage, for want of sufficient knowledge of stellar observation, or even of the simplest navigation. But he knows his limitations, and possesses a natural, and so to speak, atavistic distrust of the mysteries beyond the horizon; the intoxi-cation of distance, of depths, and the deceits of unknown seaways. All this is no reason for thinking him a fool. When it comes to getting out of a mess at sea, in bad weather and with the minimum of resources, I know some who could learn a lot from him.

As for educated seamen, such as captains of vessels, it is another matter. It would be altogether absurd to imagine that they are not in the best possible position to appreciate the dangers of the sea at their true value, and to fear them, as is proper, neither too much nor too little. They have paid for their knowledge, and have to go on paying in order to hold their jobs down. Yet this is a standard which is lacking on the one hand in the people who from pure ignorance exaggerate the terrors of sailing, and on the other in the equally ignorant lunatics who talk of 'sailing along just like a song', whatever the conditions. This is a species of valour with which I have no patience.

In the end, it is a question less of guts and experience than of ways and means. 'I am convinced', I wrote some years ago in the *Yachting World*, 'that there are plenty of men who could and would make such cruises, for the pleasure of risk, or simply to see the world in this unhampered way. What stops them is merely that it is difficult to bring together at one time all the required circumstances; one condition failing, the whole idea becomes impossible; the first requirement is the means to buy or build the right vessel; then you must have sufficient leisure; then physical fitness, which is not always enjoyed by those who have both time and money; technical knowledge (which is a sine qua non); and lastly the desire to rough it when you can so easily travel in comfort.

'Nor is this all. Having made up your mind to buy or have built a real boat, or to build her yourself (which has happened); having thrown up the daily task and freed yourself from professional obligations; having got rid of your perfectly healthy appendix (which always rather intrigues the doctors); having acquired enough practical experience—at least in your own estimation; having done all this, what then? Our hero must now face the hardest thing of all— the disapproval of his friends and the tears of his wife. (Bachelors have all the luck in this case!) His only alternative is to make his plans in absolute secrecy, which is by no means easy to do, then one fine day to say he is going out to buy a box of matches, and once round the corner, run like a lamplighter.'

These are the real reasons why the number of adventurous sailing men is so small. Yet they are very likely more numerous than one realises. For many years I was unaware of their existence myself, until the time came when certain circumstances brought them to my notice. It may be of interest to give a brief account of some of them in the following pages.

CHAPTER V

FORERUNNERS

At the beginning of 1925 I shipped as ordinary seaman (I was not yet rated A.B.) in the Polar research vessel Pourquoi Pas, commanded by the well-known explorer, J. B. Charcot. I made an initial trip to the Faroe Islands and the Greenland Coast, after which the vessel was laid up at St Servan for the winter.

When the rest of the crew were paid off, Charcot asked me not to leave, but to take up my winter quarters on board, with the job of tending the warps, keeping the wardroom stove alight, and doing the fire rounds;—in other words a very soft berth. I used to row across to a neighbouring warship three times a day for meals and spent much of my time with the crew of a Fishery Protection vessel, the Albatross, which was moored alongside us and undergoing a complete overhaul.

I had however been entrusted with the re-classification of the library of the Pourquoi Pas. My orders were to take a note of the many missing volumes, and to allow none out on loan without making the borrower sign in a special book. One result of all this was that during the subsequent cruise the officers found my system incomprehensible, and took to sending me on deck when they wanted a particular volume, hastening my steps, as often as not, with pointed remarks about people who poke their noses into concerns not their own, instead of swabbing down decks.

Early every evening, during the long winter nights, I used to light a lamp in gimbals in one of the cabins just off the wardroom, and rolled up in a pair of blankets, book in hand, would listen to the wind singing in the rigging and the rain drumming on the big skylight. My situation was retired enough, in the bowels of the 900 ton ship. Cold and deserted, she used to heave her shoulder against the quayside, and shake her chains when the lock gates opened and the swell from outside reached her. I found this way of life much to my taste. On shore I knew the local Fortnum, and the proprietor of the Hotel Victoria: enough said. I used to go to St Malo twice a week at the very most, where a banker friend of my father's would invite me to dine or take me out shooting on Saturdays. Happy times! It was delightful to stay put in my varnished pitch-pine quarters, and to keep no watch by day or night.

At first my reading was extremely miscellaneous; I dug at random into a huge pile of magazines, or into a simply prodigious collection of *Punches*. But one day, by chance in the Captain's stateroom, I came across one of Nelsons' small volumes, entitled 15,000 *Miles in a Ketch*, by Rallier du Baty. Rallier, like myself, had been one of the crew of the Pourquoi Pas some sixteen or seventeen years earlier, on an Antarctic expedition, and I knew that afterwards he had gone on his own to the Kerguelen Isles in an old Boulogne fishing smack with a crew of four. When I opened this book, I found, for the first time in my experience of nautical literature, something more than banal and empty phraseology about blue seas, enchanting vistas, and all that sort of rubbish, which was what I had expected. I would like to state here, by the way, that till then I had not been easily persuaded to read what one calls 'sea stories'. To such an extent was this so, that I was rarely able to go beyond twenty-five pages, without sending both book and author to the devil. *The Cruise of the Snark* belongs to this category, and I shall probably distress a good many of Jack London's admirers when I say that the early chapters of this book are nothing but blah and hot air raised to the nth degree of theatrical bravado, and that the whole volume is a collection of puerilities enough to give a seaman apoplexy. I would give a few typical examples of these extravagances here, but for the fact that it would mean copying out ten pages at a time.

The more trouble I had in swallowing this sort of book the more I liked Rallier du Baty. A fine man, and a fine writer, as one might expect from his inclusion in Nelsons' collection. I may add that I have never seen a copy of this book in the original French.

After a time I gave up the magazines and *Punch* as I discovered other books of the same sort, notably Captain Slocum's *Sailing Alone around the World*. I had often heard of the English edition of this book, but there was at that time no French translation, and copies were hard to come by in the libraries. Since then, Slocum has been translated by Paul Budker, who was well advised in under-

Southampton Docks, from a painting by the Author

Winnibelle Running before a Squall, from a water-colour by the Author

taking the task, as the work deals with one of the outstanding performances of this nature.

Slocum introduces himself as a retired deep-sea skipper, one of the old school. I concluded from this that even if his book were badly written, I should still find in it pertinent opinions and exact statements. And I was not disappointed, except that it proved to be admirably written as well.

Shortly before 1900, Joshua Slocum crossed the Atlantic single-handed, from Cape Sable to Gibraltar, in the extraordinary time of twenty-eight days. Subsequently he rounded the American Continent, passing through the narrows between Cape Horn and Tierra del Fuego; a thing which only one man has done since, namely Bernicot, another professional sailor, quite recently.

His boat, the Spray, was an old tub, flat as a pancake, but with very easy underwater lines. He found her in a half rotten condition, and patched her up himself, strengthening her with much new oak planking. She had a bowsprit, fitted with an immense old-fashioned jib-boom, and a sharp cutwater stem. She was rigged as a yawl, with reef points, etc., again in the old-fashioned way, and carried a squaresail for following winds. Altogether a proper little ship, though unfortunately all her stability was in her shape and she had no outside ballast, which leaves one somewhat perplexed. Be that as it may the Spray was extraordinarily fast with the wind free.

Slocum's voyage round the world lacked nothing of the picturesque. With his Winchester he fought Indians in Patagonia, and navigated the Pacific with an old alarm clock for chronometer. He was invited to lunch in the Transvaal by President Kruger, who affirmed that, as the world was flat, the Spray was making a voyage 'on the surface of the world and not around it'. During the later stages he sailed entirely without charts, his own having been worn to bits. His is such a thoroughly frank and straightforward book that as you read you say 'Oh how true!' even when you are unable to check it with personal recollections.

A few years afterwards, Slocum, still in the Spray, went down. He is believed to have been struck by a cyclone, about a hundred miles to the East of Cape Hatteras.

My next discovery was the account of Sea Bird's transatlantic passage. The Sea Bird was a hard chined, or, as they say 'diamond bottomed' boat, a type that would never have given me great confidence in bad weather. Her owner, indeed, hardly conceals the fact that he bought her only because there was nothing else available. She was much copied, on the strength of having crossed the Western Ocean, but I must admit it was with a feeling of low satisfaction ('I'm not a bit surprised! I told you so!' etc.) that I learned later that Voss had capsized at sea in a vessel of this type, off the Japanese coast. To make matters worse, the Sea Bird was yawl-rigged, a complication which, in common with many other critics, I consider useless in so small a craft. For the Sea Bird was only 26 feet overall. Nevertheless her owner, Thomas Fleming Day, editor of the American Magazine *The Rudder*, managed to ship two friends with him, one of whom, Fred Thurber, I was later to know. They crossed from New York to Gibraltar at a surprising speed: 29 days from port to port, by way of the Azores. She was a peculiar vessel assuredly, but she could move. True, she had a little Knox 2-stroke auxiliary engine, which may occasionally have served to get her out of a calm patch; but one must remember the small amount of fuel she could carry, as well as the poor speed—$3\frac{1}{2}$ knots—produced by the engine, which was frequently out of action. To supplement her inadequate tanks, Day lashed petrol drums on deck on either side of the diminutive cabin top. The obstruction and the stink must have beggared description. At any rate the Sea Bird got as far as Rome, where she was a great success. Fleming Day's account is not long, but it is absolutely masterly: a perfect example of how this sort of literature should be written.

In the story of his two consecutive ocean passages, in the Sea Bird and, more especially, in the Detroit the year following, Day has some hard, though very likely just, things to say about his shipmates. He is in fact the soul of candour, and sometimes passes equally harsh judgment on himself. This was one of the things which struck me most in his book, and I have often since had a powerful desire to make similar remarks about my own crews in ocean races and elsewhere. The story is always the same: there is the man who grouses, the man who is seasick, the man who questions your decisions, the man who is suddenly panic-stricken, and so on and so forth. Day describes them to perfection.

The next book I read was Pidgeon's. Pidgeon built himself a boat, in 1917, to a Fleming Day design in *The Rudder*. She was a larger Sea Bird, rigged like her as a yawl, and hard chined like a dory. Despite these peculiarities, it must be admitted that Pidgeon was thoroughly satisfied with his boat. He went round the world alone in her,[1] starting with a companion, who was doubtless not of the right stuff and of whom he got rid as soon as possible. Taking his departure from the Californian coast, he made the Marquesas in forty-two days, and went on by way of Samoa, the Fiji Islands, New Hebrides and New Guinea. Thereafter he called at Rodrigues, Cocos Keeling, Madagascar, Durban, Capetown, St Helena, Ascension, Trinidad, and went through the Panama Canal, finding Gerbault at Balboa. This was in 1925. Alain Gerbault, who had crossed the Atlantic two years previously, was starting on his remarkable voyage round the world. I do not find any mention of this meeting in his book. Pidgeon, on the contrary, speaks of it.

The comparison between his own Islander and Gerbault's Firecrest was, in my opinion—questions of comfort apart—to the latter's advantage. The Firecrest had more class and, though older and less comfortable, would have given me a good deal more confidence in a gale of wind. However, Pidgeon thinks otherwise.

'I enjoyed meeting this courageous seaman very much,' he writes, 'for those who have had similar experiences understand each other the better for it. However, I did not fancy the Firecrest for single-handed cruising. As a racing cutter, the purpose for which she was designed, she was probably all right, but she was certainly not designed for the comfort of the man at the helm, there being neither cockpit nor coaming for his protection. From what I learned, he had had a hard passage, one that would have discouraged most amateurs. For a tender, he had a folding canvas boat that didn't look very substantial for use among coral reefs, but I think he was a strong swimmer. After seeing the Islander he said he liked the Firecrest better, so we both parted quite satisfied with our outfit and equipment.'

Pidgeon's last run was his longest. He took eighty-five days to make his original point of departure, St Clement, near Los Angeles

[1] He has just done it again (1938).

in California. His book reveals great modesty and surprising qualities as a navigator. In point of fact Pidgeon is not primarily a
sailor; I think I am right in saying that he is a professional photographer of great talent, specialising in landscape.

I next set myself to a thorough perusal of Gerbault's book,
which I had only glanced through before. The library of the Pour
Quoi Pas only possessed the first American edition, called *The
Fight of the Firecrest* and written, it seems, before the French
version. This account in English possesses a singular force,
which I personally miss in the French text. At this date, Gerbault was still a long way from completing his world cruise,
the various stages of which I only read of in journalists' accounts
in the daily press, often so vague that it was difficult to form any
opinion.

Gerbault's first crossing from Gibraltar to New York was, as
Pidgeon says, a very hard one. The American papers of the time
speak of it as 'a man's desperate fight in a worn-out old tub'. This
is an absurd exaggeration. The Firecrest was certainly not new,
having been built well before 1900, but her teak hull was still
sound. She proved this later when, after being stranded, she
dragged over a coral reef which tore off her keel without holing her
anywhere.

On the other hand her canvas was old and the seams completely
rotten. In heavy weather they came apart one after another from
top to bottom of the sail. Her rig itself, moreover, was ill suited to
the needs of single-handed cruising. He modified it later. These
were the chief cause of his troubles. He also had the bad luck not
to pick up the trade winds where he expected to find them, and
perhaps showed a want of patience in not seeking them out in a
lower latitude. Be that as it may, he had to put up with calm after
calm, gale after gale. Then he ran out of food and water. After
that his shrouds started to work at the hounds; his bowsprit
carried away practically at the stem; and the cover of his sail-locker
was washed overboard. But this ascetic-looking man had an in-
domitable will and iron powers of resistance. When, at the end of a
hundred and one days, he entered Long Island Sound at last, he
was heartbroken to see again the shore lights, buildings and civilisation. His length of time, alone at sea, is still a record. Pidgeon

approaches it most closely with his eighty-five days from Panama to San Clement.

On first opening his narrative, I received a distinct shock: 'Adventure stories', he writes, 'were in early days my favourite reading. Some described the adventures of gold miners in Klondike or Alaska, and the name "Eldorado" fascinated me. . . .' And further on: 'It was through reading *The Cruise of the Snark* that I learnt it was possible to cross Oceans in a small boat, and I decided there and then to make that my life. . . .'

Bless my soul! *The Cruise of the Snark*! My pet aversion! How different people are. . . . To think that such fantastic nonsense, stuff which I find utterly contemptible, could be taken quite seriously by other men. The realisation of this strange fact staggered me.

Pierre MacOrlan, in his *Manual of the Perfect Adventurer*, distinguishes between the passive adventurer, who is crammed with reading but does nothing himself, and the active adventurer, who does things, suffers a thousand hard knocks, and thinks no more of them.

This is surely a very arbitrary classification, for with all his romanticism, Gerbault has proved himself beyond all question a man of action. I myself, when I look at a boat, often see visions. To be imaginative is not so very different from being romantic. . . . Who knows? Perhaps there is not so much difference, mentally, between Gerbault and me after all.[1]

Conor OBrien is one of the most caustic of characters. He has been described to me as a little man, agile as a monkey, wiry as the devil, and hairy all over: needless to add, he is Irish. His competence in the matter of small boats is beyond dispute. In the Saoirse, which he had built to his own specification and which is certainly one of the best little ships ever designed for extensive cruising, he made his round-the-world trip from west to east, by the three capes, Good Hope, Leuwen in Australia, and the Horn. He had endless difficulty with his crews, and changed them continually. He says that only once was he satisfied with them and then, at the end of their very first passage, they decamped without even waiting for their pay.

[1] Alain Gerbault died lately (1944) in New Guinea.

For hitting the nail on the head, and at the same time for bringing out the humorous side of things, give me Conor OBrien. The sly digs he sometimes makes are the right sort of digs, and his mistakes are sincere and understandable. His narrative is a perfect little masterpiece, and I can give it no higher praise than to say that I read it through three times on end without a moment's boredom.

In his preface to the cheaper edition, the only one I have, he declares: 'Since writing this book I have considerably enlarged my study of off-shore yachting and the result has been to upset most of the conclusions I had arrived at at the time the first edition was printed. Consequently, the opinions to be found in the following pages are not necessarily those I held at the moment of the occurrences on which they are founded.'

From which it would seem to follow that circumnavigating the globe has not made Conor OBrien infallible. Which is perfectly true. No one is. The real experts, the OBriens, Somersets or Paul Hammonds of the world, are never above learning. The deeper you go into a subject, the less categorical you become; and the more difficult it becomes to express your ideas in a book. I say this with feeling.

William Albert Robinson is another adventurous voyager of note. He is a particularly well educated man, learned in all that pertains to the sea, and the boat which he designed and had built, and in which he made his world cruise was (for the Svaap has been lost since then) a marvellous little yacht, handy and up-to-date.

Robinson has written two books, *Deep Water and Shoal* and *Voyage to the Galapagos*. During the latter trip, he was laid low very dramatically by an attack of appendicitis 1,200 miles from civilisation. His wife, who accompanied him, and the American Navy, notified by wireless, managed to pull him through safely. *Deep Water and Shoal* is the account of his voyage round the world, during the course of which he ate human flesh with cannibals, was taken prisoner by pirates in the Red Sea and came within an inch of losing his life in a terrific squall in the Mediterranean, a hundred and fifty miles from Nice. At that moment he believed he was really done for; which proves once and for all there are no kindly seas anywhere on the globe.

One of the noteworthy features of the Svaap was that she had a small auxiliary motor, in opposition to the rather naïve prejudices of those who sentimentalise on this point. In reality, a modern sailing yacht without some auxiliary system is an anomaly, be it only to move about in harbour without outside help, to provide electric lighting, or to enable a course to be shaped through regions of persistent calm, such as the Red Sea, which Robinson traversed. To those who object that a propeller has the disadvantage of slowing up speed on long passages under sail, I would point out, that with the system in use nowadays on many yachts, that is to say a propeller under the quarter, the blades of which fold up when sailing (Hyde or Kelvin), 'drag' is not nearly as serious as one sometimes imagines. In the bigger ocean races a handicap of one per cent. to two per cent. (no more), is allowed to boats keeping their propellers according to whether they are fixed or feathering.

Robinson had, as sole crew, a Tahitian, who gave considerable trouble at times, from which we may conclude once again, that the best way to find peace is to sail alone.

It is far from being my intention to write a monograph on the subject, but I want to bring out the fact that cruising of the adventurous sort has been much less uncommon than is usually supposed, in the course of the last fifty years. To trace its development is difficult, for there are many whose performances are only to be found in the press of the period, and others who have left no record at all.

The first such voyage of which I have any knowledge was that of a man named Johnson, who crossed the Atlantic in 1876, in a sailing dory, taking fifty-two days.

In 1891 two almost incredible Americans challenged each other to a single-handed race in craft stated to be no more than 13 feet overall! The starting line was off Boston. One of the competitors reached England in forty-five days; the other was picked up by a steamship after three weeks at sea, absolutely all-in. Spurred to new efforts by his defeat, apparently, the latter crossed to Spain from America in fifty-eight days the year after, which was not very fast, but due allowance must be made for the size of his cockleshell. Taking it all round, I think these two merry men overstepped the mark.

But what are we to say of Blackburn, of whom it is related that, although he had lost all his fingers from frost-bite in the Arctic, he rowed to Ireland from the Newfoundland banks. As good a rowing story as you could wish. Yet even Blackburn has had his rivals. Two men set out on a West to East crossing in a whaler called the Richard Fox. They had of course inadequate stocks of food and water, and relied on such ships as they might meet to keep them going. Naturally they had no real instruments to find their position. They succeeded in getting across, but disappeared somewhere in the Channel or the North Sea. So much water is not really needed to drown a man; the Seine estuary would do.

But the masterpiece, the most fabulous of all these feats, was the crossing of stout Captain Brude, a Norwegian, who pinned his faith to a sort of steel egg, an affair with a round top and bottom, a little steel mast, and a trysail! For getting in and out it had a sort of conning-tower something like a submarine, and indeed I imagine the whole contraption must have resembled the famous 'sailing submarine' dear to my humorous friend Francis André. Brude's idea was to demonstrate the unsinkability of his apparatus, which he believed would revolutionise the design of the life-boats carried by transatlantic liners. He shipped two live passengers and set out from Bergen for New York. His was the most interminable voyage hitherto recorded: 251 days from port to port! At the end of this time, the Vraad—so the sailing submarine was called—was cast up on Long Island beach, her steel mast bent at right angles by the winter gales she had encountered. Her crew were safe and sound, but much to the indignation of Captain Brude his invention was not taken up. How those poor devils survived seven and a half months in their metal egg, which cannot have carried much in the way of provisions, is an unfathomable mystery. Visions of murder and cannibalism must surely have flitted through their minds. At any rate their record is safer than most.

I could cite plenty of other examples, including many whose departure was announced, but never their landfall: such as Blythe, who disappeared with his companions, in a boat not unlike the Spray, no one knows within a thousand miles where.

Winter passed quickly. The wind sang more sweetly in the rigging. Grass began to sprout on the deck. I expected no compliments, and got none.

By April the Pour Quoi Pas had refitted and was on the way to the Arctic.

Now and again, in the forecastle or on deck when my watch was off duty, I used to tell the stories I had read, which gave me quite a reputation as the biggest liar on board. One day, M. Charcot asked me for Slocum's book. It had disappeared. A search through the file of receipts produced the signature of one of the officers of the pilots' school-ship, who was away at work off the Norwegian coast, and had forgotten to return it. This was the crowning triumph of my career as librarian, nor can I recall it to this day without feeling a cold shiver down my spine.

I served for seventeen months as A.B. and No. 1 of the whaler, on board the Pour Quoi Pas. She was the last French three-masted barque. Ten years later she foundered off the coast of Iceland, in a bay I know well. Captain Charcot went down at his post, and with him perished more than fifty souls, leaving only a single survivor. It is unnecessary to say with what emotion I recall that ship, her master, and the comrades I knew.

CHAPTER VI

ENDEAVOUR

ON my return to France I held an exhibition of off-shore marine subjects, mostly depicting Arctic waters, which resulted in my being able to acquire a small cruising cutter. I paid heavily for her, or at least what the vendor asked; but I had no choice. The boat was no other than the old Holiday II, almost unrecognisable now, with a pole-mast and lengthened by a false canoe-stern; but it was her all the same. I rediscovered in her a thousand and one details which had thronged my childhood, including a notch cut in the mahogany saloon table by my penknife (how well I remembered being locked up by way of punishment).

The vendor must have realised how irresistibly I was drawn to her, for he stuck to his figure, which was 25,000 francs, quite a fancy price at that time for a 40 foot boat with no auxiliary. I was quite well aware that my father had bought her for 5,000 francs in 1908, and sold her for 9,000 seven years later. Since then she had passed through many hands, and 18,000 had been paid for her by her latest owner, the very man who was now asking 25,000 francs. There was nothing for it but to pay up. I may add, however, that I sold her again a year later for exactly double, though not without completely re-conditioning her hull and gear.

In her I made a cruise of about 1,500 miles through the Irish Sea, with my wife, to whom I had recently been married, and Henri Maubert, then about nineteen or twenty years old, and studying for the School of Navigation, as crew. Naturally, having no motor, we were frequently becalmed, besides being caught out more than once by hard blows in difficult and enclosed waters, such as Ramsey Sound, near Milford Haven, which we cleared stern first at surprising speed, amongst breakers the like of which I have never seen (the Wild Geese), and over reefs of rock which we could see only a little below our keel, without being able to do anything much about it except get ready to abandon ship as quickly as possible.

We had another bad moment in Carnarvon Bay, which is un-lighted, when we tried to make the entrance of the Menai Straits in the middle of the night, using the lead, and in dirty weather. The boom goose-neck broke off and the mainsail, although brand new, started to tear. Finally I decided to let her take the ground on a sandbank in the shelter of Llandwin Island, as I was afraid of being set ashore before having time to rig a trysail. In the morning, when she floated again and we were preparing to heave to quite comfortably under the lee of the island, the Port Dinthlaen life-boat suddenly appeared. She had been warned by the local pilot vessel, which was itself unable to put out owing to the state of the sea.

It was blowing really hard, so I decided to accept a tow up the Carnarvon entrance channel, which we should have found beyond our powers to negotiate in the then state of the tide.

Having read of our plight in the morning papers, a large number of inquisitive people came in cars from all over the county to give themselves the thrill of witnessing so dramatic a rescue. Personally, I did not find it so very entertaining; particularly when the Life Boat Association demanded 5,000 fr. for its help.

Contrariwise, at Liverpool, I had the pleasure of beating to windward up the whole twenty-five miles of the channel (we tacked more than a hundred and fifty times between midnight and 8 a.m., across a stream of cargo steamers) and then stood off and on for four hours in the Mersey between Birkenhead and the Albert Dock entrance, waiting for the dock gates to open at mid-day. Finally, much to the amusement of the lock keepers, we passed through I don't know how many basins still under sail. Luckily the Holiday II had lost none of her former gyratory talents.

Here we embarked a passenger, Mr Collins, who was an enthu-siastic supporter of the 'Midnight Race' from Liverpool to the Isle of Man, which we had in any case intended to visit. When the time came to leave, there wasn't a breath of wind, but the tide was on the ebb, so all we had to do was to keep in the centre of the fair-way by means of sweeps.

I remember a topsail schooner which had drifted down help-lessly on to one of the light-buoys, fouled it with one of her bow-sprit shrouds, and stuck fast. Very late that night we could hear the thud of sledge-hammers as the crew tried to cut the chain shroud to get clear. It is no laughing matter to touch a Liverpool buoy: the Port authorities are a serious-minded set of people. . . .

By seven in the morning a nice air from the south had worked us over the seventy miles to the Isle of Man and we were off Douglas Harbour again in 'a dead calm sea and never a breath'. After waiting twelve hours without making twelve lengths, we decided to use the sweeps and enter by man power. Towards 2 a.m. as we hove and pulled away against hell's own current into the outer harbour, I swore a mighty oath that my next boat would have some sort of a stink pot as auxiliary. Ridiculous to have been caught out as I had been among the Wild Geese; absurd to have had to pay 5,000 francs for nothing more than a couple of oar-strokes; mad to remain fifteen hours just outside harbour, and finally to be hailed by a kind-hearted fisherman chugging back to port in a nondescript 3½ h.p. contraption, who, out of sheer pity, passed us a rope's end and towed us alongside the quay.

I am not denying that lack of power may have its romantic and picturesque side. It conjures up visions of big ships returning from sea (and perhaps also of swarms of tug-boats fussing round them). But the case is different when it comes to new boats. We are all agreed that there's nothing like sailing. But to-day you pay your penny and you take your choice. If you decide to sail as they sailed in the old days, why, the least you can do is to put up with the consequences and refrain from being a burden to others, so it seems to me.

The season was pretty well advanced (October) when we set our course southwards for home. With the rocky outcrops which fringe the East coast of Ireland abeam, and being about level with Dublin, we had another incident. My wife was laid low by a sudden attack of appendicitis without the slightest warning, just at the moment when she was bringing on deck our usual bread and milk—which flew through the air in a flash and was all over the cabin floor. We had to make Wicklow, a small harbour that dries out and which by now was just abreast of us in the mist and darkness. A little way off the entrance we were welcomed by half-a-dozen natives in a ship's boat, who, seeing our navigation lights, rowed over to us and gave us a tow in.

They sought to dissuade me from venturing into the town at that hour of the night to get a doctor. They said Sinn Fein agitation had broken out. There was sniping going on from windows, they assured me. However, I set off all the same to dig out brave Doctor O'Something or other, whose address they gave me, and who refused point blank to venture out of his house. A pleasant evening. . .

Later I had serious thoughts of using this excellent vessel, the Holiday II, for more ambitious cruises, but she was not so very new and I should have had to cut off her extension; a thing I would have done long before if the canoe-stern had not been so useful for stowing the crutch. The deck also wanted renewing, without taking into account the fact that one of her less scrupulous owners had sawn through the two centre beams to give more cabin room. In addition to all this, her mast wanted replacing. So I preferred to sell her and wait for another bargain.

Realising that I might have to wait years, I contented myself in the meantime with a small twin-engined launch, designed by myself, which was amply sufficient for everyday use in Chausey. There was always plenty of sailing to be had with friends, and from time to time I was given a boat to take round the coast from one regatta to another. In this way, I got in the way of taking part in such races as the Plymouth–Santander and the Cannes–Dinard every season.

One day, a shipyard in Northern France asked me to come and give my opinion on a boat under construction. In the main it was a question of assessing her value for the Company's balance sheet, as to which the directors could not agree.

I disembarked at Boulogne and, on entering the palace of draughts (which is every shipyard), found myself peering at a newly planked hull, coated with white lead, and not yet completely decked. She was eleven metres over all, with a Colin Archer sort of profile, though on looking closer you saw that was all she had of the Norwegian type; the mid-section floor bearers were much raised, the beam moderate, with as a consequence a relatively large draught. She had a $3\frac{1}{2}$ ton lead keel.

Such work as was done was remarkably well finished, and the accommodation carefully thought out and just right; nevertheless, my valuation was a great deal lower than the yard had anticipated.

I took into account the slump which was already (in 1931) making itself felt in the yacht market.

Meanwhile, I was boatless. And the question was, to buy or to build? How often had I not taken part in endless and almost meaningless discussions about 'fast cruisers'. In such talks, those who bang their fists on the table and shout the loudest are generally thosewhose opinions are ready made and founded on little experience. I had my own views, of course. I was well past thirty, not so agile as I had been. . . . Was my enthusiasm beginning to flag? Enthusiasm is a grand word, but mine is not a fanatical nature. I like to see things at first hand, to sum them up by trial and error, and I was in a peculiarly favourable position for experimenting. If in the end my experience cost me too dear, I could always as a last resource re-sell the boat. In fact, there was nothing to prevent my taking the plunge.

Nothing . . . except making the actual decision. The thought of having to face the innumerable people who would give me good advice, or lift their arms to heaven in horror, filled me with dread.

People have often reproached me for making sudden decisions; but the truth is they are not always as sudden as they seem to the onlooker. I have an instinctive dislike, almost a physical incapability, of sharing my pet problems with anyone else until my mind is made up. Approval and encouragement are all very well, but in reality they bring solution no nearer. As for the other thing, when you meet with nothing but objections, the selfsame objections you have faced and overcome or got round in the course of much hard thinking; the only way to convince the objector is to lead him laboriously through the long, long trail of your own reasoning, with interminable detailed explanations, and I for one find life too short for that sort of thing.

This may seem a little ungracious towards people who are not in a position to appreciate the number of pencils one has sucked, or the number of miles one has paced back and forth before making one's mind up; but that is how I am made. And at the time of which I am now writing, I did a great deal of thinking before I eventually made my choice.

Instead of settling down to design a boat, with the help of the mass of material I had collected and stowed in drawers and port-

folios, I started by having a good look round to see if there were
not the vessel I wanted on the market. One judges sometimes better on the slipway than on the drawing-board. And then again,
there are risks in building, and unexpected items (how many!) in
the estimate. This, at least, was the excuse I gave myself, with the
idea of gaining time.

I should have been quite glad to buy back the Holiday II for the
second time, despite all the alteration she needed (for I had no
qualms about her hull, the essential thing), but I learned she had
been lost off the Spanish coast.

Penboch was not on the market, and anyway she was not an
easily handled boat, and had a large boom, just the reverse of what
was wanted.

There was, of course, the boat Philippe Dauchez was building
with his own hands; a small cruising vessel of 7·50 m. He had
begun by making a scale model of her which had pleased me.
Philippe first of all made his own yard, in reinforced concrete,
against a gable of his father's house at Lesconil. He felled by himself all the timber required for the main beams and frames; hauled
the cast-iron keel into place across the dunes by some shrewd work
with tackles (the lorry being unable to get as far) and had hand-
sawn, hour upon hour, her planking from the actual pitch-pine
logs.

Her construction was faultless and already sufficiently advanced
to presage an excellent result. But I knew that Philippe was hardly
disposed to sell or even lend his child, whom he had christened
Mordicus and to whom he clung truly 'mordicus' (tooth and nail).
No, she was quite out of the question.

I then remembered the eleven metre cruising boat I had seen the
year before in the Chantiers de la Liane in Boulogne. After all, she
mightn't yet be sold, or even finished (which would enable me to
complete her as I liked).

I called up the manager of the yard, who told me she was indeed
finished, but not yet rigged. She was going to be on view in Paris
at the Salon Nautique. No; she was not yet sold. I made an offer
of the amount of my old estimate, which was accepted in principle. It was thus I bought Winnibelle in three minutes on the
telephone.

I recall the moment when I again found myself in the lift on the way to my flat. A shaky cage of a thing, subject to sinister creakings and of a proverbial slowness. Morning and evening I had the time, between the ground and fourth floor, to open and read all correspondence, glance at prospectuses and run through the papers.

This time it seemed to have an uncalled for sprightliness. I was unable to fix my attention on a letter which I had read at least three times before; and I began to regret the fact that I had not come up by the stairs to give me a little time to think. An indefinite atmosphere of hostility seemed to float in the air; the sort of thing that lies in wait for husbands when they have just shaved off their moustaches without warning, or have bought a car, after spending the previous evening running cars down, or have found in their coat pocket an urgent letter handed to them a week previously addressed to their better half, or when they realise they're unable to say 'truly rural' properly; or again, when they've just bought a boat for 150,000 francs for which they have neither the slightest need nor the first 'sou' in cash. In a word, my conscience felt like the back of a stove. The shadow of the landings kept passing over the frosted glass. It would have taken very little to make me press the return button. Finally, I seized my bunch of keys with the determined gesture of one prepared to sell his life dearly, and with my throat dry, got off in front of my door.

My wife has an excellent recipe, which I well know is most unusual in her sex, for making one eat the bread of repentance, or at least preventing one from savouring the full pleasure of doing what one likes; this simple recipe consists in putting on a bright smile; in seeing your point of view at once; and finally, in declaring that one's decisions are stamped with the utmost apropos, especially when they don't hold water. To lay you low, there's nothing like pulling the obstacle away just when you are going to jump.

I asked her, with a most casual air if, in the event of my buying another boat, she would be very much against it. 'Not at all,' she replied, 'Why?'

Had I perhaps some idea in my head? Yes? How funny! She suspected it! But what sort of one? As big as that? Magnificent! What yard? Well I never! Oh yes, she had heard me mention them! And what are you going to do with it? Oh, yes! Naturally! To America? How foolish of her! She knew already! No, no, quite useless to protest. No, she couldn't come with me! She had a whole lot of other things to do! And then, possibly that sort of boat wouldn't be so comfortable. Yes, she did feel she might be seasick. Keep it a secret? But, what did one take her for? Oh, yes, she was sure everything would go well—absolutely on ball-bearings.

And, by the way, I must get busy with stores and medicines. One cannot be too careful. She'd look after that herself, and at once.

I was staggered. Everyone has their own sort of courage. I haven't got that sort.

From that moment, I was up to the neck in a series of trials and complications which I had never for an instant foreseen.

I had to put up with the shoulder-shrugging of the yard foreman who thought me a madman: my ideas must certainly have seemed outlandish to him from the moment I was unable to explain my reasons for them.

When the doctor came to the flat, to examine me and make all sorts of blood-tests for my life insurance, there was a tempest of whispers behind the door.

When the English architect, Laurent Giles, saw the layout of my shrouds, he raised his arms to heaven and said it was 'ridikool'. From his point of view he was right, except that my system had been worked out for all sorts of other ends which escaped him; such as using wooden ratlines and a special rig for following winds.

Henri, my sailor friend, whom I had asked to come and keep an eye on her completion, was in an excellent position to see through some of these 'mysteries', but not being of an inquisitive nature simply kept a heavy silence, which depressed me much more than any questions.

My son was by no means the least astute, in another kind of way. When I returned to Boulogne he heard us talking of the sea: he saw clothes he knew well being taken out of wardrobes. He had a good look at all the photographs on the table. He realised something was in the air and finally began to question me with annoying accuracy.

It is much more difficult than one imagines to put a boy of five off
the scent.

I had to bring my notary into the scheme. By a curious coincidence he was also Alain Gerbault's, for we both hailed from the
same part of the country. However, this most excellent man did
not call it a coincidence at all, but a fatality, nor did he refrain from
shaking his head in sorrow.

We decided to name the boat Winnibelle II. There was already
a ship's boat called Winnie Belle in Chausey, after my daughter
Winnie and Bonnie Belle, a Ramsgate smack, whose derelict hull,
hard aground just by the house, had formerly been used as a store
for fishing gear.

But, by a bookish influence that I now regret, I telescoped it to
make it more like Dulcibella, the name of the little boat in *The
Riddle of the Sands* by Erskine Childers, a book I love.

I was anxious to get her copper sheathing completed before the
Salon Nautique, but had no time to get them to instal the engine.
Winnibelle reached Paris nevertheless, at the highest speed she has
ever logged, dragged by the nose behind a tractor.

Halfway there, she managed to knock her stem against the arch
of a bridge. I mention this to show her toughness—the bridge it
was that fell. I was not in Paris myself when she arrived, but someone wrote to me at the time, saying that he had seen a cruising
vessel of about fifteen metres coming round a street corner, 'a boat
to go round the world in'! Ha! ha! Doubtless he exaggerated her
size somewhat, for on land boats always look enormous: once at
sea the impression one gets is far otherwise. . . .

During the Salon, she was more than once criticised on account
of a certain twist in the after-deck, and for her absence of bulwarks;
two things I always meant to alter.

In the long run, quite a number of alterations had to be made.
The accommodation was perfect; french-polished mahogany (even
in the fo'c'sle) with white enamel panels. The upholstery and
cushions came from the workshop of some decorator then in vogue.
She was really too luxurious for the uses I intended to put her to.
(But as the boat was being shown in this way as an exhibition
model, I naturally benefitted.) On the other hand, the skylight
fastenings, ironwork, bottle-screws, bolts on the drawers, etc. were

not made for really serious cruising. The cockpit was too wide and not deep enough, the boom much too weak, and so on. . . . As the season was too advanced to hope to be able to fit out that year, I had all the time I wanted to study these details. The Winnibelle, therefore, again took the road to Boulogne, just as she had come, and resumed her place under the shed in the shipyard. . . .

CHAPTER VII

REALISATION

I HAVE not the least desire to force a description of my pocket cruiser on the reader, who, if he is bored by such details, can skip the whole of this chapter. I am going to turn the cock full on in the matter of technical terms, so as to be able to do without all that later on, at least, if the pressure's not too great.

I never knew exactly where the Winnibelle's plans came from. I imagine originally they were American, more or less rehashed. I wrote to the architect whom I thought responsible; he replied that he had indeed designed a very similar vessel, which had shown good results in speed, particularly to windward.

It did not seem to me, however, that Winnibelle would be a very fast boat. She lacked nothing in character, but would have, very manifestly, the defects of her qualities, as always when one has character. For example, by virtue of her draught, which was considerable, and her narrow shape, she would make headway close-hauled in steep seas; but as she had a narrow bilge she would heel rapidly and would roll a lot before the wind.

This lack of inherent stability of form was compensated by her keel (more than five tons) which made her a boat almost impossible to capsize. For me, this was the essential thing.

Her great length of keel would prevent her being flighty, that is to say, it would be a comparatively simple matter to keep her on her course with the helm lashed. On the other hand, this same great length of keel and the small amount of difference in her draught, bow and stern, would give her a slow helm. She had a small rudder, bound solidly with iron, which removed any fear of damage at this spot, but it was more than probable that she would be sluggish, not to say troublesome, in going about.

One could equally foresee, with the sail plan I laid down, a well balanced, but rather stiff vessel: hardly the thing for racing, but much to be preferred for offshore work in hard winds. One can't have everything: but one must know how to get over certain dis-

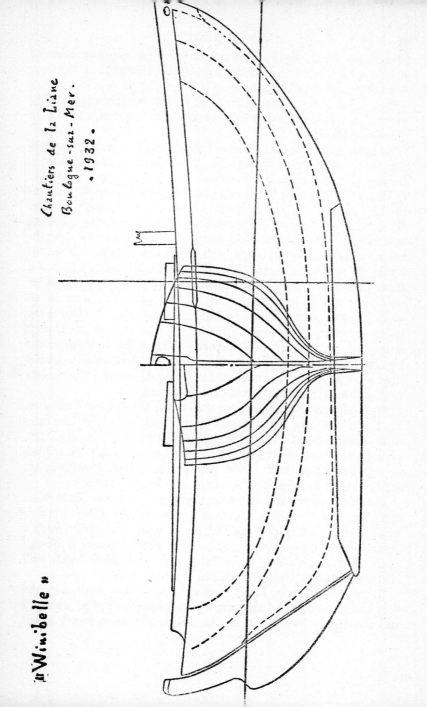

"Winibelle"

Chantiers de la Liane
Boulogne-sur-Mer.
. 1932 .

advantages. If one only wants comfort and the greatest inherent stability, then one had certainly better buy a barge. . . . My boat was not for fair-weather sailors.

Take a modern lifeboat of 30 to 40 ft. for example, and costing more than a half-million francs—well, I don't recommend it as a pleasure craft.

As to Winnibelle's construction and accommodation, the former was first-class; bronze fastenings, copper bottom and riveting—the latter could not be more practical.

There was plenty of headroom in all cabins and even in the fore-castle, a great thing, and moreover unusual in a vessel of this size. Working from the bow aft, the forecastle contained two comfort-able bunks with drawers underneath; then came the W.C., wash-basin, and hanging cupboard; amidships the saloon, with settee bunks on each side, centre table, racks and book-shelves as usual; aft of that, at the foot of the companion on one side, a small galley with sink and a stove in gimbals, so that one could cook in all weathers, and on the other a roomy bunk, the owner's. Having the galley and the best bunk well aft is a thing I consider essential, as it is there pitching is least felt—what's bad for the cooking pots is bad for the sleeper, and what upsets the cups and saucers equally upsets the stomach. In ocean racing it should never be necessary to sleep a man in the bows, except in flat calms.

Right aft was a separate compartment for the engine. I installed a 9 h.p. two-stroke Diesel made by the Societe Lilloise (the only small French Diesel then in existence). Her tanks held 180 litres, giving a range of about 280 miles at an average of 4 knots. Quite enough for what I wanted (on trial her maximum speed was 4·2 knots and her cruising speed 3·8 knots at 900 revolutions).

The deck appeared comparatively clear, with no deckhouse, cabin top or other useless impedimenta; from bow aft were the fore hatch, simply a trap-door closing down on rubber bands, with a central screw (the only really watertight system I know); a fife-rail at the foot of the mast; the cabin skylight; the main hatch, and lastly, the cockpit. Everything in the accepted style.

In the matter of rig, I had espoused, not without hesitation, the very simple solution of adopting a pilot vessel's sail plan, with gaff and completely loose foot, i.e. no boom. The controversy about

Marconi rig and the old-style peaked sails has raged too long to tempt me to put my finger in the pie. The Bermudian sail was never without disadvantages from the beginning, but it has swept the board. If I refused to adopt it, it was in no retrograde spirit, but simply because the pilot rig, the principal advantage of which, like the Marconi, is in eliminating one spar of two (although here it was the boom instead of the gaff), gave for equal sail areas, certain advantages in my case—particularly and categorically:

1. To allow of a very short mast, so that in consequence one had nothing to worry about in the matter of shrouds, particularly regarding stretching.
2. To be able to drop the sail in a twinkling, without leaving the helm; without even heaving on a down-haul. (The two halliards led into the cockpit and I had only to let them go without moving.)
3. Realising I would often be running before the wind I feared accidental gybes, which can be catastrophic when one has a boom, but are not in the least dangerous when there is only a gaff.
4. With an eye to the possibility of breakages, I wanted to carry a spare spar, and I had room to stow on deck a gaff, but not a boom. On all counts, I preferred to keep the lighter of the two spars. In a cyclone I could unbend the mainsail completely, stow the gaff on deck, and make the best of it.

I must add that I do not like roller booms, with which I have frequently had sensational troubles. Even with a crew it isn't always easy to roll up a sail correctly in reefing. And one knows what a job it can be single-handed. It is by no means as practical as people always make out. Let heavy weather come, and it's a question of rolling, rolling, more and more till it's a positive nightmare. Eventually, if it gets worse still, one usually has to get a storm try-sail out of the locker, get it ready for hoisting away, stow the mainsail, make fast the boom as well as one can—and all that b——business.

I find it a great deal simpler to ease the mainsail down gradually as I want, thanks to halliards within arm's length, pass a lashing ready to hand, a gasket through the earing, and tie up half a dozen reef-points without hurrying. If it comes on to blow really hard and I am reefed down completely, she is just as if under a trysail, that is to say, the third reef band runs diagonally, with gaff well peaked up and no boom to worry about.

Consequently I didn't even have to order a trysail, for I should never have had any use for it.

From photographs I have of Winnibelle, this rig, without being elegant, gives her quite a workmanlike look with her old-fashioned reef-bands.

The question remains whether such a rig is good to windward. To this I would reply frankly, no. It is not up to a Bermudian sail, at least, if the latter is of normal size—and that means a tidy bit of canvas to look after. Not everyone realises that a boat the size of the Winnibelle, if Marconi rigged, would have a mast about 50 ft. high, that is to say, the height of a fourth floor flat in Paris: I speak of normal height for cruising.

Anyone single-handed, if he is wise, should content himself with much less, unless he likes trouble. For that you only want a nice stormy night, black as your hat, rain driving horizontally like bullets, a savage pooping sea and a jammed track, and then, adieu la musique!

If he knows his business he will have a shorter mast and in consequence a Bermudian sail of smaller area. And then, when the bad time comes, he will hardly be any better off, from the point of view of sail area, than the man who chose (as I did), a pilot's sail-plan of normal size.

When sailing single-handed, one must consider, before all else, ease of handling, which makes it possible to maintain consistently a sail area to suit the force of the wind. Unless of course, in uncertain weather or during the night, one is persuaded to take in a reef in advance, through sheer funk of work later on.

Remains the very real inconvenience of having to set up—and handle—a topsail. I must admit I never satisfactorily overcame this problem. After a time I gave up using it altogether and found myself encumbered with a topsail yard stowed on deck, which was never much use to me. There were undoubtedly times when I could have done with some sort of light topmast, on which I could have set a jib-headed sail.

My mast was of very moderate height. Made of two pieces of Oregon pine glued together, with a hollow centre, it was bound in four places by collars of high-grade steel which I had designed myself in such a way that they might serve at the same time as hounds, for the shrouds and backstays, and to take the hooks of the halliard blocks. All my shrouds were immediately interchangeable. The bobstay was in one piece; simply a thin bar of steel, without bottle-screws or any sort of complication. At anchor the chain could chafe on it without harm: if I hit any flotsam it made a fairly good shock-absorber.

I evolved a simple system of halliards by which I was able to work the tiller from the saloon. I found this arrangement most useful throughout my voyage. I could fix the helm without going on deck.

I also designed and fitted a device calculated to keep the boat on her course with the wind dead aft, but I will return to that at the right moment.

I may say that all Winnibelle's gear was of the best quality and that there was plenty of it: anchors, chains, lights, instruments, spare sails and warps, etc., etc. . . .

To sum up, the Winnibelle hardly differed at first sight from any number of other cruising vessels, except in the details I have outlined previously, viz.:

1. Loose-footed sail with 3rd reef-band running diagonally (balance reef).
2. Peak and throat halliards leading into the cockpit with hand winches.
3. Double fore-stay, allowing one to change foresails instantly and also making it possible to set two fanwise, braced out square, with the sheets led out on two booms, in following winds.
4. The braces of the foresail booms led to the tiller, working it automatically.
5. Halliards on the tiller, allowing control from the saloon.
6. Interchangeable shrouds; bobstay of bar steel.
7. Closing cockpit (sliding cover).
8. Propeller under the quarter, without external wood seating.

A large horse of tubular steel, built into the stern, supported the extremity of the gaff when the mainsail was stowed. It was very strong, and proved most useful to hold on to when standing in the stern-sheets, or as protection from the main sheet blocks when they banged about at head-level in going about. I also used it to take my stern light, a small searchlight and a cine-projector; in short, it was by no means the least valuable part of my lay-out.

CHAPTER VIII
THE CHANNEL

THE Winnibelle II was launched in February 1933, in the presence of the Administrateur de la Marine, and the Inspecteur de la Navigation, as well as Lloyd's and Veritas' agents. My wife broke the traditional bottle of wine, not without the usual two or three mis-hits, and Winnibelle took the water bow first, well and truly.

That evening it blew hard, and the following day the deck was covered with a foot of snow which froze solid almost at once, greatly hampering the final work afloat. However I was well content. I got on very well with the people in the yard and now and then we met for long yarns in an inn on the bank of the Liane, run by a certain Charlie, an Englishman, who made excellent tea, and put us up in an enormous room heated with a stove, which was always red hot.

Henri slept on board and was nearly frozen stiff with the cold during the first night. We got hold of a stove, and as a result in the mornings found the snow melted on deck just above the saloon, though nowhere else.

Meanwhile I had to return to Paris, and only managed to get back a fortnight later in time to get under way.

Winnibelle looked very good with her burgee flapping at the masthead, but was too light in the water, and I had, at the last moment, to load a ton and a half of lead waste sold to me at an astronomic figure. Everyone was most curious to know what my boomless mainsail looked like. Early in the afternoon the compass was swung, as usual by the Principal of the School of Navigation with two pupils, whilst we sailed about in the outer harbour in a bitter wind. It was a long time since I had been afloat and the cold got at me at first, though formerly I had never really noticed it.

Following immemorial custom, the carpenters were still working on board. I have never seen yard workmen get their tools together otherwise than under the threat of sailing off with them. I dashed ashore, bought a bottle of rum while they got the dinghy inboard, and we were off to Cowes. . . . Night was falling as Henri took the helm. He heaved a great sigh; everything was going well and in a little while we should know more about her.

The running gear was very stiff, but although her sails were not yet stretched they inspired confidence. Ever since her launching she had made a certain amount of water, but this did not worry us much. A forgotten fastening, no doubt, as sometimes happens in newly built vessels. Nevertheless we had to keep pumping to stop the water flooding the cabin floor when she listed—giving us a first subject for recrimination. Water also came in through the sink drainpipe, which had to be blocked up.

We made our landfall in thick fog the following evening off the Nab Tower, after having had to make a long board to clear Beachy Head. The enormous tower of the Nab is surmounted by a foghorn, which emits a mocking sort of toot like a child's trumpet. It carries excellently nevertheless. It was here I got into the most ridiculous mess imaginable. I was under the impression that the tide was setting us steadily on to the tower, and that I was only getting past it very slowly, in spite of a fresh breeze which gave us about 6 knots through the water. Suddenly the sails started shaking, and I shouted to Henri that the wind had shifted; then I had a look at the compass and was dumbfounded; in the fog, as though hypnotised by the Nab, which was very close, I had managed to put her completely about—a sort of vertigo in the horizontal plane.

On the stroke of midnight, just as we were letting go the anchor in the roads, a violent squall came down on us, and Henri had to go aloft to free the mainsail as the throat halliard had jammed. This little affair lasted half an hour; the usual thing with new rope. We had to change two halliards which were too big for their sheaves, and certain blocks.

I got at Pascall Atkey's in Cowes the remainder of my gear, mostly things only procurable in England: certain special sorts of cleat, a Primus stove in gimbals, a pair of hand winches for the halliards, as well as a lot of other odds and ends. Atkey is a most engaging sort of chap, a real individualist. He is a little ship enthusiast and his own vessel was the only one in commission at Cowes at that time of year. We used often to warm ourselves at the coal stove in his saloon, where he liked to spend entire afternoons. His talk was a mine of information on little details of equipment. Sometimes he came on board the Winnibelle to have a drink of real French coffee, which he firmly believes only a Frenchman can make.

He and I were no strangers, as I had several times competed in the Cowes-Dinard race, usually in the Minoru, and was a member of the local club, the Island Sailing Club. Atkey has the art of telling sea stories, of which he has an inexhaustible fund, and he would sit the while, winking slyly and sucking a clay pipe, hardly ever properly alight. In a general way he has a 'chic' altogether his own, thanks to an assortment of berets and pea-jackets, the like of which I have never seen on anyone else.

Every Sunday, when the shop was closed, this delightful fellow used to get under way and take the papers to the keepers of the Spit lightship, which lay some distance off. From there he just used to let the tide take him under short canvas up and down the Solent, sometimes to the east, sometimes to the west, and would lunch peacefully under way, with his one old hand.

'One day', he confided to me, 'I made a present of this boat to my son, but he likes cars better. So I bought it back from him.'

The day after our arrival we made two rather disagreeable discoveries. First, we found that one of the propeller blades had been buckled during the launching, which explained the lamentable performance of the motor, which had greatly puzzled us. And then the topsides had a deplorable appearance: the magnificent enamel paintwork, of which I had been so proud on the day of the launch, was coming off in flakes as though she had leprosy. The last coat must have been put on in frost. And now it never stopped raining, which prevented us repainting, and friend Atkey did not spare his sarcasm.

He kept us company as far as the Needles on the day we left; he used never to go further.

'I have never succeeded', he said, 'in getting round the Isle of Wight in a day, at least under sail.'

Passing alongside we threw him a kilo of sugar. He was short of it, and the matter was as serious as if he had been single-handed in mid-Ocean; tea without sugar, on the stroke of five, is a tragedy to an Englishman. From Cowes to the Needles we had made it a race, and he beat us so easily that it was positively laughable. It certainly was a fact, as we had already thoroughly confirmed, that Winnibelle was hampered by her propeller and that her small mainsail made her sluggish.

We re-crossed the Channel in thick fog. I remember a tanker that practically shaved us, and also a large motor vessel, probably a passenger boat, whose powerful compressed air fog-horn I heard for over an hour, each time louder and louder, as she came straight at us. Finally I heard her engines and felt her so near that I called Henri, who had turned in below. But he confined himself to remarking that he was not asleep, that he heard her just as well as I did, and that 'she'd give us plenty of room'. Room she did give us as it turned out, but there was none to spare.

We made Alderney just in time to escape an equinoctial blow. I shall not easily forget that night. Sheltered by the mole, Winnibelle rode it out at two anchors, the cables veered to the last link and stoppered to avoid snubbing. We had to keep watch all night in a deluge of rain, booted and in oilskins, determined to get under way, if the anchors began to drag, rather than let her drift at high water to the bottom of the anchorage. At every gust she lay over as if she were under sail. The sea beat against the mole with a noise like thunder and the spray rose to a prodigious height. The noise was fearful, we had to shout in each other's ears to make ourselves heard.

During the night I had one of the nastiest frights of my life. I had gone below to make some tea on the Primus, which was swinging gently in its weighted gimbals. Henri had gone forward to keep an eye on the anchor chains, which were chafing against the bobstay. As he could not see very well in the dark, he had dropped down till his feet were on the steel bar of the bobstay, the water coming halfway up his boots at each plunge. He was there for perhaps five minutes. When the tea was ready I came up the companion to call him . . . the deck was bare!

To relieve my conscience I jumped below and looked everywhere, even in the forepeak and engine room—nobody! I came up on deck again, and as he certainly was not anywhere there, I believed he had fallen overboard, which meant quite clearly that he was lost, for one could not handle a dinghy in a storm of this sort with any hope of success, or in fact, do anything to save him in any way whatsoever. Suddenly I saw him come up from under the bowsprit and clamber calmly on to the foredeck. I was in such a state of fright that I couldn't say a word of reproach nor, I hardly know why, did I ever refer to the incident subsequently. In a later chapter I shall have something to say about the practical disadvantages of being only two on board a boat.

During a period of calm which preceded a shift of the wind to the N. E., we were able to enter the inner harbour, which though small is well protected, and there we had peace. The gale lasted a week.

In these waters, where tides and currents run strong and the dangers of the coast are never far off, a sailing vessel, however seaworthy and whatever her tonnage, should keep in harbour during the equinox. It was on the coast and not out at sea that ships used to founder, nine times out of ten. The great barques and full rigged ships which used to sail the ocean from the Indies, America and all over the world, commonly ended their career on the rocks of Cornwall, Southern Ireland or Brittany. After rounding Cape Horn and the Hope, scraping past icebergs in the Atlantic, weathering typhoons in the China seas and battling successfully against all the perils of deep waters, they came to grief at last near their journey's end, at home, as you might say.

Alderney is as curious and original an island as any I know. As the crow flies it is but 250 miles from Paris, and nine from Cape La Hague. The Channel traffic all passes in sight of it; all the great transatlantic liners on their way to or from New York are in a sense familiar with it; yet its population of some 1,600 souls was literally cut off from the world until quite recently, when the planes linking Southampton and Jersey took to landing there. Even today the Island has very little connection with France, not only because Alderney is under the British flag, but because the Raz Blanchard, which one must cross to reach Cherbourg, presents a more or less impassable barrier to the sort of small craft used by the local fisher folk.

Twice a week only the Courier, a small steam vessel, brings letters, freight and passengers from Guernsey. There are very few tourists, as one may well imagine. To get from Cherbourg to

Alderney you must take the cross channel packet to Southampton, then take another to Jersey, and then wait for the Courier's sailing date.

For this very reason Alderney is to me a blessed land, where I often dream of spending a winter. Except for a few retired English officers, who go there for peace and quiet and to play golf or prop up the bars (according to the weather), the inhabitants live by their work, and have a social system rarely found elsewhere. I had visited the place more than once with my brother, and we very soon got to know people. Chausey is barely sixty miles away, and people who live on little islands understand each other very quickly. At the dances and parties to which we were invited, we were surprised to meet chaps in immaculate evening dress whom we knew well by day as lorry or bus-drivers (there are excellent motor buses in the island), or it might be some shop girl, perfectly gowned, from whom that very afternoon one had bought a dozen handkerchiefs. This may be usual enough in New York, for example, but is not quite the same thing in this corner of the old world. At the same time, such differences as there were in social levels seemed to be solely a matter of the length of the family tree, without reference to money. Amongst them were some who could trace their descent to the time of the Conqueror; these usually spoke Norman-French as well as English.

Parliamentary sessions, for there is a Parliament, as in Jersey or Guernsey, are opened and closed in Norman-French. The lawyers and teachers usually study and take their degrees at the Universities of Caen or Rennes.

The arrival of the Winnibelle at this unwonted time of the year attracted some notice, and we were cordially welcomed at Marais Hall, one of the hotels in St Anne, the little town perched on top of the island.

One evening when we were there later than usual, a chimney caught fire, which Henri and I put out more by luck than cunning, water being scarce at the top of the hill. From then on we were not allowed to pay for a meal.

The Chief Magistrate, Mr Mellish, was courtesy and kindness itself. Whenever there was any sort of a meeting I was regularly invited to appear on the platform in company with the parson and

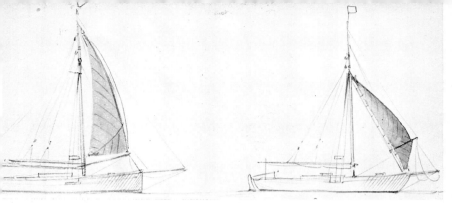

Twin Spinnakers   Twin Staysails

Twin staysails will give a better lift in a sea-way

Under Way

The spinnaker drawing

The tiller working by itself

curate. Below the town, at Port de Bray, we used to have interminable talks with the pilots. In Alderney half the fishermen are pilots. There is a fair amount of traffic, for every day small cargo boats come in to load crushed stone (which is particularly durable here) for roadmaking in England. The Harbour Master was an old sailing-ship captain of very commanding presence, always dressed smartly in a frock coat with gilt buttons and always preceded by his dog carrying his stick or paper.

Notwithstanding all the charm of this peaceful spot, with its pubs by the harbour where we used to play skittles or shove ha'penny from morning till night, the time came when we had to leave. Cigarettes at Alderney are cheaper than elsewhere, about half the English price, as there is no tax, so I laid in a good supply before setting out for Chausey, with a head wind, of course.

Once again it was brought home to me that the Winnibelle was an indifferent performer to windward, by reason of her small sail area. In the middle of the night this fault very nearly put an untimely end to her career just south of Jersey. Try as we might, she would not come about; there was nothing for it but to wear her round, in the course of which manœuvre, while the wind was aft, we were carried much too near some very unpleasant-looking rocks. They were just awash, and the broken water was distressingly visible despite the darkness.

At last the Winnibelle was on her mooring at Chausey, a few cable lengths off my home.

Her arrival was a local event, and the fishermen, most of whom, as already mentioned, had been my friends from childhood, lost no time in sizing up the new boat. The mainsail came in for plenty of criticism, nor did her sluggardly helm escape notice. We left again shortly for St Malo, where I took on board food, paraffin, and endless parcels and packages. The customs officers, intrigued by all this loading, kept me under close observation wherever I went.

I had her out of the water at La Richardais and ripped off several square metres of her sheathing in an endeavour to find the famous leak, but the caulker himself was baffled, and we only half succeeded. Water still came in, though much less. It was maddening.

I was stung by the Customs for a log bought at Cowes, and had

c

endless difficulty in getting them to seal the tobacco from Alderney. The douaniers were not the only people to be intrigued by what was going on. Henri himself could not understand it at all. He did not know where to stow all the stuff I was bringing on board; the saloon was full up, forecastle likewise; 100 cases of condensed milk, 150 litres of oil, 140 kilos of sea-biscuits, and everything else in proportion. At last one day he was given an enormous roll of charts from Paris; as usual, he undid the parcel, and saw with stupefaction charts of the coasts of Africa, Guiana, Mexico, the Bermudas. . . . To crown all, a case arrived at the same time with a complete collection of Pilotage Instructions for these waters. I found him in the saloon, in the middle of examining this consignment.

'Well, well. What's the bearing of all this?' he asked in a meaning tone.

I pretended they must have been sent by mistake, and kept my secret.

It was at St Malo that I met Capt. Amicel, whom we shall come across again later. He turned up one day at a little café by the harbour, where we were having lunch, sat down with us and told us that he had just lost his ship, the Teresa, in a most fantastic way. She was a fine three-masted schooner, fitted out for the Newfoundland fishing. The day before, as they were leaving for the banks, she had been jammed in the lock-gates by the buoyage-vessel which, in trying to get past her, had stuck fast. As the water-level sank, the two ships settled down further and further into the lock chamber, and it was not long before they broke each other open. Amicel, still shaken by this drama, had come to St Malo to make his report to the Marine Superintendent and the underwriters.

'Ah well, so much the worse,' he sighed. 'For twenty-two years I've always been on the banks at this season of the year. For twenty-two years I've never seen the strawberries ripen. Not having a ship now, I shall see them this year, whether I like it or not.'

One does not realise that these people see their own country only in winter time.

The Winnibelle was baptized officially at Cancale, on Easter Sunday. My friend Rochard, who was going to live aboard with me till I took my departure, came on the Paris train just in time to

join us. At Cancale also I said goodbye to my wife, who was returning to Paris, where she would stay until I set sail. We had made this
decision quite mutually: I was not very keen, and nor was she
either, I believe, on a scene of actual farewell, waving handkerchiefs and all that sort of thing. There was a crowd of fishermen
and other onlookers, whose presence, apart from anything else,
prevented us prolonging our adieux. My boat lay right alongside
the pontoon, with everything set. I only had to sheer her off and
the Winnibelle began to move ahead at once.

Two mornings later we dropped anchor in the outer harbour at
Douarnenez, having made the passage at an average of seven knots,
passing the Vierge light to the north of Brest. I had a new mainsail,
which seemed to give better results, and kept the old one as a spare.
From here Henri returned by train to St Malo as his classes at the
School of Navigation were starting the day after. When we separated on the Douarnenez Station platform he looked at his feet for
quite a time. The engine whistled, and just before he jumped in,
he embraced me. I was both surprised and deeply touched.

Since then we have often sailed together, but I have never re-
ferred to this incident any more than to the other one at Alderney,
when I thought he was lost overboard.

I jumped into a taxi at the station and got on board as quickly as
possible, having realised that I had forgotten to wind the chronometer, a lapse that was to recur more than once before I accustomed
myself to the necessity of winding it up every day exactly at the
same time.

It was very difficult to get on or off the ship where we lay at
Douarnenez. I no longer had a boat for the purpose, as the dinghy
had been left at St Malo, to Henri's great indignation.

That night we had to get aboard, and Mr Marcel Laurent, a very
obliging fishmonger, lent us a punt so small that it was hardly big
enough for one man. We squeezed ourselves into it with anxious
care. I am not exactly thin and Rochard is almost as heavy. With
the two of us together it made quite a good balancing turn, as
there was only about a quarter of an inch of freeboard.

Regretting that we had dined far from wisely, and hardly daring
to breathe, we somehow, by means of infinitely delicate paddle-
strokes, regained the ship, amid the cheers and groans of half a

dozen sailors. To complete the picture there was quite a lop in the roads and the Winnibelle lay well out from the shore.

I accordingly decided to up anchor next morning and make fast at the other end of the town, alongside the coasters' quay in the river. This had its disadvantages as well, for we took the ground at each tide and had to watch her all the time to see she didn't list outwards when she touched; but at least we could get ashore straight away.

CHAPTER IX

THE OCEAN

I HAD selected Douarnenez as my point of departure, with New York as my goal. In New York I had arranged for an exhibition of my pictures to be held at the end of the summer: *they* would go by liner. The manager of the K. gallery in Paris undertook to announce my own shipment, though I could easily see that he was sceptical of the success of my voyage. At bottom, he was sure I was mad, or that I should change my mind at the last moment, or else that I should find a watery grave.

Never having been to New York was an additional attraction to my project. I should have an opportunity of exploring the market for marine prints, a thing I had long wanted to do. It also tickled my fancy to give a little of the character of a 'business trip' to a crossing which was in reality about as far removed from such a description as could well be. I tried to convince myself that 'it would not be altogether a waste of time', but all the same I had to laugh whenever I saw my face in the glass.

The distance which separates Europe from the United States of America is one of the greatest that passenger boats have to make without intermediate ports of call, and the companies who make the run boast of offering their clients 'the longest gang-plank in the world'. The transatlantic liners are, as is well known, the biggest and most powerful liners in existence, and go straight across the ocean, more or less.

For a sailing vessel it is an entirely different matter. From America to Europe she can keep a direct course, for the prevailing winds are favourable at all seasons, but going from Europe to America a sailing-vessel must make a considerable détour, far longer in actual distance, but quicker on account of the prevailing wind systems. There are two possible routes, Northabout and Southabout.

If your starting point is Gibraltar, or any port below the latitude of Vigo, there is no question of going Northabout, as you are

already close to the region of the Trade Winds, which blow
steadily towards America. You follow a wide southerly curve as far
as the neighbourhood of the Antilles, thence turn northwards
again until close to the American coastline, level with Bermuda,
where you pick up the Gulf Stream.

But he who sails from the Channel or the coasts of Britain may
be forgiven for hesitating. And I did hesitate. For example, to
strike the trade winds, on leaving Brest, you would have to get
down to the latitude of Casablanca, a strong test of patience, particularly as the Bay of Biscay is not always good-tempered or the
Portuguese waters as amiable as could be desired. Once there, you
reap the reward of your trouble; but many miles have gone for
nothing.

Northabout, the course is much shorter. It is hardly 2,000 miles
to St John's in Newfoundland, and a little more than 3,000 to New
York direct. By the South, you can reckon 4,000 miles from Gibraltar, or more than 5,000 if you take your departure from Douarnenez; say 2,000 miles further. On the other hand, the northern
route has many drawbacks: the seas are heavier, the wind, if not
dead contrary, keeps more or less regularly in the western sector,
so that a sailing vessel is close-hauled all the time, with the list, the
pitching and the discomfort, which inevitably result. Moreover,
the Gulf Stream, comparatively feeble though it is in the north,
runs contrary to your course.

In 1933 the little yacht Dorade, belonging to Rod and Olin
Stephens and designed by the latter, went north-about from England and successfully crossed the Atlantic in the wonderful time of
twenty-one days. The brothers Stephens, it may be added, had
just won the Atlantic Race from New York to Plymouth; before
long they were off again in the Bermuda Race, which they also
won, as well as a number of others during the ensuing year, notably
that to Honolulu. Dorade is but eighteen metres overall, and had
a crew of only six, but she is an extraordinary vessel and was in-
comparably handled.

What led me to flirt with the idea of choosing the northern passage, was not only that it is the shorter distance, but also because a
boat will sail herself without trouble close-hauled, so that one can
leave the helm for considerable periods; whereas running free or

with the wind dead aft, the problem, strange as it may appear to the landsman, is much more complicated.

However, three main considerations prevented me going North-about, all concerned with safety. First, the risk of collision along so frequented a route; second, atmospheric conditions, rain, mist, etc., which augment the above risk; and thirdly, the crossing of the Newfoundland Banks, where, far offshore, I should run into the fishing fleet, trawlers, sailing vessels, dories, etc., in incalculable numbers. To sleep in such waters was too heavy a responsibility. This problem is far less acute when there is a crew to keep permanent watch. The advantage of a quick trip in exchange for more prevalent bad weather, marked on the Pilot-charts by symbols showing percentages of winds greater than force '8' (Beaufort Scale), counted for nothing with me.

Finally, I preferred to abide by the Pilot-Charts rather than to follow my own whim. Based on the experience of our forefathers, they indicate the track of the trade winds for sailing vessels leaving the Channel for New York, or indeed for any other Port in the world. They are marked in thin blue lines, with here and there branch lines like railway tracks. For example, one line bifurcates on each side of Madeira, to indicate that you can go either side of the island, then bends towards the west, rejoins another line, coming up from the South Atlantic, and goes up towards Canada; and so on.

I have a great respect for these Pilot Charts, which in France are still called 'Wind Charts'. Some are published in England, others by the Weather Bureau of Washington, and they are issued monthly. Procurable in all ports of the world at very little cost, they are within the reach of all.

The big companies issue them to their ships in spite of their being less obviously necessary for steam vessels than for sailing-ships; for they not only show the direction of winds with their symbols of frequency, force, the percentage of calms and storms (for more than 120 areas spread over each Ocean), but they are kept up to date, with the tracks of cyclones, drifting ice, all reported wreckage, the annual change in magnetic variation, and a mass of other indispensable information; not to mention the tracks of steam-ships both slow and fast (in black) and sailing vessels (in blue).

These charts are the most instructive, I would even say the most thrilling in the world. I know no treatise, for example, in which the theory of cyclones is explained so clearly as it is on the back of these charts, however difficult it may be to put the said theory into practice.

CHAPTER X
DEPRESSION

THE open sea was not visible from the quayside at Porz Rhu where my boat lay alongside. Even if the island of Tristan had not blocked the horizon, one could only have seen the bay of Morgat, itself land-locked. But it had begun to blow hard immediately after our arrival, and the sky was a sufficient indication to make a sight of the sea unnecessary. Ragged clouds chased one another in quick succession, rising into view from behind the wooded hills and rushing across the sky. The glass could hardly have been lower, and fully bore out the opinion of the local douanier that the gale would be at least an all-night affair.

I had no intention of getting under way under these conditions. This may seem a little strange in view of the fact that a boat like mine is able in principle to tackle the heaviest weather; but it would have been lost labour. The wind was south to south-westerly, and I could have only made towards the west, which would have been no progress at all.

I had few weather reports. However, this sort of depression, the so called 'Depression over Iceland', is well known in our waters. It begins with a falling glass and south-east to southerly winds, which veer gradually towards the south-west. At this stage there is commonly a lull followed by a jump to the N.W., with the glass rising. If the rise is rapid the wind is more than likely to back, and the bad weather recommences. These cycles of depression some-times succeed each other for weeks on end.

Nevertheless, with summer coming on, I might reasonably have looked for an improvement, but for certain 'mares' tails' and little woolly patches which I could see high in the sky; pretty to the artist's eye but ominous to the seaman. The barometer stopped falling, then rose very sharply; the signs were quite unmistakable.

Day after day I stood by to clear, until the local population began to regard my continually deferred departure as a joke. . . . I used to say goodbye to them, and the day after they would come across me again, clumping along in my sabots on the uneven cobbles of the town, with a piece of cast iron or a coil of wire-rope in my hands.

'What, not gone yet?' they would exclaim. I laughed to avoid explanations.

I was in correspondence with Robert Somerset, who had recently sold the Jolie Brise, and bought the Nina, Paul Hammond's old boat, the winner of the New York–Santander transatlantic race. He wrote to me from Nassau, in the Bahamas, stating his opinion that it would be wise to leave not later than the beginning of April, in order to avoid the cyclones at the end of July in the Gulf Stream. And here I was at Douarnenez in May, with persistent bad weather which began at last to get on my nerves.

I read in one of his letters, dated March 5th:

'I'll try and answer your questions as well as I can, and give you all the advice that comes to my mind. Remember that when I say anything it is only my opinion of the moment; at sea one is constantly learning, and changing one's ideas; but I'll do my best.

'I recommend Antigua as a port of call in the Antilles. The island is conveniently situated; it's a magnificent place and you will find a spot there called English Harbour, where I was last year, and which I consider the finest in the world. You can tie up alongside the ruins of Nelson's old arsenal, and except for Dr O'Mahoney and his wife, who are friends of mine, you won't find a soul for miles around. However, I've no doubt you'll prefer a French colony.

'If I were you I would touch at Madeira to lay in fresh food, water, etc. At about 20° N. you should be sufficiently south, but if you don't find steady winds then, don't be afraid of going down to 2° or 3°. It pays every time. Take a pith helmet and a small tent with you; and one of those porous earthenware jars you hang up to keep your water cool.'

He went on to tell me many other things, such as the state of the sea in the trade wind belt. He told me he had encountered winds of more than 35 m.p.h. lasting for more than a week during the Jolie Brise's crossing. Regarding rig, his ideas coincided with mine: 'In general I don't believe in any special rig for following winds, such as a squaresail. I used two spinnakers, port and starboard, which worked excellently.'

I am not a squaresail enthusiast myself. Their gear is complicated, nor does their use enable the helm to be left for any considerable time. My experience in big square-rigged vessels has convinced me that the only method which really works is the old one with clew-lines, the sail being clewed to the yard. All the labour-saving devices, such as roller, curtain or other systems of stowing are, *pace* Conor O Brien, too tricky and unreliable. Moreover, O Brien always had a crew, which alters the problem in no small degree.

A squaresail looks very pretty and simple from a distance; seen close to, it is full of complications. It has to have a yard halliard, with tackle of course, a pair of sheets, a pair of tacks, a pair of brails, a pair of clew-lines, foot-ropes, reef-points, gaskets, etc. To dispense with any of these is asking for trouble. In addition the yard adds considerable top-hamper to the mast, and has to be lowered when your boat is close hauled.

O Brien says, truly enough, that he chose his course so as to carry favourable winds: but there are places where it is quite impossible to avoid variable winds, for example in the vicinity of the Bermudas, whither I was bound. No; a squaresail in a cyclone is definitely not my cup of tea.

Besides, I had settled on another idea, not exactly double spinnakers, but somewhat similar. Meanwhile, there was plenty to do in the way of minor details of internal economy, such as fitting tool racks, making shelves with holes to take every shape of bottle, or marking the heads and tacks of the jibs and foresails with red and black paint so as to distinguish them easily.

Rochard and I passed our time hammering, nailing, sawing, re-arranging and making inventories. Now and again we stopped talking to listen to a particularly fierce squall: nothing interrupts a conversation more effectively than that sudden howl in the rigging followed by the machine-gun rat-tat-tat of rain on the skylight. A shake of the head: 'Well, old man, as I was saying . . .'

We got a lot of fun out of a gramophone made almost entirely of cardboard which produced a noise the like of no other gramophone known to commerce. We had bought it for eighty-five francs in the bazaar at St Malo. The shop-girl was most indignant when I said:

'You see, Madame, the thing is I want to be able to throw it overboard with no regrets.' It never reached the end of a tune without running down and finishing on a most lamentable note, unless you made a dash to wind it up again. One day we bought some new records, and after hearing them on board, came to the conclusion, in absolute good faith, that they were not the ones we had tried in the shop. It was the turn of the dealer to be indignant when I asked for my money back. We got to know all our records almost by heart, so that after a time certain passages in 'Les vignes du Seigneur' or 'Marius' became positive catchwords, all the more so as the sound of our phonograph heightened the comedy of the lines. In this way the depressing atmosphere, the rain and the unpleasant smells of the quayside were kept at bay.

On every tide, more and more windbound coasters crowded into harbour, and poor Winnibelle eventually found herself squeezed into a corner rendered charming by the fragrance of a nearby sewer. One very wild night, when the gas lamps flickered uncertainly and she was bumping harder than usual against the stone quayside, I heard the beat of a heavy Bolinder engine. Then came the sound of voices and oaths, among which I thought I caught a rude remark directed at my vessel. I was accustomed to this and jumped ashore, barefoot among the puddles. A man half asleep had landed from a ship's boat and was trying to heave on my stern warps, undeterred by the fact that the bow ones were still fast. At the same time he was struggling to bring across an enormous hawser without noticing it had fouled my mast. The vague mass of a sailing vessel, her auxiliary motor vomiting sparks, could just be made out. The voices only reached me in fits and starts: the skipper of the coaster, deafened by the noise of his engine, could hear nothing. Frightened of grounding before he could tie up, he was beside himself with rage, and before long I was in the same condition. He was threatening all and sundry with violent death and had no idea of the true state of affairs. In the end I had to slack off his hawser myself and pass it, not without difficulty, under the Winnibelle's keel.

I found my man the next day in Mother Le Meur's bar and we became the best friends in the world after a few rather stormy introductory words on the subject of the night's happenings.

'That c. . . . of a boat of yours,' he had said.

'I should like to know in what way my boat is more of a c. . . . than yours?'

He had been trying to make Audierne from Brest and had kept at it for two days without success. The coaster skippers are a tough race. They sail with small crews, sometimes only two hands or even only a man and boy for a thirty to forty ton vessel. I take off my hat to them.

Their knowledge of the French coast is so thorough that they often dispense with charts and are content with a tide-table and almanack. We listened one day with awe to two skippers arguing about the buoys and lights at the entrance to Roscoff. The chart they used to make their points, and which was nailed in fact to the cabin bulkhead, was neither more nor less than a map of Britanny, published by the Crédit Lyonnais, with a lot of blue circles on it which, far from denoting the position and visibility of lights, merely indicated the offices and branches of the Bank. I leave to the imagination how roughly the coastline was marked on this un-expected document. . . .

The Winnibelle, compared with these vessels, seemed very small. She attracted plenty of interest, as few yachts are in com-mission in the Channel at this time of year. Groups of sailors used to stand on the quay alongside and discuss her. I could overhear them perfectly well from the cabin, particularly when the hatch was closed and they thought I was away. Certain things particu-larly intrigued them: for example the sheet winches, the cockpit cover, and the double forestays. Generally they appreciated at a glance the fact that here was a deep sea vessel. They observed the spare gear, not only lashed but secured as well by wrought iron straps bolted to the deck; the copper bottom and the unusually heavy standing rigging. There were always a few who made caustic remarks, which sometimes did and sometimes did not amuse me. A frequently repeated comment was: 'He'll swallow more water than wine!' I am no water-fan.

There were often arguments and even blows on the quayside, I was always afraid some drunk would fall, not into the river. which would be a small matter, but on to my deck. Again and again I urged the disuptants to have it out elsewhere. Their wives used to run up from every point of the compass and drive the fighters off with hefty swipes of their sabots, clouting guilty and innocent alike. An hour after, the row would start all over again.

'Look,' one man would say, 'in that thing you could be in Marseilles in a brace of shakes; twenty-four hours and there you are!'

'Go on, listen to him! Marseilles! Why, I wouldn't even cross the Channel in her!'

'Oh, you wouldnt? And since when has it been necessary to cross the Channel to get to Marseilles?'

'Well, anyway I tell you it would take more than twenty-four hours.'

'More than twenty-four hours?'

'Yes, forty-eight at least!', etc., etc.

In point of fact eighteen to twenty days would be a fair estimate, and no time wasted.

I had let it be thought that I was on my way to the Mediterranean by way of Gibraltar. The Harbour Master, Captain Mainguy, knew that I intended to sail single-handed. Every other morning he used to arrive alongside on the quay, with his umbrella, which he always carried rolled even if it was raining. Deep-sea skippers affect umbrellas. This one had been in command of the Vincennes three-masted barque for eighteen years. He made no attempt to conceal his disapproval of my not shipping a hand, but provided we kept off that subject, we could yarn happily for hours on end about the old clippers, ships like the Versailles, which I had known well and which was a sister-vessel of the Vincennes. Were we right or wrong to regret the days of sail? 'I have known men who had no regrets for all that,' says Francis André, adding, 'It is true they lacked the poetic touch.'

I filled up my watertanks regularly every day as they emptied, and used to repair to the street fountain with a couple of buckets. Fresh bread had been delivered for the third time, thrown with a crash on deck by the baker's man from his van.

As I wanted to be able to get away without delay when the time came, I used also to go now and then to the public wash-house to avoid having to entrust my linen to the laundry, where it would have been kept for several days. There, surrounded by peasant women in 'coiffes' chattering in Breton, I washed my shirts and handkerchiefs, and did my best to dry them afterwards strung on a line on board. In general, women dislike seeing a man do his own washing, and more than once the affair was taken out of my hands by some gnarled-fisted, lynx-eyed old person of deceptively terrifying aspect. I had already had similar experiences at Reykyavik, in Iceland, when the crew of the Pourquoi-Pas? went by watches to the hot springs which served as municipal wash-houses, just outside the town. The Iceland women and girls watched us with good-humoured contempt, and it must be confessed that we hardly shone at the game: the water there is literally boiling, so that washing can only be managed with the help of certain wooden contraptions with which naturally we were unprovided. In the end they took charge and washed for the lot of us, to everyone's complete satisfaction.

There was also the question of bread. Faddy or not, I prefer bread to biscuit, and very hard baked bread, the sort they make specially in fishing ports for boats leaving for a spell of work, which keeps a fortnight without going mouldy. I ordered a consignment regularly, but at the end of a week had to renew the order and throw the old lot overboard, it being then unwanted by anyone even for chickenfeed.

As we had to tend her at each tide, we were practically confined to the harbour. One day the Winnibelle took the bottom and listed outwards. This gave us plenty to do; we had to prop her up well and truly with oil drums and an old telegraph pole we were lucky enough to find close by.

The glass of my large compass was cracked. I had trodden on it. Of course, there was no specialist in the place, nor was there time to send to Paris. So I had to resign myself to a leak which would have to be made good from time to time.

The fishing harbour, as I have said, is on the far side of the town. We spent hours there, watching the huge round-bellied ketches with their massive spars getting under way for North Africa or returning with cargoes of eight or ten tons of crayfish. There were Channel trawlers too, regularly discharging their tens of thousands of mackerel and other fish for canning, and sardine boats of every shape and size, old and new. The activity of the port is unbelievable, and the bars are all packed with hard-swearing men in patched brown overalls.

We had lost no time in renewing contact with Marcel Laurent, the fishmonger who had lent us the little punt on the day of our arrival. We got to know him well, and through him were received into the little circle of people who represent the yachting fraternity of Douarnenez. Some of them knew me of old, and I even came across an old school friend, the director of an important canning factory at Quimper. I had several offers of tinned goods, and later regretted not having shipped a cargo to the Antilles, where they are worth their weight in gold.

We planned revenge, during the long days of waiting, on Marcel Laurent, who had evidently taken us for cockneys, for the good of whose souls he had prescribed a ducking. To this end I inserted an advertisement in the local paper, to the effect that Dr Laurent undertook to cure a somewhat unusual complaint, red noses (enclose stamp for reply). Our unfortunate victim was overwhelmed with applications, some of which we penned ourselves in a disguised hand, attaching strange and fearful photographs by way of evidence. The poor chap was driven completely out of his wits, but we let several days go by before we gave him the true, secret and simple recipe, which is as follows: 'If you have a red nose, it's because you drink claret. Drink Burgundy and it will go purple!'

This was the start of a regular little war. Returning on board that night, I found my port light halfway up the mast and a broom flying at the masthead: but what I had not seen in the dark was a huge notice-board fixed to the shrouds, informing the world at large that I sold peinture (=painting or paint) of the highest quality—flattering enough so far for an artist; but by the pound, which was less to my taste. It worked so well that I was roused early next morning by several fishing-boat skippers demanding my price list.

However, I was not the only painter in Douarnenez. In the dining-room of the hotel an artist namesake of our fishmonger friend was holding an exhibition of his work; admirable work it was, by the way. The similarity in name gave us a new idea: a discreetly placed notice, which the manager of the establishment did not at first see, promised the hotel clients a reduction of twenty per cent. on the pension rates if they bought one of the pictures on view. Some of these good folk, after making a brief calculation, easily saw that the market was exceedingly favourable, bought a picture and claimed the rebate on their bills. There were heated explanations and thereafter the management kept a sharp eye on us. In addition to the above-mentioned notice, I designed a somewhat fanciful menu card, on which the hotel cook, a tubby little person, was depicted in the act of concocting her masterpieces on a Primus stove in gimbals. We substituted for the existing menus new ones of our own composition, comprising such exquisite jests as dog pâté, and others perhaps a shade more subtle, like shin of turkey, spaghetti polonaise and devilled crimpies, a marginal note declaring that all cooking was done with mobiloil. Naturally we lay low and were the first to ask for crimpies and dishes à la polonaise. The unfortunate proprietor more than half believed in the existence of crimpies before we had done with him, as we insisted on seeing them being served at neighbouring tables, and assured him they were all the rage in Paris.

On looking back, these witticisms do not seem to have been very brilliant. Nevertheless they helped to mitigate the boredom of those days of waiting, which was the main thing.

Nearly every day there were elaborate and interminable peasant weddings with a great array of Breton costumes. They often lasted three days on end, and we had no difficulty in slipping in amongst the guests, drinking the bride's health right and left, and getting showered with invitations to other weddings. A true land of cockaigne, if only the wine had occasionally been drinkable. In farthest Brittany the most unnameable substitutes and horrific liquids pass muster as wine. The fact is they drink so much that nobody has time to think about it.

Every morning I used to telephone to Paris, first to my wife and then to the Observatory for the exact time by which to adjust my chronometer. At that date the automatic time signal at the Observatory had only recently been instituted and the number Odéon 8400 was unknown in the provinces. When they noticed that I called this number every morning, that I locked myself in the telephone booth with Rochard, who had a reliable watch, and that without uttering a word we simply listened for a 'pip-pip', excitement ran high. Doubtless our reputation as jokers had begun to spread, for I was the recipient of much backchat from the girls on the local exchange, not to mention Quimper, Rennes and all sorts of other places; every five seconds they would exhort me to 'speak up' or finally, thinking I was pulling their leg, they would cut us off. It was well that I had never breathed a word to a soul about my destination on leaving Douarnenez. No one would have believed me for a moment. This is an example of the disadvantage of possessing a sense of humour. Let me counsel you, sir or madam, good doctor, learned master, and you too, heroes after your fashion, whatever it be, if you would impress fools, above all be serious.

However, the moment came when the bad weather eased and I began to scent the possibility of getting under way.

I called at the harbour-master's office for my ship's papers, which were endorsed 'Crew: nil' and 'Destination: the high seas', for I was indeed unable to specify in advance my ports of call. I asked Rochard to sleep on board so as not to have to call him at the hotel if I decided suddenly to profit by a favourable slant; and so, everything being pretty well ready, I awaited developments.

CHAPTER XI

DEPARTURE

At seven o'clock one fine morning I got under way for New York. It was the 10th of May.

When I say 'one fine morning' I speak figuratively. At dawn, about 6 a.m., when I came on deck, it was raining as usual.

The wind had eased hardly at all, as far as could be judged, but the glass was appreciably higher than of late.

After walking up and down the muddy quayside in bare feet for some minutes, thinking hard, I jumped on board again and started up the stove for coffee.

'I rely on you to telephone to my wife as soon as the Post Office opens,' I said to Rochard, while I operated the Primus plunger with a violence that made every pot and pan in the galley rattle.

He leaped out of his bunk and had a look at the sky himself. When he came below again his expression was not noticeably enthusiastic. All the same, in a few moments he had his gear packed and had begun to take in the warps. Meanwhile I sent up the mainsail with two reefs in it and my smallest jib, the number three. Sounding with the boat hook, I found there was hardly a foot of water under the keel. The tide was taking off rapidly and there was not a minute to lose. I certainly did not want to wait for the evening tide, which would have meant going through the Raz de Sein in the middle of the night. We said good-bye to each other. A warm handshake, 'I'll say good-morning to your wife for you.' Winnibelle moved slowly away and drifted down river with the tide, scarcely feeling the wind as yet.

I was far from cheerful, and a racking cough did nothing to raise my spirits. I can still see the melancholy deserted quayside, and Rochard alone on the little stone jetty, trying to take photographs in spite of the bad light.

Once clear of the Isle de Tristan I hoisted the single-reefed foresail and the boat began to feel the wind and swell. In the bay of Morgat I found a stiffish westerly breeze, just what would be

73

wanted outside though unfortunately dead ahead for the time being. Going about off Morgat the main sheet knocked my cap overboard. My efforts to retrieve it were in vain, for it sank almost immediately: my oldest and most cherished cap, the only one I had which really fitted me.

Shortly after noon the weather cleared and I was able to set my No. 2 jib and shake out a reef in the mainsail. Fishing craft began coming out of Douarnenez, Camaret, and all the other harbours. A large fishing launch passed me in a flash, exactly as though I had been hove too. The effortless ease of her progress and the way she attacked the crest of the waves filled me with admiration. Such vessels have become a class in themselves, and the fishermen do not hesitate to venture two and three hundred miles to sea in them, going even as far afield as the Portuguese and North African coasts.

Ushant was in sight by the time I judged it advisable to go about and head for the Raz de Sein, which unfortunately I reached just as the stream began to turn foul.

It was out of the question for a vessel as slow as mine to make this narrow passage against the stream.

The Raz de Sein has a very bad reputation. With the possible exception of the Raz Blanchard it is the worst race on the French coast. The waters of the Atlantic and the Channel pour through it alternately as they sweep round the coast of Brittany, producing violent disturbance at all times, and, in heavy weather, mountainous seas. At such times, and particularly when the tide is running hard, navigation becomes virtually impracticable even for big ships. The race is then an awe-inspiring spectacle. You can look out over it from the high ground of the coast, with your heart in your mouth and keeping a firm hold on your hat.

Over there you can just make out the Isle of Sein, half hidden by the spindrift which whirls over the roofs into the streets and fields. You can picture the good wives raising their arms to heaven as though they had never seen such a sight before and their opportunist husbands firmly ensconced in the snug bar-parlours. Over the long line of rocks, known as the Chaussée de Sein, hangs a vast cloud of spray like white dust in suspense.

Immediately below you, just beyond the point of the headland, in the midst of the maelstrom loom two towers, the two light-houses of La Vieille, whence there comes to your ears some seconds after you see it, like a distant gunshot, the dull thud of each huge wave that crashes against them.

It is just outside the smaller, more distant lighthouse that vessels pass when they can, not for pleasure, but to save the owner's coal by cutting a corner. For many of them, large and small, this tide-way is a graveyard.

As the weather was still unsettled, I was anxious to leave these waters behind me as soon as possible; but for six hours Winnibelle gained not a fraction of a mile, in fact, she moved backwards, as though in the presence of royalty. Maddening, but inevitable; there was nothing for it but to hang on, losing as little ground as possible. Then, when at last the coastline began to slip by, slowly at first, then faster, I knew that the tide had turned, and we were free. It was not long before the Isle de Sein, which nowhere rises more than a few feet above sea level, sank out of sight astern.

Hurrah for the open sea! They tell me there are people who find comfort in the nearness of the land. . . . Of such am not I!

A steamer's smoke, then two, soon ten; I was approaching the line of vessels whose course takes them round As-Men. This is a route much used by boats making for the Mediterranean, the Far East, and South America or homeward bound to Southampton, London, Havre and Hamburg: altogether too crowded a thorough-fare to be healthy by night.

I had already, whilst clearing La Veille, passed close by an old cargo tramp in ballast. Her sides wept rust, a small jungle of green weed sprouted from her cheeks, her propeller, half out of water, churned up the white foam with rhythmical beats, like a whisk making mayonnaise. She was a 'Pinardier', so called because this sort of vessel carries Bordeaux or Algerian wine (pinard). The officer on watch, a lonely figure at one end of her bridge, waved a friendly hand to me. Further off shore the Aurigny crossed my bow, one of the Chargeurs-Réunis line; her superimposed decks, open to every draught of air, made one think of the heat of the Red Sea, deck chairs and drill clothing. Her passengers, unused as yet to the cold, had migrated to the saloons; in any case it was dinner time. Not so much as a cat was visible on deck. Above the dodger on the wing of the bridge, I could just make out the head of an officer having a look at me through his glasses. Then he too raised his arm in greeting, just as the other had done. They were feeling good those two, not a doubt of it: they would be in port next morning, and the night promised well.

I had begun talking to myself, as is my habit when sailing, painting, or writing. 'Time to put the log over. . . . How far off is the shore?' It was quite a job to look back over my shoulder, with yards of thick wool muffler wound round my neck, for the wind had turned bitter with the sinking sun. 'I'll make a start with the old Massey, there's no fear of the sharks getting it here.' I set the pointers to zero, carefully lowered the apparatus and paid out the line, which being quite dry floated on the surface in a series of fantastic kinks. It seemed an age before it at last made up its mind to straighten out properly.

'Cheer up, it's not worth getting annoyed. Plenty of time for that before you reach New York!'

I made the end of the line fast with great care. Having only two logs on board, the loss of one would be a serious matter. Chafing against the gunwale or rudder head must be avoided at all costs; the stoutest cord can be worn through in a single night in this way.

That done, I felt a nice cup of tea would go down well. I had still to light and fix the navigation lights. They were of galvanized iron, of the massive type used by the Boulogne fishermen, primitive enough, and I must admit hardly decorative. But what they lacked in beauty they more than made up in effectiveness.

The lamps inside had neither glass funnels nor, what is even more to the point, cones, which get smoked up too often. The coloured globes themselves were in one piece, without magnifying striations or prisms. Magnifying glasses are designed to spread out the light in horizontal planes, and it is a mistake to use them on a sailing vessel, which hardly ever keeps an even keel; this means that the luminous plane on one side points to the sky, and on the other side is lost in the sea.

Masters of steam vessels complain of never seeing sailing ships' lights: this is to a great extent due to the above cause. Plain glass, rightly tinted and as large as possible, are certainly the best solution for small sailing boats.

By nine o'clock in the evening I felt comfortably clear of the big steamship lines and the shore, where the lights had already sunk below the horizon. The quick fanlike flash from a lighthouse here and there was all that indicated the coast. Two or three ships, separated from the main procession, still showed their mast lights, but they were far astern, and I decided to set a course for Finisterre. Lowering the mainsail, I let the boat steer herself under her fore-sail and the big balloon jib well hardened in.

At 1 a.m. I made out the dark mass of a fishing vessel showing no lights, and at 6 a.m. saw a schooner far to the N.N.E. For a moment I hoped that she was sailing parallel, but in reality her course was oblique to mine and she disappeared to the S.E. without my being able to approach her. At this moment the balloon jib sheet parted. Already!

I had slept for very few hours, but now made ready for another day at the helm, one of those endless, stupid days with one's eyes rivetted to the compass; impossible to read or do anything but keep her more or less straight with the help of an occasional glance at the wash astern. On such a day a numbness settles on mind and body.

I soon found myself experiencing an old sensation which I had quite forgotten: that of the length of a watch at sea. In my days before the mast the seemingly interminable silence of the ship's clock behind me had, so to say, stabbed me in the back. Now the same sensation hit me in the face, for by leaning forward a little I could see the binnacle clock without leaving the tiller. How often, too, in the old days I had sworn never again to let myself in for such long tricks at the helm. It is a game which loses its charm when one has had a belly-full. Yet here I was, of my own free will and with no one to please but myself, and never a relief to look forward to. In the old days I would be looking out of the corner of my eye through the wheel-house door the moment the ship's bell struck the hour, and if my relief was a minute or two late in shewing up I used to tell him how I felt about it in no uncertain terms. Observe that the prospect of remaining at the helm all day of my own accord did not stop my grousing in the least: there's all the difference in the world between 'the delights of sailing' and hanging on to the stick from morning till night. I reckoned on having my own back further south; but at the start, that is to say, in the Bay of Biscay and until Portugal was doubled, and likewise at the other end of the trip, when nearing New York, I was resigned in advance to several rather hard days and even nights because of variable winds and the necessity of travelling fast. In the trade winds it would be different; for that I had my plan.

I tried to divide up the hours as well as I could. At such a time I would have a look at the log, at such a time I would make a cup of tea, and so on. At dusk every evening I set myself a definite time for turning in; yet sometimes I hung on for an hour, sometimes even two when I was not too dazed. This was in truth mere folly, for nothing obliged me to do it. But human nature is such that I used to prolong my watch quite mechanically to the extreme limit, I do not say of my strength, but of my patience.

I decided to give my second log, an Excelsior, a trial, in order to compare it with the Massey. It showed a considerable error, of about twelve per cent. Log makers always say that the blades of the apparatus must not be tampered with, and warn one not to let them knock against the side of the ship when being hauled on board. Yet I have known old sailors who thought nothing of using hammers and wrenches to adjust their blades with, and got excellent results by such rough and ready means. I never tried this method, but confined myself to making the requisite correction in my calculation of distances run; all the same it is an indisputable fact that some logs work accurately and others do not. In my own particular case while the Massey registered more or less correctly down to the low limit of two and a half knots, the other remained sluggish even at six knots, though mounted absolutely correctly.

Just before sunset a robin came on board. The poor creature was too exhausted to stand; at each lurch of the vessel it rolled about on deck like a little ball of feathers. After a while it went below, and instinct guided it to the gimballed stove, where it found a more stable perch. Then it fluttered to a basin which had a little water in it and drank a few drops. I began to hope that it would settle down on board, and avoided the slightest movement which might alarm it, but suddenly it flew off, zigzagging away, I much fear, towards the open sea.

Next morning I found the wind south-westerly, and Winnibelle, close-hauled, looked after herself. A day without incident; wind light, variable.

On the 13th I had a pleasant surprise. Through the morning mist I saw the dim shape of a sailing vessel about a mile off. She turned out to be a Camaret fishing yawl bound for the African coast. I approached to within hailing distance; she had left the same day as myself, but about noon, and had come through the Raz de Sein directly in my wake. I had hardly lost any time against her. Her log showed pretty well the same figure as my own: 180 miles. All her crew were asleep except the man at the wheel . . . and I'm not sure about him. However, he roused himself sufficiently to ask me if I was alone, and when I told him it was so, he shook his head and assured me with considerable vigour that he had no desire to be in my shoes. Neither would I have changed places with him, so all was for the best. By nightfall she was out of sight.

To check my course I worked over again towards the shipping lane, and found it at once. A number of lights showed up, always in single file, a marvel of precision. I had misgivings about the accuracy of my main compass, which had begun to leak and now revealed an abnormal variation. Fortunately I had made a point of frequently comparing it with the saloon compass, which had led me to suspect this divergence. I had already taken two meridians, according to which I must either have benefited by a favourable current or else my two logs had a common lag. On the 14th I got a direct reading which confirmed this and enabled me to shift my dead reckoning another twenty miles to the S.W.

Time dragged interminably. It is impossible to sit down in comfort for long on a small sailing vessel on account of the incessant motion; standing and lying at full length are the only satisfactory positions.

The Winnibelle's tiller had a way of kicking—in light airs the Norwegian type is, I fancy, apt to develop back lash. I usually steer by leaning against the tiller with the small of my back or thighs, or when standing on deck, by holding it between my legs, so as to keep my hands free. Hence, before long, a beautiful array of bruises, and the impact was always on the same spot. I cannot be blamed if I gave vent to certain expressions of a lurid kind. Anyway, there was no one to take exception to my antics.

I was still far from the Spanish coast when I ran into fairly stiff contrary winds, which obliged me to lay a westerly course, and lose some of the distance made good the day before.

In the early morning of the 15th May I was awakened by the blast of a siren close at hand. In one leap I was out of my bunk and on deck, with a vague idea that a patch of fog had come down and that I was on the point of being run down. But no; the weather was fine and clear, and silhouetted against the dawn light, within easy hail, I saw a big cargo vessel. She had stopped. Observing a little yacht so far out to sea, with no one on deck, she had come to investigate. I had already consigned her to perdition when I recognised by her funnel that she belonged to the P.L.M. Company, whose managing director is Raoul Van Der Kemp, President of the Association of Deep-Sea Captains, and a very good friend of mine. 'Love to Van Der,' I bellowed to the Captain. After a moment's hesitation, during which his bewildered expression was laughable, he made a sign that he had understood. After which he got under way again, with a parting hoot, and two minutes later I had resumed my interrupted doss.

My mistrust of the Bay proved to be well founded. Hardly had my first week at sea passed before the barometer began to fall rapidly and I had a taste of what a hard easterly blow can do in those waters. It lasted thirty-six hours. In a sense I could not have asked better, for an E. wind was favourable; but I was afraid it might go round to the S. or even W., and so make an uncomfortable lee shore of the Portuguese coast. In such an event I decided to run for the Carogne, which I knew well, rather than make a board to the N. thus losing all distance made good, or let myself be driven into the bight of the Bay.

About this time of year, in 1929, I had been in a large ketch, the Black Swan, in these very waters. We had to heave to for three days, by the end of which we had been forced back to just off Ushant, although we had been on the point of clearing Ortegal. That little breeze had left tender memories, and I was taking no chances this time.

I changed my jib, according to the book, as the wind increased, and took in first one, then two reefs in the main and foresail: all this during one of those pitch black nights that are made to measure for folk who have to get out of their troubles by themselves. The headlamp was a tremendous help, and reefing down proved so easy with my boomless mainsail that from that moment I ceased to have the slightest apprehension about repeating the performance in any weather.

All that night I drove her hard, lighting cigarette after cigarette which the slashing rain put out a few seconds later. From time to time the top of a wave hit her side with a dull thud, shot half way up the mainsail and then tumbled back in phosphorescent cascades. The powdery foam to leeward shone a magnificent emerald under the starboard light.

In the half light of dawn I was passed by a Breton lobster boat, similar to the one I had fallen in with earlier. I had watched her coming up astern, and had at first taken her for a steamer. For a long time I hoped to see her pass close by me, and she seemed bent on doing so, taking me no doubt for a colleague; but when she saw her mistake she quickly altered course and stood off a mile or so. She was afraid I might want something or other; small yachts are often given a wide berth by working craft for this reason.

Thus I doubled Finistère, about fifty miles off, which is to say, out of sight. I began to get seriously tired, and consequently dispirited. It had taken me more than a week to reach the Spanish coast, much too long, to my way of thinking. I was soaked from head to foot. I was aching all over, having first tripped over something below and fallen heavily on my back, then nearly broken my leg during the night by falling into the cockpit, which I thought was closed, when actually the slide was just open. Also my eyes were beginning to smart unpleasantly; they were encrusted all round with salt, and I was afraid to rub them.

What with one thing and another, I began to lose my sense of humour, as I always do on such occasions. The reaction is, I find, bound to set in sooner or later, and is the more acute in proportion to the length of time one has been away from the sea. Its origin is purely physical.

Automatically I began to ask myself what lunacy could have possessed me, that for no reason at all I should be indulging in these ludicrous antics four hundred miles from home, when I might have been comfortably asleep in a real bed, or standing by the window, quietly watching the pouring rain.

Then ill humour turned to rage, and I hurled great oaths into the wind, which promptly and unceremoniously cast them back into my throat.

CHAPTER XII

THOUGHTS ON THE SEA

IT always amuses a sailor to observe how little bad weather means to people who live in towns.

Time and again on coming ashore at a Channel port during a really hard blow, I have been glad to cross the cobblestones at the quayside and relax in some little bar, my face still glowing and my boots full of water; and invariably I have been amazed by the calm which reigns in the sheltered streets, where the puddles have hardly a ripple on them and the sound and fury of the storm are completely stilled. If I happen to remark to anyone: 'Filthy weather outside!' I see a raised eyebrow and get some such reply as: 'Yes, indeed, just look at the rain.'

On shore, rain is the only thing that counts, as one realises from the newspaper and wireless weather forecasts. The vital thing is to know whether to take an umbrella or not.

It is far otherwise with those who have been 'vaccinated', as sailors call it. They remember, and always will, even if only at intervals. You cannot for ever be thinking of the sea, you even forget it very quickly; and indeed the worst ordeals you have been through are the quickest to fade, in this as in other spheres. If it were not so, sailors would not sign on again. Sometimes all is forgotten by next day, sometimes in a couple of hours. You will often hear sailors declare that never in all their lives have they seen such weather—no, by God they haven't! The phrase is classic, and shows that they do not, at the moment of speaking, remember the last time. Next time they will say it again, word for word, myself as much as any of them.

But just let the wind whistle under a door, and all sorts of half-forgotten memories revive! A flapping blind, a splash of rain at the corner of the street, and immediately the sailor will raise his eyes to the little square of sky which is all he can see. Sometimes he is not thinking and the glance is purely mechanical; at other times he says to himself 'It's not so good outside!'

There have been occasions when I have said this aloud, and the person with me has answered: 'Outside? But we are outside, aren't we?'

Agreed; but what I mean by 'outside' is out at sea, off the Casquets, the Pierres Noires, Finistère . . .

And there are times when the sailor ashore says to himself: 'It's your turn now, you others, so make the most of it! It can't catch all of us out all of the time; it just happens to be me that's enjoying his pipe and his glass in comfort now, and very nice too, thank you!' The words, or the thought, are devoid of ill-feeling; they merely express the moment's intimate satisfaction, and implicit in them is the speaker's awareness that he will be 'there' again himself, sooner or later. Under these conditions, as I well know, rain and wind are among the profound satisfactions of life.

A moment ago, while getting these notes into shape, I made a discovery: a flying fish's wing, hardly bigger than a fin, pressed between two pages of an old Brown's Nautical Almanac, and, a little further on, between two other pages, a small bit of sargasso weed. I do not remember putting them there, and in any case heaven only knows why I should have kept the out-of-date Almanac; out of respect perhaps, for all the books which have followed me from one boat to another, and whose deplorable broken backs are at the same time a disgrace to my library and its most precious feature.

The chance discovery let loose a flood of completely dead memories. I saw again the little fish, stuck fast to a hot deck, blistering under the vertical sunlight; I saw the long wisps of golden yellow sargasso weed in an indigo sea; the schools of tiny fish leaping in mad myriads as they fled from beneath the Winnibelle's gaily advancing bows, and diving all together, after their miniature flight, with a splash like a whiplash on the surface of the sea, not forgetting at the last moment to perform their little ruse, their famous lightning right turn, to put their pursuers off the track.

Of all this I had retained no conscious memory, although those hours were well worth living. I remember now that once or twice in the early stages of my voyage I said aloud, for my own benefit, while the loneliness was still a new sensation: 'No one can understand, who has not tried this.' And now, a certain torn jib comes to my mind. I found it in the loft at Chausey. It had been to America with me, and I laid it out on the grass in front of the house, where the sailors came to see it. I had never examined it so closely before; only the bolt ropes and seams remained, so knotted and twisted and entangled that it was a marvel to behold. Even the small strands of frayed cloth were ravelled up with each other in a thousand complicated knots impossible to untie. I had completely lost sight of that jib, and would have said I had thrown it away long before. But no, it had been dragged out of the chain locker with a lot of other rubbish which I had never sorted or bothered about. Nothing could be more convincing than this exhibit as a means of bringing home the strength of a tropical squall, the very sound of the sail splitting, like the report of a gun at close range.

And, little by little, as I work my way back up the stream of memory, all sorts of things came back to me; things forgotten because they were impossible to explain to anyone, but which, now that I have taken my courage in both hands and shut myself off from the world to write, fill my brain as they did when I was alone on the waters of the deep.

I left off at the point in my story when for the first time I asked myself the question: Why?

At that moment I was struggling only for the sake of the struggle, against no one, against nothing, simply for my own personal discomfort. I was in a bad way: eyes hurting, barked shins, bruises all over my body. Oh, I knew well enough that I should reach my goal; I felt no apprehension of the open sea, no pang of horror at the thought of the vast distance which still separated me from New York; on the contrary, I had a very good boat under me, the best probably that anyone ever had in similar circumstances; and all the fever of departure, the worries and difficulties, the telephone calls, arguments with the yard, wrangles with the Authorities, disputes with Life Insurance Companies were over and done with; the pictures that had to be finished before I could be free to leave, had been finished; the mud of the quayside and the harbour smells were forgotten; fled too was the ever painful moment of goodbyes, so full of false pathos.

But what I asked myself was, why all this trouble simply to be here, clinging by my eyebrows to the tiller, with a sea increasing from minute to minute, a perfect sod of a sea, to be exact? And that cow of a lobsterman who had just gone about for no reason at all except to avoid me. . . . And my peak downhaul which had cunningly unrove itself and gone overboard, at least seven fathoms of beautiful new signal halliard. . . . And my favourite record, one of Sophie Tucker's, a record of records, on which I had sat down heavily half an hour ago in a particularly sudden lurch—crack! . . . And half my crockery already overboard, so much so that I seemed to be spending practically my whole time chucking out the broken pieces. . . . Well, damn the crockery, anyway, but what about my mattress, soaked through and through with salt water, soaked so that it will never be dry again to all eternity?

I see myself stretched out on my bunk, having decided to let her look after herself. I was clear of the dangers of the land and the weather could hardly get worse: I had stowed the mainsail, not without difficulty, as it got into the water in lowering away, and the names I called myself at the top of my voice had done little to relieve my feelings. The Winnibelle was riding nearly at right angles to the sea and climbed up the steep walls of water like a little gull. The wind must damned well moderate while I rested.

With a watchful eye on the deck beams, not being fond of banging my head, I wedged myself in the bunk as tightly as I could between the leeboard and a stretcher. The gleam of the stern light danced on the bulkhead opposite. Again and yet again I asked myself, 'In God's name what am I doing here?' It was impossible not to laugh and equally impossible to hear myself laughing, so noisy is a small boat when it blows hard. . . . I pulled the blanket over my shoulders, turned my face inboard . . . and was asleep.

In point of fact I should have done better to look at the other side of the question, to ask myself why the devil I should deprive myself of an interesting experience, following the lead of the celebrated Claude Bernard, who tried everything once, 'just to see what happened'. What more natural than to come face to face now and then with my own pet subject, and what could be more beneficial to mind and body, to say nothing of the art of marine painting? And then, too, I was not sorry, after having heard so much, and talked so much myself, about the experiences of 'single-handed cruisers', to be in a position to find out how much was true

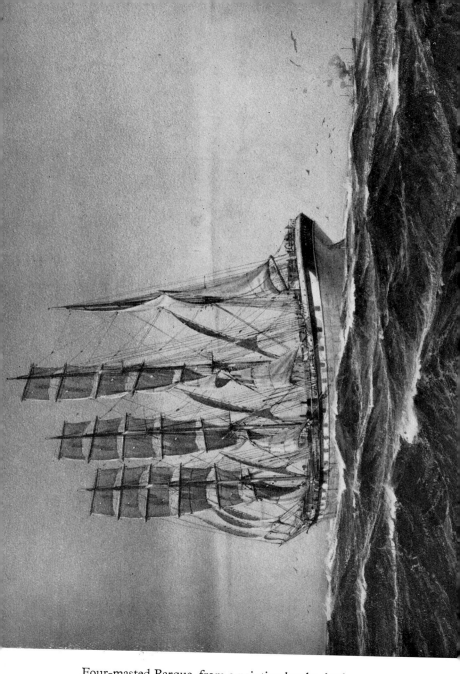

Four-masted Barque, from a painting by the Author

(1) Spray
(2) Saoirse
(3) Firecrest ⎫ New
(4) Svaap ⎭ rig
(5) Svaap
(6) Sea-bir
(7) Winnib
(8) Tilicum

Small boats that made long voyages—different types of rig

and how much false in all the stories. I knew that the professional deep sea sailorman, in his unrefined way, simply called them by a vulgar name, with nothing complimentary about it; the same name by which he describes the ship that leaves the convoy and shapes a course off the beaten track for purely selfish ends. Well, if anyone deserved the epithet, that man was I.

Having said which, I might as well set down 'love of the waves'[1] as one of my chief motives. After all, why bother to go any deeper into the matter? The phrase covers everything, surely.

Perhaps not quite everything. Let us consider what the phrase really amounts to. In reality its meaning is both complex and vague, having regard to the fact that it varies with individuals; I think it belongs to the same family as love of mountains, or love of the open road, that hoary old cliché. The only difference is that love of the waves has a rather more impressive sound about it.

I have so often heard old ladies declare that I am 'passionately in love with the sea', that in sheer desperation I have had to plead guilty. It is, after all, only a question of vocabulary, and the dear old creatures who clasp their hands at the idea of the perils of the deep are too charming for me to want to hurt their feelings. True, to talk of 'loving the sea' when one means loving the beauty and size of it, or the colour of it, or loving Jules Verne novels or sub-Jules Verne novels, or even loving hot sand and bathing costumes, is, from my point of view, beside the point. It is open to everyone to find what they like in the sea and to love it after their fashion.

For myself, the phrase implies above all a taste for boats and sailing; and that does not prevent me from having a more contemplative passion for the sea, which properly belongs to my profession of marine painter. And it is precisely through my work that I have come to realise how many people there are who only see the sea through what floats on its surface. I have sold paintings in which there was literally nothing but a ship and its reflection, with untouched canvas for sky and horizon; in other words, nothing that could properly be called sea, yet what the buyers

---

[1] An expression read the other day in a book, and which I do not much like.

D

found in those paintings was essentially the sea, the sea as they saw it.

There remains what is known, in the novelists' vocabulary, as 'the call of the ocean', and 'danger for danger's sake'. As for the call of the ocean, there is poetry in it, and good poetry too; in the modern world a little idealism is not out of place, far from it. . . . It may be no more than the very natural desire to step ashore on the other side of the water, in other words a taste for sea travel, but a 'taste for sea travel' smacks a little of Cook's, the words conjure up a vision of many-labelled suitcases; 'call of the ocean' is decidedly more euphonious. As to 'danger for danger's sake', that is simply sport. It is enough in itself to justify all the voyages which are undertaken for the sake of the difficulties they offer, and which serve no other end (such as the one I am relating). Utilitarianism is the negation of all sport. Did not the Committee of the 'Cruising Club of America' decide to award its 'Blue Water Medal' for the voyage of the year which should stand as the best example of amateur seamanship and the spirit of endeavour?[1]

Unfortunately—there is always an 'unfortunately'—the lust of adventure is found as frequently among fools as among sensible people, hence a good many foolish adventures. That is why so much has been said and written, quite unjustifiably, about the madness of all long ocean voyages in small boats; the truth being that immense funds of prudence and forethought have to be drawn on, if the thing is to be done well.

It will be agreed, then, that all sorts of sentiments such as these, and many more, make up what we call love of the sea. . . . As to love of the sea pure and simple, talk of it to a professional, to a seaman who makes his living out of it, and you will get an edifying answer. He will explain that his life is one long struggle against the sea, not for the fun of it, but in the full consciousness that he must never lose the upper hand. To this fight he must bring all his intelligence, nor for a single instant can he afford to forget the respect due to a formidable foe: respect, not adoration; far from being desirable, her kiss to him is fatal.

---

[1] In 1936 the Blue Water Medal was awarded to M. Marin-Marie for his single-handed Atlantic passage in the Arielle. (Publisher's Note).

'When the sea possesses you, so much the worse for you. You may think you're winning sometimes, but the sea knows better, and just laughs. The dice are loaded against you, and the sea always has the last word, even if it's only a question of giving you the rheumatics.'

Such is the answer you will get from the man who really knows the sea through and through, in all her moods.

CHAPTER XIII

HEAVY WEATHER

ONCE clear of Cap Finistère I had decided to go below and lie down, and I proceeded to put my plan into execution in spite of the hard easterly blow which had come on.

I soon found that lying down was one thing and resting another, for the wind showed no inclination to ease off. Rolled about in my bunk by increasingly violent shocks and lurches which threatened every moment to tumble me out, I took the initiative and philosophically shifted my mattress on to the cabin floor.

At dawn, as it was impossible to sleep, I stuck my head on deck and had a look round for any sign of smoke on the horizon. I had no wish to see any, and if I had I should immediately have altered my course further out to sea, but fortunately there was none in sight.

The sea presented a superb spectacle. With your eye at water level you suffer a good deal of inconvenience, but the viewpoint is much finer than from the lofty bridge of a steamship. In the trough of the waves you are dominated by a colourless sea entirely overspread by a sort of white powder which is driven by the wind across the heaving surface. From the crests you see an ocean of foam; from time to time the top of a huge wave topples over and bursts into an unforgettable cloud of spray, shot with pink in the early light. Facing the wind it is difficult to open your eyes.

Still more striking are the extraordinary patches of indescribable green, 'electric green' as I always call it, which appears on the slopes of the larger waves, those which break or at least try to break, before they are decapitated by the fury of the wind. This is an 'effect' which marine painters find almost impossible to reproduce, as it is essentially luminous; not that there are many who have really seen it. Sea-water, permeated as it is with active phosphorescent organic life, from which its colour is derived (for sea-water is coloured, as you may see by pouring some into a big wineglass), glows through and through with an inward light. On the flanks of the waves oily tracts gleam lividly, mixed with patches of whipped foam.

And the noise.... The noise is what impresses you above all. A gun could be fired twenty yards off and you would never notice it. I have sometimes shouted at the top of my voice without being able to hear myself. Not that this is peculiar to small boats: the rush of sound in the rigging and bridge of a liner is equally deafening. Officers on watch know well these sudden blasts which assail the eardrums, like an express train coming the opposite way when the window of your carriage is wide open. The only difference in a small boat is that you are at sea level, sometimes rising high, sometimes sinking low, and that you only dominate the scene or see any distance now and then, just before you take a tremendous slide into the trough again.

Normally in this sort of weather a small boat can make no headway. She lies usually with the wind on the beam, and when I speak of 'slide' I mean she first climbs sideways towards the crest, where more often than not she gets nearly knocked down; then comes a dizzy drop down the far slope, still sideways. I have seen slides of this kind which literally resembled a downward rush on skis, powdered snow, tracks and all; only instead of a man's weight, what is slithering down is a displacement of ten or twenty tons, and I can assure you the effect is impressive. In a well found craft this kind of thing no doubt comes under the heading of sport; but it is no fun at all to be caught out in such conditions in a 'bargain'.

Slocum disappeared far out at sea off Cape Hatteras in a blow of this sort, and it is generally held that his shallow-draft Spray simply foundered, although she had circumnavigated the globe. Gerbault's Firecrest made a big hole in the water in less than ten minutes, to everyone's astonishment, after having lain for a year in the inner harbour at Le Havre, where most likely she had gone rotten. Voss disappeared without leaving a trace.... These are the kind of thoughts that are apt to intrude, as your boat sinks into the abyss between two waves.

But taking careful note of the Winnibelle's motion, I began to reproach myself for giving way to a certain instinctive apprehension when the descending lurch was particularly steep and long or the upward surge exceptionally dizzy. Because, in reality, my vessel, brand new and consequently sound, with her deep draught and ample ballast, presented the maximum of security; while her light, hollow mast, supported by extra powerful shrouds, gave me boundless confidence. Had I not deliberately envisaged the possibility of capsizing and being rolled over in a big sea without having to worry about the ballast falling on my head, or the boat being dismasted or even shipping enough water to sink her? Which was why Winnibelle's original hatches had been condemned, and were now almost waterproof. (Almost, I say!)

For some days past I had been trailing over the stern a tunny-line, given me with all sorts of tips regarding its use by the skipper of a Douarnenez tunnyman. In the course of the present blow it had got mixed up with the line of my Excelsior log, and I spent at least half a day in the cabin disentangling it. This little job, which required patience and close attention, restored my equanimity, in the sense that I entirely stopped questioning myself about the reasons and aims of my voyage. For the rest, the most violent phase of a gale, that which comes immediately before the end, is always the brightest, just as the premonitory signs and portents, which tell you a gale is on the way, are the darkest. When the fight is on, the fight is on; it is the ten minutes before any difficult test which are the most painful; later, under the stimulus of action, you cheer up. So it is with the test of a hard blow at sea; and the moment the wind shows signs of moderating you find life good again.

I know of nothing more exhilarating than fair weather when it comes as suddenly as foul. The feeling generally translates itself into the luxury of a wash, dry clothes and an exploration of the food locker. In point of fact, I had my programme all mapped out for great occasions: a little Muscadet, three eggs from the box of table salt in which they were stowed, and a small tin of Libby's asparagus, the ends of which I cut off, to make *œufs brouillés aux asperges*. I had a marvellous enamel pan, a pan with an excellent character. A very precious thing is a good pan, wherefore I nursed it with tender care, lest any ill befall it. With this pan never a fritter, never an omelette had been known to burn. On great occasions such as this I considered lard, provided it was of the best quality, a better cooking medium than salted butter. Two or three cups of tea, and all was right with the world; there was no question of crowding on sail, I had no extra sails to do it with, and I felt capable of keeping watch for twenty-four hours on end. The morale of a crew has always depended on small, ordinary details such as these, as is well known.

It was in this mood that I wrote in my log, under date 17th May: 'Heavy weather, but not unenjoyable. First glimpse of sun. Not cold. Twelve hours on watch without leaving the helm. At 11 p.m sighted liner, apparently on same course.'

And this: 'Hoisted mainsail with two reefs and foresail: no jib. Day's run: 59 miles.' Fifty-nine may not be very brilliant, nor is a double reefed main and foresail exactly what used to be called a press of canvas; on the other hand twelve and a half hours without leaving the helm is something accomplished. I was content with very little.

I wrote a later entry: 'Midnight. Handed mainsail', which again has no very heroic ring about it. But I was happy, for I had overcome that physical depression, which was no less real for having been foreseen.

To tell the truth I was beginning to wonder whether my powers of resistance were as good as the next man's, for I had given way to the extent of steering the whole of one day from the saloon by means of the tiller tackles, indifferent to everything that happened on the horizon. A large tanker had passed not far away from me, one of the 'O' boats of the Ophelia, Omphala, etc., line, identifiable by their vertical black and red funnel bands, and I had hardly looked at her.

I took refuge in reading. I had brought with me certain books which I had never had the courage to read ashore, because I found them too anecdotal. These were narratives of experiences similar to my own, and in almost all of them I found mention, more or less undisguised in proportion to the courage or frankness of the writer, of some small crisis such as I was going through myself. Did not Slocum, the toughest nut of them all, openly confess to having one day 'given way to his feelings'?

I had thought to find a counter-irritant in fiction, in novels of adventure; but it was so much time wasted, for such tales have no attraction the moment you begin to live an adventure yourself. You feel very keenly the false and artificial side to all this class of literature, and you wonder how the authors could have the face to set down in cold black and white astounding occurrences of the true nature of which they have not the least conception.

This reaction of mine is one of the things that struck me most forcibly, for ashore I often revel in the most imbecile detective story before going to sleep, while at sea I am unable to read such a book for five minutes on end.

Once the bad weather was over I hardly had time for casual reading: it was necessary to make the most of every air and get as quickly as possible to the zone of fair winds. This meant about twelve hours a day at the helm.

Ship's log, 19th May:—'Nearly all the bread is already mouldy (after 9 days!). The sardines also (they were salted). The sausages look pretty queer. At 10 p.m. picked up liner's lights, moving parallel, but in the opposite direction. 10 hours at the helm today.'

The following day:—'Dull, grey day, milky sea. You would think you were off the Faroes rather than near the latitude of Lisbon. 12 hours on end at the helm: run, 80 miles.'

On 22nd May:—'S.S. Mount . . . ? On same course as myself, gave me 3 blasts on syren. I showed my colours, she showed hers. . . . French, to my astonishment. What rotten glasses I have! At 7 p.m. liner approaching from ahead. When abeam she stopped, had a good look and then proceeded on her way. She was at least 6 miles away, I could only see her bridge above the horizon. Lot of play in tiller.'

The fair weather accompanied me, conforming to the data on the wind chart, until I was very nearly on the latitude of Lisbon. Then it came on to blow from the North, and I had a taste of the discomfort of steering with the wind dead aft. Gybes were not infrequent, as I could not keep on an absolutely straight course from morning till night, but fortunately they entailed no damage or serious jar.

It was then, on 18th May, that I decided to try out my pet gadget, which was to enable me to leave the helm completely while continuing to travel at normal speed. I had passed many hours at home thinking it out, drawing plans, making models, etc.: the job now was to heave all the gear out of the locker and see if it was good for anything.

CHAPTER XIV
AUTOMATIC STEERING

T HERE are plenty of people who think that a man who sails alone stops at night. No, I am not exaggerating. . . . The question has often been asked me: 'How do you manage about sleeping? Do you let the anchor down?' Or again: 'Do you just let her drift?'

Not necessarily. It is quite possible to hold one's course without staying at the tiller. But to begin with, before explaining how a sailing boat can keep going automatically, it may be well to clear up a point which worries a good many professional sailors.

'Granted', they say, 'that your vessel steers herself, no watch is kept, and she therefore runs the risk of collision with other vessels. Apart from the danger to yourself you are a danger to navigation, like icebergs or derelicts. How are you justified in your action?'

This is a manifest exaggeration; a vessel of the Winnibelle's size cannot be a danger to the liners or cargo vessels one meets on the high seas. They are much too powerful: in other words, in the event of a collision the Winnibelle would be sunk out of hand, and no serious damage would be done to the other party. I am the first to admit that it is wrong to subject one's own life or the lives of others to the hazard of mere chance; but if we examine a little more closely into the question, we shall find that in practice things work out as follows. I do my sleeping almost invariably in the daytime, and then only when the weather is clear. A big ship at sea in clear weather, seeing a small sail, is not going to run it down for pleasure. Mere curiosity, as likely as not, will induce her to stop and, if no sign of life is visible, she will give a few blasts on the syren, when the mystery will very quickly be solved by the appearance of the owner or crew of the smaller vessel. This has often happened to me, and I have given more than one instance. In these conditions, then, danger is non-existent.

During the night I am generally on the look-out, and if it does happen that I sleep a little when the horizon is clear, there is still the protection provided by the regulation lights. In our time sailing ships are almost as rare as the dodo on the high seas; a sailing ship's lights are characteristic and entirely different from those of a steamship, and thus easily recognisable. By the maritime law of all nations a sailing ship has priority, and as soon as her lights show up it is the steamship's duty to avoid her. The risk of collision with another sailing ship is for all practical purposes nil.

Other sailors, again, raise this objection: In thick weather it is often very hard to make out the lights of a small sailing ship in the trough of the seas. Besides, these lights are red and green, colours which have a very mediocre range and power; moreover, their play is practically limited to the forward sector. An overtaking steam vessel cannot, therefore, see them, and it is necessary to have in addition a white poop light, as bright as possible. I used formerly to keep a heavy binnacle light made fast to the galvanised iron gaff-crutch.

But a white paraffin lamp does not amount to much. It is laid down that when in danger from a big approaching vessel, one should indicate one's presence by means of what is called a flare or a maroon. This is lit only when needed, and throws a violent light on to the sails, which at once reveals the whereabouts of the little vessel. Up till a few years ago it was customary to use an iron rod with a rag soaked in petrol wrapped round the end of it, which used to burn brightly for several minutes. More recently powerful electric torches have come into use for this purpose, both among yachtsmen and fishermen.

For myself I procured a small car headlight and had it wired to my accumulators and clamped to shine on the sails like flood-lighting. The effect was remarkable. From a distance of several miles a white silhouette stood out, perfectly defined, or, from the opposite direction, a luminous halo with the silhouette in black. I used to leave this headlight burning whenever I went below or slept at night, and I can affirm that it would be impossible for a steamship anywhere in my vicinity to miss seeing me. In fact, so illuminated, the Winnibelle was more conspicuous than in broad daylight.

The case of fog remains. According to the regulations, the captain must remain on watch on the bridge personally as long as it lasts. On a passenger liner, in the middle of a gala dinner, the

officer on watch passes the word to the commander, 'Fog'. Immediately the latter puts down his napkin, makes his excuses and disappears. With limited vision, everyone is equally affected; the
danger is the same for all.

It remains to be added that along the course I was following fog
is exceptional and visibility generally good in comparison with the
North Atlantic.

And lastly, as the course was also an extremely unfrequented
one, the risk of collision was reduced to a minimum, save at certain
well-known and dangerous 'cross-roads', where it is wise to keep a
sharp look-out, and where you may be sure I kept one.

Under these conditions, then, it is permissible to leave the helm
and let the vessel sail herself during the day or on a clear night.
The reader will agree there is everything to be said for keeping
going at normal speed rather than heaving to, drifting or anchoring
(in 4,000 fathoms!). And anyway, a stationary vessel is just as liable
to be run down as one moving at five or six knots.

So much having been said, I come now to the ways and means of
sailing happily along while fast asleep.

In order to steer a sailing vessel automatically, it is not enough
simply to lock the tiller and set the sails in a particular way.
Generally she will keep her course when close hauled, i.e. with the
wind well forward of the beam, and constant. In very favourable
conditions it can be done with a beam wind, but only with considerable difficulty. With a following wind it becomes practically
impossible, however queer this phenomenon may seem to the un-
initiated, for a sailing vessel seeks all the time to ride up into and
face the wind: there is no rig in the world that has not this tendency. Now in my crossing I relied entirely on the trades, which
meant a following wind day in day out practically the whole way.

Slocum, when he wanted to sleep, stowed his mainsail and
hardened in his jibs as strongly as possible. The fore part of his
boat then fell away from the wind by itself, like the tail of a weather-
cock, and in a sense achieved the desired result, as she no longer
pointed into the wind. But he also made hardly any progress. I
had done the same thing myself by way of experiment, in the Bay
of Biscay.

What is the solution? Quite simple. Make the sails control the

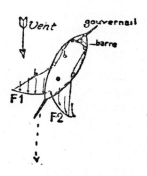

rudder; that is to say, make them alter the angle of the tiller, pro-portionately with the pressure exerted by the wind on one sail or another; just as small model boats have done for a long time. The manufacturers of these model racing craft were in fact the first to hit on the idea. A model racing boat must of necessity do without a helmsman, and she races over considerable distances quite by herself, her builders having, so to speak, given her intelligence. I had not neglected to acquaint myself with their methods and profit by their experience. The exact layout of a model is impos-sible to apply in a real boat, but, the broad principle being estab-lished, I evolved an adaptation suitable for the Winnibelle.

I firmly believed at the time that I was the first to make the attempt. Later I discovered that Capt. Otway Waller had been before me, although his method took an altogether different form. It is interesting to compare his apparatus with mine. Gerbault employed Waller's system, slightly modified, on his second voyage. Paul Hammond wrote to me, after my crossing, asking for details of mine, as he wanted to use the idea on his new cutter Barn-swallow. But eventually he found still another solution. And there may well be others of which I have not heard.

The object was in all cases the same: to sail before the wind without steering. There is no point of sailing more tiring for a helmsman than when the wind is dead aft; the vessel 'doesn't feel the helm', and yaws about on the slopes of the waves which, moving in exactly the same direction as herself, continually over-take her. With some boats it is quite impossible to run directly before the wind, using the mainsail; half a second of inattention, however skilful the helmsman, gets her by the lee and produces a gybe all standing. Many a boat has lost her mast through such a gybe, which sends the heavy boom crashing from one side to the other, carrying away backstays, runners and shrouds as it goes. I had not this to fear with my boomless mainsail, but all human resistance has its limits, and four hours at the tiller in such con-ditions is more than enough for any man.

I had accordingly made up my mind not to use my mainsail at all in the trades, but to replace it with two symmetrical foresails, run-ning up a double forestay and boomed out nearly square on either side. The booms would be trimmed slightly forward, i.e. in a wide

V, and their braces would lead directly through blocks and be made fast to the tiller.

With the wind exactly aft the pull on the two braces should be equal and keep the helm amidships, but should the vessel yaw to left or right, one of the sails would have more wind and the other less. This would pull the tiller the requisite way to keep the boat on her course.

My chief worry was lest the vessel should yaw continuously from side to side, or again, lest the pull on the tiller should not be sufficient to correct her in a very steep sea.

Here I was plunging into the unknown, but since I had often fought with the sheets of a sail full of wind, it seemed to me that the pull on the helm would be equal to any that the toughest of helmsmen could achieve.

The advantage of the system was its extreme simplicity. Instead of having special triangular sails made, like Waller, I utilised my ordinary balloon foresails and could, if necessary, in very heavy weather, use my No. 2 pair. The iron shackles could be instantaneously fixed on the forestays, which had been made double for the purpose; they were of the usual type, and there was neither Wykeham-Martin roller gear, nor anything of the Waller or Hammond reefing system, to reduce sail. No traveller, no sheet, no unlashed tack, nothing but screw-shackles fitted permanently and a little length of chain. To reduce canvas was the simplest thing in the world; I simply slacked off the two foresail halliards and the sails slid down and, so to speak, stowed themselves; and the squall once blown over, I had only to hoist them again.

Another advantage of my sail plan was that an oblique or 'lifting' surface was presented to the following wind, tending to raise the bow, the more so as it was all well forward, compared with the straight, vertical surface presented by two spinnakers much further aft, indeed almost abreast of the mast.

Meanwhile the boat was making such good progress under mainsail in the fresh northerly wind, and the weather was so fine, that I put off till next morning the inevitable loss of half a day's sailing which the change-over would entail. I was not quite certain yet whether the wind would hold, and did not want to lose the benefit of it, but as in the morning it showed no sign of shifting, I decided to delay no longer. It proved to be quite a business, but fortunately I was prepared for that. I had had no opportunity of trying out the plan in the Channel or the Bay; all I had been able to do was to satisfy myself, by rigging all the gear, with Henri's assistance, one fine day while lying in Cowes Roads, that nothing was missing.

By way of a start I took in all sail, jib, mainsail, etc. . . . The vessel lay to, under bare poles, as usual with the wind more or less abeam, and made the most of it by giving way to an orgy of rolling, which did not help matters at all. I set to work and fitted wire braces to the tiller, with return sheaves placed athwart the bulwarks. I spent two hours with my legs entangled in cordage, battling with bits of rope, chain and shackles. I was banged in the face two or three times by the sheet blocks. The rolling was so fierce that I had to work on my hands and knees. I swiped my hand with a hammer in trying to cut a chain link with the cold chisel, broke two saw blades and dropped a spike overboard. And all for nothing. When everything was fixed and the boat put on her course, nothing worked. The booms lifted up in the air, the foresails ballooned in every direction, and nothing, absolutely nothing, functioned. It was a grotesque mockery. I just stood there at the helm quite dazed and trying to make out why it would not work.

I began again by changing the braces, and replaced the wire by some manilla that I luckily had in reserve. I rigged guys, which necessitated climbing the mast, and led two fore braces through blocks at the bowsprit end. I was astride the bowsprit well over half-an-hour on this job, and reached considerable heights of eloquence in the swearing line, as may be imagined, while I was at it.

The second attempt succeeded hardly better than the first. All that it established was that, as I lessened friction, so I began to get vestiges of a result. Sometimes the mere effect of a roll produced a pull strong enough to move the tiller; unfortunately this movement was followed by no reaction in the opposite direction, as the rope jammed in the lead blocks which I had had specially made in St Malo. During all this time the Winnibelle never ceased for a moment from jumping up and down and pirouetting wildly as the seas dictated.

I unshipped everything for the second time, in such a rage by now that I lashed out as hard as I could with my fist at one of the blocks. Naturally I hurt myself abominably and my hand was swollen to double its size for several days. The effect meanwhile was sobering, and pulling myself together, I dived into the bosun's locker and got out four good blocks with roller bearings, two pots of tallow, a drilling brace and some iron wire.

I fixed two ringbolts in the gunwale just forward of the shrouds and hooked on two of the blocks. I fixed the other two on the stern hoop and passed the braces through these two sets of blocks and carefully tallowed their bearings. There is nothing like a good big block for giving a minimum of friction, provided it can move about freely with the action of the rope; by its own weight it exerts a regulating action on the pull of the latter. This is readily apparent on big sailing ships, where the brace blocks have to be as big and heavy as possible, though at first sight one wonders why.

The moment came when everything began to function: the booms no longer lifted, as they were held down by the blocks on the gunwale, and now the braces slipped through the leads with perfect ease. I stayed where I was for a quarter of an hour, covered with sweat and filled with amazement.

It is curiously impressive to watch something working for the first time which you have designed and rigged and guessed at and made mistakes over, and which, in spite of everything, really and truly works! And it did work, that was the essential thing. It remained to be seen what would happen in bad weather, or on the other hand, in light airs, but that could be attended to later. I preferred to meet difficulties, should they come, in my stride, rather than spend whole days standing at the helm with my eyes fixed on the compass, unable to move.

Thereupon I went peacefully below to the galley and, by way of a success-signal, heated up an enormous tin of American prawns, glancing from time to time through the hatch at the silent movement, back and forth, of my tiller. Then I treated myself to seven hours sleep, during which the log chalked up thirty-five miles; a mean of five knots. When I grasped this, I danced a jig on deck: it was miraculous, there was no other word! As the wind was not exactly in the required quarter, I had, it is true, deviated slightly from my course, but one must not be too particular. The problem now was to make the boat sail 10° to port or starboard of the wind's axis. To attain this was only a matter of easing one brace and taking in the other. There were limits to this method, however, and with the wind on the quarter she at once began to show herself definitely refractory. Then I managed to increase the desired inclination by checking the swing of the tiller on one side, so that all her yawing took place in one direction only. This adjustment was a fairly delicate business, but I could do it without being disturbed, from the inside of the saloon, by setting up one of the tiller ropes which I have already mentioned.

Decidedly, life was good!

CHAPTER XV

MADEIRA

Everything was going according to plan, and progress was normal, but I was beginning to worry about my rudder head, which felt the effects of the excessive play which I mentioned earlier. But for this I should not have put in to Madeira, despite Somerset's recommendation. Now I felt that it would be as well, before reaching the trades, to have an iron strengthener made and fitted, so as to avoid serious trouble later.

On the 23rd May the mainsail lacing, worn away by constant use, parted at the gaff. The frapping of the second peak cringle was also in a bad state, so I repaired it.

The rudder head opened up more and more. I entered in the log:

'Made a wire bridle. Vile weather. Winnibelle is rolling continuously and excessively. All my tumblers are smashed except the two unbreakable ones. Very difficult to fix the side lights. The boat is *overballasted*. Run 96 miles.'

The following day:

'85 miles, made another bridle of hoop iron for the rudder head.'

I had too much weight under the floors and the Winnibelle, once she had started rolling, oscillated like a pendulum, the wind being strong and dead aft.

On the 21st I had spoken an oil tanker, the Zorroza, bound from Texas for the coast of Southern Spain. She had skilfully given me a lee in the heavyish sea then running. I generally like to give large vessels a wide berth for fear of accidents, but it was easy to see that this skipper knew his business. When I first sighted her she was crossing my bows some miles ahead, but shortly altered course towards me, evidently intrigued by a small sail so far out at sea. Nor was I sorry myself to hoist the signal 'QZK'—(Please give me your latitude and longitude).

She approached and came round in a half-circle under my stern, keeping just sufficient way on. When she was quite close I saw a black board at one corner of her bridge with the latitude and longitude chalked up, a method which I very much appreciated, as it saved me the trouble of burying my nose in the code book to interpret her signal. The captain then hailed me through the megaphone, asking where I was bound for.

'Madeira,' I shouted.

'Do you want me to report you?'

'Yes, to the Yacht Club, Paris.'

Three blasts on the syren, a dip of my ensign, and the Zorroza was on her course again. Later on I sent the captain of this ship a short account of my voyage. He wrote back from Sevastopol and thanked me very charmingly, enclosing a photograph of himself, which I am glad to have.

I made the land at Porto-Santo, thirty miles to the North of Madeira, on 25th May, at 5 p.m. Madeira itself being very mountainous, rising to some 6,000 feet, I had hoped to sight it a long way off, but I was wrong. It is impossible to unravel from the French Nautical Instructions what the average visibility in this locality is. Never in my life have I read a document through so carefully with so little profit. 'In these waters', I learned, 'visibility is rarely less than a mile.'

Well, well! What are normal weather conditions here? Misty? It is up to you to guess. The sky was quite clear, yet I had the impression of a kind of yellowish haze over the sea, but could not estimate how much it would hinder visibility. I could make out the line of the horizon, but the horizon is no distance away in a small boat, three or four miles at most.

Towards noon I began to get nervous. I felt land was quite near, yet I could not help wondering if I had made some error in my calculations. After all, Madeira is not the biggest island in the world, and has plenty of open space all round it.

At 3 p.m. I thought I saw something astern, a hill of some sort with houses on it. I was on the point of going about, thinking I must have got between Porto-Santo and Madeira. In the luminous and deceptive atmosphere I soon began to realise that I was seeing hills and white houses in all directions. I shut my eyes and then opened them again quickly, trying to make certain of some particular point. Truth to tell, I was beginning to feel the strain.

This feeling is quite familiar to the lone navigator making a tricky landfall; he loses patience, scratches his head, checks his course for the hundredth time, goes over his calculations, calls himself every name under the sun. There is no one to talk it over with. Suddenly, he feels lost, and begins to doubt whether the land exists at all, and whether he will ever find it. Two weeks at sea without sight of land are quite enough to induce this frame of mind.

The Winnibelle was sailing herself, close-hauled, leaning nicely in an ideal sea, making about six knots. I climbed into the throat of the mainsail and looked round with a sort of foregone conviction I should see nothing, so disconcerted was I by not having found what I sought at the correct moment. Perhaps my chronometer was out of adjustment. . . .

'If I see land tonight,' I said aloud to myself, 'I'll uncork a bottle of champagne. Be damned if I don't!'

Suddenly I thought I saw something straight ahead. The sun was in my eyes. I opened and shut them two or three times; each time it was still there; the outline of a mountain, greyish yellow and no great distance away. I came down from the mast, went below and forced myself to stay there for half an hour. The hands of the cabin clock turned slowly, very slowly, while the Winnibelle sailed on.

On the tick, I again clambered up the ratlines and settled once more in the throat. The outline of the island of Porto-Santo stretched in front of me clearly defined. I took a sight as well as a bearing of the summit and end points of the island, from which I learnt that I was much nearer than I would ever have believed: only four miles. And I had counted on picking it up from thirty miles off at least.

From aloft the spectacle was a marvellous one: steep, majestic peaks, bathed in the glow of the setting sun. Not a sail, not a ship to be seen. I shifted the Winnibelle's course, went below and wrote:

'Was in the rigging from 4.30 to 5.40 p.m. 6.10, land in sight 4 miles off. Patches of mist hiding the land from time to time. Headed for Fora. Compass bearing, 6.30 p.m., S. 63. W. Sighted Sao-Laurenço light at 8.0 p.m.

As I did not want to reach Madeira before morning I took in a couple of reefs and pulled down the foresail.

Funchal attracted me. My brother had touched there when serving as an officer-instructor in the cadet ship Jeanne d'Arc, and I had on board a photograph of one of her seaplanes taking off, with the serrated outline of one of the steep island mountains in the background.

For spring it was abominably cold. At 5.0 a.m. I cleared the islet of Fora at a few cable-lengths, pushed along by a stiff breeze and covered with spray (the two reefs were not at all too much) in a setting I shall long remember. The clouds, hurrying from the north-east, gathered about the island pinnacles, where for a time they writhed and swirled in grey masses; soon first one wisp, then another would detach itself, sweep halfway down the other side, glowing in the pink light of the dawn, and then vanish like magic into thin air. The side of the island exposed to the trade winds was bare, deserted and wild; one might have been looking at the Lofoten Islands.

Suddenly, not far from the rocky islets of Desertas and Bugio, I ran into a belt of calm. These islets rise abruptly from the sea to dizzy heights, like the blades of a knife; they are reputed to be inaccessible, and neither boasts a lighthouse, so that they can be exceedingly dangerous to mariners. My sails began to shake and I found myself in a dead calm, just as the warmth of the day began to make itself felt.

I decided to start the auxiliary and motor the remaining eight or ten miles to Funchal, which was still hidden behind a projecting headland, but on trying to swing the starting-handle I found the engine completely seized. I injected petrol and oil into the cylinders, I pulled, I pushed: it was no good. Finally, in a spirit of desperation, I resorted to heroic measures. Rigging a purchase to the mast and taking two turns round the flywheel, I heaved on that purchase, alternately fore and aft, with every ounce of energy I possessed, putting my whole weight into the job. Nothing moved. Then just as I was abandoning hope, a jet of water shot from the compression plug; the piston had just uncovered the exhaust vent and the sea water in the crank-case (where the compression takes place in two strokes) had spouted up.

I knew at once that sea water must have got into the engine through the exhaust pipe during bad weather. . . . Needless to say, it was my own fault. I had insisted on the makers fitting a stop valve, against their better judgment, but . . . I had left it open since Finistère. Just the way things happen; you raise hell, you insist, you get your way . . . and after all you're caught out like a mutt.

The engine being a two-stroke diesel I had naturally to change the crank-case oil, which by now was a sort of soapy emulsion with all the salt water in it. I had to turn the motor over for nearly half an hour to clear it out completely, then wash out with paraffin and fill up again with oil, after which it started at the first turn. On the whole it was an excellent little engine which never afterwards gave me a moment's trouble, and had the great advantage of starting from cold on a quarter turn.

There was not a breath of wind under the lee of the island. The clouds remained perched on the high mountain tops . . . and the sun beat down.

Visitors only stay on the southern slopes, hence the legend that in Madeira it is always fine. . . . The devil it is! Once the liner gets clear of the roads, fine is hardly the right word. (They always tell you they ran into a storm shortly after leaving.)

Very soon I made out liners at anchor in the roads, then the town, the signal mast, the hillsides dotted with innumerable white houses. I headed outside the liners to give myself time to inspect the anchorage.

I remember a man who leaned over the rail of one of the vessels with one arm out towards me and his thumb raised, evidently asking some question. At first I thought he wanted to know whether I needed help, and I shook my head and smiled. Then I began to understand; he wanted to know whether I was alone. On learning that I was, he began to clap. Meanwhile, a number of gaily coloured rowing boats were heading in my direction, a regular regatta. 'Here', thought I, 'begins the plucking and diddling of yours truly, just dropped from the sky. God help me when they come alongside. . . . My poor white paint!'

'Clear out, you . . .! Hands off! I don't understand your blasted lingo! English? No, not a word. Oh, go to bed!'

All the same I had to bring up somewhere. I let the mainsail and foresail come down with a run, without leaving the helm. A ripple of curiosity. The natives had never seen sails stowing themselves before. . . . And then what? Where can I put her? Here? There? Two natives clambered on board. The anchor was ready to let go, and there were two warps coiled down in the stern. One of the pair tried to tow me in one direction, the other had different ideas altogether. Heave! Now comes the tug of war! The confusion was indescribable. However, better let 'em get on with it, I thought. No point in losing my temper. Here I am, anyway. I'll go below and start the primus.

'Captain', (they say Kep'n) 'you let down anchor?'

'Well, I'm not dead set on it. I prefer being moored fore and aft, if it's all the same to you.'

'Oh yes! Very good here, anchor.'

'I say NO!'

'Very good here.'

'!!!!!!'.

'Me all savvy, y'know me, harbour master he tell me . . . me all arrange for you, y' know.'

'Oh, all right, have it your own way, but for God's sake make a tripping line fast to the anchor; otherwise with all the other anchor cables there must be at the bottom here, I'm bound to hook one of them, and then where'll I be?'

He saw what I meant; there was evidently some sense in his unpromising skull. 'No, no, nev' mind, me get it all right, me diving man, y' know? Me dive' . . . (He went through the motion of diving.)

'Is that so? A guinea a dive, I suppose? Do you take me for a Rothschild? Get along with you!'

'Yes, yes. Very good, let go . . . me dive' . . . and splash! There went my big anchor over the side. Nothing I could say would have made any difference. And after all, there was plenty of time to straighten things out.

CHAPTER XVI

IN PORT

For better or worse the Winnibelle eventually found a berth at La Pontinha, with one stern warp made fast to a motor tender—one of the numerous pretty little varnished craft which convey tourists to and from the liners—and the other to a grubby little steam vessel belonging to Blandy's, the Lloyds' agents. The place is about a thousand yards from the town, but is the only sheltered anchorage, the rest of the coast being steep to. The big ships stay in the roads off Funchal, relying on fine weather and such protection as the island affords. In the not very likely event of an on shore gale they can always up anchor and steam out to sea. It is three generations since such a gale last occurred, I believe, and they still talk of it in Madeira with bated breath.

Pontinha, being on the edge of very deep water, suffers from an incessant swell, which unfortunately corresponded exactly to the Winnibelle's tendencies in that respect. She was soon rolling gunwale under, while her masthead described semi-circles in the air. However, there are worse fates than rolling in harbour. I had a look at my surroundings. The fierce sun beat down on tiled roofs, white walls and strange-shaped belfries and the air was heavy with the scent of flowers. Some food, then exploration, seemed to be indicated.

I was breaking some eggs into the frying pan when I realised I æas not alone. Watching me from the top of the companion, where he sat in a free and easy way, with bulging eyes and a general air of detachment, was a youth of about twenty. He seemed friendly, and I passed him a glass of Douarnenez cider and a slice of ham between a couple of biscuits.

'You wait for doctor,' was all he said.

True. The sanitary inspection. . . . I passed him up a yellow flag to hoist, according to the best traditions.

'Where have your pals got to?'

He laughed. 'Calaboose, hop!'

There is no more international word than 'calaboose' on earth. But why, I asked him, had they put his friends in jug? What was it all about?

'They came on board before Doctor, very bad, calaboose!'

Well, that was their own look-out. They need never have boarded me. I hadn't asked for them.

'Me too, calaboose!' he insisted. 'Kep'n, you speak to Doctor, me no calaboose, eh?'

'We'll see, we'll see. Meanwhile talk about something else.'

At two o'clock the doctor, dressed in khaki, came alongside in one of the port launches, twice the size of the Winnibelle and making enough disturbance for a destroyer. No, he didn't want to come on board. He looked like Franz Joseph of Austria. He was in a rage. He heaped objurgations on my goggle-eyed friend. It went on and on.

'Papers! What, no health certificate?'

I began to feel that I should be joining the others in the lock-up. He looked through every document I possessed, and was only too obviously mystified by all he saw. To save his face he read the whole way through the ship's papers, white, yellow, red and green, at the top of his voice, starting with 'République Française, Minis-tère de la Marine Marchande. Première région maritime ... Quartier de ... Acte de francisation provisoire ... au nom du peuple français,' etc., etc. Not one word did he understand.

I wanted to laugh so badly that I very nearly choked. And my coffee was on the point of boiling over on the stove, and I dared not budge. At last he made ready to go, magnanimously agreeing not to commit Rojado (the name by which goggle-eyes went) to the calaboose this time. But if it occurred again, chrm, brr, hm ... etc. Impossible to express my gratitude; my cap swept the deck again and again.

'Thank you, dear sir, I like you very much, gracias, senhor, thank you, merci. Pas du tout au contraire. Bonjour to your lady. Yes. Yes. Understood. Yes. That's it. Adios! Agreed! Au revoir!' I hastened to save what remained of the coffee.

Hunger appeased, I went ashore, and had myself rowed over to the new jetty, then recently completed on the town side of the anchorage. I took the ship's papers with me to deposit them at the

Consulate. They were in a metal tube painted green. A Customs man, full of zeal and suspicion, stopped me immediately to ask what it was. When I opened the lid and showed him the contents he remarked, 'Ah, bueno, papelar!'

'Exactly,' I said, 'papelards' (whatever that might mean).

At the Consular Office an exceedingly tall man whose face I liked accepted my documents without remark and gave me the address of a good ironsmith. I was now free to wander as the spirit moved me in the brilliant sunlight.

The sea front of the town, which is remarkably fine, is entirely occupied by the Steamship Companies' landing stages: a short slope, shaded by beautiful trees, leads to the principal square and the shopping quarter. Any sailor finds his way there by instinct.

Before I had gone far I began to feel the ground moving under my feet; perhaps it would be more accurate to say that the soles of my boots seemed to touch the ground either too soon or too late. Fifteen days of dancing about from one foot to the other had their effect.

I chose a restaurant in the main square for dinner, and quickly learnt to order 'bisteck con patatas fritas'. When I got back to the Winnibelle Rojado introduced the two other sailors who had hailed me in the roadstead, and who had been let out of the calaboose. Their names were Domingo and Escorcio. Escorcio was a pleasant-looking fellow; a conspicuous scar decorated Domingo's dial, which was perfectly round, and his right hand was minus two fingers.

I slept late next morning and was roused by the sound of bare feet on deck. My three retainers were busy washing down the varnished work with fresh water; they coughed with due discretion and conversed in whispers. I may say that in general I look on un-solicited aid with a good deal of scepticism, but in this instance I decided to postpone judgment till later.

The Winnibelle was still rolling incessantly. The sun's rays penetrated down the hatch into the cabin and the temperature began to rise. My men refused a glass of white wine, but brought lemons and taught me to concoct 'sangria', a kind of lemon squash made with red wine and soda. Presumably it is called 'sangria' on account of its blood colour; at any rate it suits the climate perfectly. Here was good evidence of the sobriety of Domingo and Co., nor had I ever to complain of them in that respect, or indeed in any other.

Domingo spoke a little English, and I used him for all sorts of things. He fixed the iron collar on the rudder head; lapped a sheet of copper on the mast at the jaws of the gaff; tallowed the leather on the jaws; washed the topsides, and scrubbed the bottom below water with stiff, long-handled brooms which he managed to borrow from somewhere.

There is no slip at Funchal, and scarcely any tide, so that hauling out or careening for a proper scrape down is impracticable; barnacles of various sorts take hold very quickly, even on copper. In fact, the marvellously clear water there, through which the bottom can be seen quite clearly at two and a half fathoms, is as unhealthy as any in the world, especially for wooden hulls. The teredo worm will penetrate a hull, if not coppered, in a few days, and once it has got into the planking the damage is irreparable. I was told that no amount of anti-fouling mixture will keep the pests at bay for more than a very short time.

The teredo is a worm with a hard head and a tail like a gimlet. It leaves only a single small hole to mark its actual entry into the vessel's side, and then ceaselessly digs out galleries without once breaking the surface, so that very often its presence is quite unsuspected. Only a trained ear can hear them at work, when everything else is still; then you can detect a rhythmic sound like that of a hand auger being used: crack, crack. . . . I have heard it myself on some vessels; a most sinister sound. It is quite useless to try and locate the spot, or to trace the tunnels by picking with a knife; owing to some curious sound-effect the worm is never where you look for it. I have several times had in my hands pieces of planking attacked by teredoes: outwardly they were intact, with no visible mark on either surface, but if pinched or squeezed they crumbled away into dust, so completely were they eaten up and hollowed out in a thousand galleries. From this it will be realised how difficult it is to assess the condition of a hull so attacked. It is sometimes said that it can be done by holding a watch against one side of the suspected part of the hull and putting your ear to the other. Only if the wood is sound will the tick of the watch sound clearly. I cannot vouch for the effectiveness of this somewhat primitive method.

In Madeira all vessels are copper bottomed and the sheathing is even brought up as much as a foot above the water line, whereas it is the general opinion, at any rate in our own home waters, that the teredo will not attack wood out of water. In Madeira they think differently, and as the Winnibelle's sheathing stopped at the water line, I decided to scrub her for some distance above it every day. In spite of this I more than once spotted teredoes *in flagrante delicto*, enormous brutes, as thick as pencils.

About noon I was hailed, much to my surprise, by the Consul, who asked if he might come aboard. He was much interested in the Winnibelle's voyage, and explained that it was only after I had left his office, when he came to examine my papers, that he realised I was single-handed. He took me off to lunch at his home, a delightful house with a wonderful garden, and we soon found we had many mutual acquaintances. Mr da Cunha, Madeira-born himself, had married a Frenchwoman. A first class tennis player, agent for the British Elder-Dempster line, and a man of many parts, he soon acquired French sympathies. Early in the last war he recovered and sent home, at his own expense, the bodies of the French sailors who lost their lives when the sloop La Surprise was torpedoed. Nobody in France showed any particular sign of gratitude, which is no doubt in accordance with the best tradition.

I next turned my attention to the replenishment of stores. The water I had brought with me, over and above what my tanks held, was carried in badly galvanised tins, and had gone rusty. On the advice of a ship's chandler, named Coelho, who had served under Scott in the Discovery, I simply bought fifty bottles, which I stowed in various parts of the boat. This method I have used ever since; it has the merit of extreme simplicity, which I suppose is why I had never thought of it before, and experience has amply demonstrated its advantages. In the course of several years I can only remember having broken three or four bottles.

I needed wine also. I thought it would be easy to buy some inexpensive young local wine, but what I was offered was peppery and undrinkable, with an exceedingly off flavour. As the only home grown alternative was old Madeira, which is above price, I had to fall back on some indifferent stuff imported from Lisbon.

No one knows the maturing limit of real Madeira; there is some in existence a hundred and fifty years old. It reaches fantastic prices when it is authentic. The vines, which grow on the very steep hillsides of the island, require a great deal of attention; huge cement reservoirs are necessary, and strong and expensive walls have to be built to retain the soil. The peasant is becoming discouraged and tends, little by little, to abandon the vine in favour of the sugar cane, which thrives anywhere, and brings in almost as much. Hence the scarcity of Madeira wine, and the rising price of it. The grower brings it in bulk to the firms which undertake the treatment of it, for Madeira, be it understood, is always artificially 'treated'. Natural maturing no longer takes place, unless perhaps in a few private cellars. In the past it was noticed that a sea voyage greatly improved a Madeira, and certain wine merchants used to ship quantities in the wood to the Antilles and back, for example. It was really the heat of the 'tween-decks, coupled with the ship's motion, which caused it to 'work' at the right temperature and accelerated the process of 'madeirisation'. Nowadays the wine is merely steam heated by means of coils of copper tubing, and movement is imparted by electric pumps which draw it from one cask into another. In spite of all this I imagine the result falls short of the product of the natural process; but it asks a lot from human patience to wait twenty or thirty years to drink what would still only be a young Madeira!

The time drew near for my departure from this perfumed, colourful, sunlit island, an island of eternal spring, and a little enervating on that account.

As at Douarnenez, I insisted on having some hard-baked bread. I had repeated over and over again to all the bakers 'bene coquito', and not one of them took any notice. They said 'Yes', promised, and then completely disregarded my instructions. The fact was they could not understand my wanting this kind of bread, and thought it just a foolish whim on my part. No liner buys bread; it is baked on board: on the other hand, no Madeira fisherman will risk going as far as the African coast, although it is no great distance.

When my arrangements were nearly complete, Rojado, Escorcio and Domingo redoubled their attentions. The cockpit-cover guide got more and more difficult to open on going below, so that I had to force the hatch open with my feet. Domingo and I spent a whole afternoon tallowing and sandpapering it, without much result. I asked the harbour-master, who often used to read the papers in the pilot-launch alongside the Winnibelle, how I ought to settle with my three sailors. He told me that they had been working to please themselves, and that I had done quite enough for them. Nevertheless I did not feel quite happy about it, and was glad when soon afterwards a chance of repaying them occurred.

As the Winnibelle was carrying too much ballast, I had decided to unload rather more than a ton of lead pigs. I asked permission of the Customs to take the pigs ashore: they refused. I said it was essential: they were prepared to waive their objection provided I paid duty of one shilling per kilo landed; the price of loose lead being hardly a quarter of that amount, I returned to the attack and said I would assert my right of throwing the lead overboard, when it would become a dead loss, but I offered to give it away for the taking, rather than chuck it away. The authorities remained inflexible: an admirable example of official stupidity.

I did not want to throw it overboard at sea, as nothing is more tricky than handling ballast or stowing it properly in a moving vessel; a pig may easily slip through your hands and fall, and serious damage to yourself or the boat may result. So I decided to drop my ton of lead in the water where I was: that is to say, sixty pieces of lead ballast would go to the bottom of the harbour. It was done at night, very silently. The following day there it lay, clearly visible in a beautiful heap. I was afraid someone might see it from the quayside, when I could have been charged with dumping rubbish, and heavily fined. But it was no affair of mine what my good chaps did with the lead, and indeed I do not know to this day whether they got it all up. But the very next morning Domingo said to me: 'Captain, will you bet me I can't get up three bits in a single dive?'

He boasted of his prowess as a high-diver and claimed to have dived more than once from the top of the tower on Fort Pontinha, which is about sixty feet high. I did not doubt his talent, but I know from experience that one man cannot possibly get up three lead pigs, if indeed he can manage a single one.

At any rate Domingo dived in. . . . After a time he came up, his face wreathed in smiles, but empty-handed.

'There you are,' he spluttered, and from a near-by dinghy Escorcio could be seen hauling a basket on a line to the surface. For form's sake I questioned the validity of the bet. . . . Domingo, on reaching bottom, had merely to put the pigs into the basket.

I felt I had been too long at Funchal, and began to worry, as the season was getting on.

'For the love of Heaven', Mrs Brown, the wife of the British Consul, had entreated, 'don't hang about the coast of Florida in August!' Serious enough advice, since Mrs Brown was born in Miami and knew well what she was talking about.

So on the 9th June I got under way.

Winnibelle as she appeared at the Salon Nautique in Paris (with bulwarks) 1933

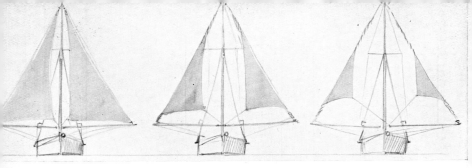

Otway Waller

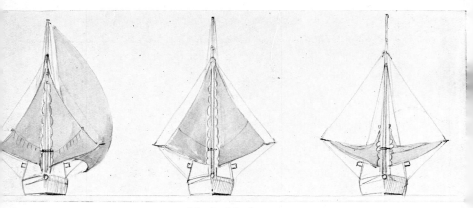

Marin-Marie

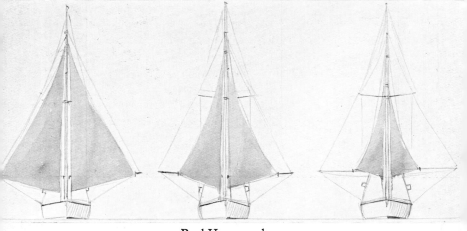

Paul Hammond
Different ways of reefing double-wings

CHAPTER XVII

THE TRADES

From Madeira to the West Indies is 2,830 nautical miles as the crow flies—or rather doesn't.

As I was following a big circle in the very heart of the trades, a magnificent sweep, a true curve of nature, my actual course was longer, though not as much longer as might be thought, the difference only being about fifty nautical miles. In addition, a small boat naturally makes frequent zig-zags, big and small. The small ones occur when you go below to get a packet of cigarettes; rather bigger ones when you sleep well and the wind shifts meanwhile; the biggest happen through cross currents, gales, misadventure or simply through error, when you may be off your course for twenty-four hours or more. Then it is necessary to correct by taking a sight.

All these sinuosities have to be traced as one tries to keep in the main direction of the arrows on the wind chart. The 3,000 miles may become 3,200 or 3,500, depending primarily on how carefully you sail.

Needless to say, a single-handed boat will always sheer off her course more than another, and be slower on a passage, simply because she so often sails herself. Shortcomings of one kind and another, careless watch-keeping, delay in making good an error, all come into the account. And after all, what does it matter? As long as you have food and incur no shipwrights' bills, why worry? True . . . yet there is always the old instinct that takes command: it is not 'the thing' to sail just anyhow, deliberately, any more than it is to go out of your way from sheer neglect.

Joking apart, the fact has to be faced that fatigue, or lack of alertness, will inevitably cause a lengthening of the course; fatigue itself being often the result of lack of alertness, or of mere laziness, whether physical or mental. Therefore, no excuses.

Progress, then, is a series of yawings. This is true even of big liners, though less obviously. It is often amusing to look over the

stern at a big ship's wake which, due to the great speed and enormous displacement, goes back almost to the horizon. You can see
quite clearly, thanks to the long perspective, how her course shifts
and wavers. Such a wake is called a 'sea-serpent'.

We often navigated by dead reckoning when I was with the
Pourquoi-Pas, as the northern fogs prevented solar observation.
For this reason the officer of the watch took particular care that the
helmsman kept a good course. Very often, after involuntarily yawing away, I used to glance back anxiously over my shoulder at the
wake, well knowing that I should be called to order if the 'serpent'
was too apparent.

I now had in front of me my longest run, the real passage of the
Atlantic. It was a new experience. I lay in my bunk on the eve of
my departure, under a deck still burning from the day's sunshine,
endlessly turning over in my mind the distance, my possible average speed, the essential things I might have forgotten. . . .

Today I am quite accustomed to this sort of thing and it never
worries me in advance.

Da Cunha was even more anxious than I was myself. During my
two weeks on the island we had got to know each other well, and
indeed it seemed as if the whole of Funchal was interested in the
Winnibelle's departure. No one had ever before come single-
handed from Brittany, or even from Lisbon; nor had anyone set
sail for the Antilles in so small a boat.

They had shown me, in the Funchal Sports Club, photographs
of the first Portuguese seaplane from the mainland to come down
in the roads; it was at the end of the last war, and they still spoke of
it with enthusiasm. In this respect the islanders have a peculiar
mentality, and the interest shown by them in all movements of ships
in the harbour is much greater than in most coast towns; which is
quite understandable.

I was awakened as usual on the morning of my departure by one
of my three musketeers. He began, without any fuss, to take in my
anchors and coil down the warps which he had already cast off
from the quay. We drank a last tot of sangria. Domingo had
brought a mass of things on board, amongst them a string of
onions. They hung, throughout the voyage, in the galley, and before the end had scraped away an appreciable amount of the paint

on the bulkhead, as they swung to and fro like a clinometer when she rolled.

The C.L.M. representative was at hand in his dinghy. The Harbour-Master came much earlier than usual to read the morning papers in his launch. When I saw an enormous bunch of flowers come off I thought at first it was a final assault being delivered by one of the numerous orphanages which had pestered me for subscriptions, and was on the point of refusing them without ceremony, as I had changed all my local money. But this time it was my three faithful henchmen. The flowers were from them. It is always rather embarrassing for a man to accept flowers; but their friendly gesture touched me deeply.

Da Cunha decided to stay on board until we cleared the roads, when his launch would take him back. I let Domingo get her under way. He greatly enjoyed holding the tiller while she began to feel the soft land breeze and slowly forged ahead.

Meanwhile I wrote a few telegrams, and cracked a few last jests with the Consul. He undertook to cable Paris for me as well as my brother, who was then lying at Fort-de-France in the cadet ship Jeanne d'Arc. What a pity that I could not have arranged my programme so as to join him there.

As the launch carried da Cunha away, I shot a few feet of film, then turned round and found myself at the helm again, just as before. I had the impression of having hardly left it. As there was a great gathering of people at the end of the pier, I ran in as close as I could and dipped my ensign in salute, doing my best to perform the evolution smartly while going about. The affair did not pass off without difficulty, as the sennit down-haul which I had formerly used as a flag-halliard had been lost at sea, and was now replaced by a new line which was full of kinks.

I then proceeded under the stern of a German steam-yacht which had arrived during the night, and which was painted an appalling sky-blue. I have never seen a boat painted such a colour before or since.

It was 12.30. Almost at once I ceased to think of the land and resumed my habitual little soliloquy.

The breeze hardened the further I got away from the island. By 6.30 p.m. Madeira had already disappeared behind its cloudy haze of mauve and rose. My first recall to reality was when I felt the tiller knocking against the old bruises which I thought had gone for ever. At midnight I was still on deck, half dreaming under the pure and marvellously starlit heavens.

I saw a liner pass on her way to the Canaries, and calculated she would reach them next day. It seemed fantastic. Around me the sea was as thick as soup with phosphorescent jellyfish, and when I brought in the log-line, their glowing tentacles still clung to it. As I took no precautions my forearms and the backs of my hands were stung as though by nettles. A few days later I was to be stung again even more unpleasantly by nautiluses.

I watched the liner's lights get fainter as she passed southwards and thought it would be long before I saw any others. At night such lights seem companionable, and would be a welcome break in the monotony of a long watch were they not generally attended by anxiety as to the risk of collision.

From time to time, as is the habit of all coastwise navigators, I had a look round the horizon, searching for lights, particularly astern for Madeira's, which were high enough up to be still above the skyline. But the island's warm haze absorbs the most powerful electric lights anywhere beyond a range of twenty miles. One whole month of seeing nothing around me, near or far, day or night, from week's end to week's end, that was what lay ahead of me. Ejnar Nikkelsen, who was cast away in Greenland for more than a year, used to tell me that he would plant a stick about ten paces away 'just to have something to look at', so depressed was he by the utter lack of all objects to relieve the white monotony of the immediate prospect. It was less hard for me, as I had plenty of foreground, say sixty yards of it, and beyond that I no longer strained into the infinite. No doubt the smoke or lights of distant vessels sometimes passed within range of my vision without my observing them.

The following day I picked up on deck nine craches. These little fish, which are a species of cuttlefish, leap out of the water with an arrow-like flight of some five or six yards. I cleaned them carefully, rinsed them several times (what an amount of ink a cuttlefish holds!) and put them in the frying pan, well dusted with flour. I did not foresee that the flour would effectively block up the hollow ink-sacs. The consequence was that they swelled up like balloons and finally burst, throwing sheets of burning oil about, before I had time to do anything about it. Only three survived the explosion; the others had been thrown out of the frying-pan, so I had only three small mouthfuls for my pains.

The sea began to get warm as soon as the wind failed. I ran into a patch of dead calm and started up the engine, but soon switched it off again, preferring to keep my fuel for later on. You never know the extent of a calm patch.

On the third day a faint air, a possible forerunner of the North East trades, deigned to ripple the calm surface. I immediately set up the double foresails. I had greatly improved the apparatus during my stay in Funchal, and though the wind continued light, made good eighty miles in twenty-four hours and seventy-two the day after.

After a time I noticed that the two stays carrying the foresail boom goose-necks had a tendency, under the thrust of the latter, to twist in relation to each other. The tension was not sufficient to keep them straight. I evolved a method of keeping them parallel by means of short chains leading to the fife rail at the foot of the mast. Then I came to the conclusion that the sail area presented under this rig was too small to give sufficient speed in light airs. The alternative would be to hoist a spinnaker and keep at the tiller the whole day, except for my trick below, when I could leave her under the double foresails. Even so I should not be able to get any rest until there was wind enough to give her more than four knots.

Very reluctantly I got the spinnaker out of the sail locker and set up its boom. It filled, pulled steadily on its sheet, and the sea began to froth past. I hauled the sheet in and jumped to the helm. I had not the least idea of the pleasant surprise which awaited me; the boat had not shifted her course and showed no inclination to do so. By all the rules she should have begun to luff. But it was not so. I let her carry on for a quarter of an hour ... twenty minutes ... an hour! The Winnibelle held her course.

As always when I am particularly pleased, I indulged in a little celebration. I treated myself to a very choice dinner, had a luxurious wash, lit a cigar, came up on deck to find the first stars appearing in the sky, went down below again to get a bottle of old

Madeira, and once back on deck began to feel as happy as a king. The explanation of this phenomenon was simple enough, but I was not yet sure whether it would always work without trouble: time alone would show.

Actually it was easy to see what was happening by merely observing the respective pulls on the two pairs of foresail braces. The port foresail, masked by the big spinnaker, hardly pulled at all, and so no longer counterbalanced the action of its opposite number, whereby the latter was easily able to pull on the tiller enough to prevent the boat luffing.

I lit the navigation lights, lay down and slept. I was a passenger. I no longer had anything to do all day long but twiddle my thumbs or attend to odd jobs. As yet I did not believe, in spite of everything, that I would make the Antilles under this same rig. Nevertheless, it so befell. I know of no other yacht owner who can boast of having run 2,600 miles at a stretch without touching the helm.

If the wind shifted a few degrees I did not worry: tomorrow would compensate today; now she had hit the North East trades, I let her carry on. If the error became momentarily too pronounced, I was content to limit it by adjusting the tiller tackles from the saloon, thus preventing the free play of the rudder for the time being.

The 13th June is for me a day of note. That day I felt full of optimism and took some photographs of the sky. The sky is one of the things I contemplate most readily. It seems that I have a mania for looking up suddenly and saying: 'Look at that beautiful cloud formation!' When I am driving a car this makes the passengers a little nervous, so one of them once told me.

For me a beautiful sky is a picture in itself, though skyscapes pure and simple are not in vogue. There is a good reason for this, namely, that it is a most difficult thing to paint the sky. And then again, the painters of street scenes, or even landscapes, never show more of it than just a little corner, whereas at sea, two-thirds of everything is sky. One must admit that there are countries where skies are virtually non-existent, or just downright ugly. For example, I am not very fond of the sky in the Antilles: it is sometimes leaden and sometimes a crude blue, like those smeared on daubs in Montparnasse.

One of the reasons I enjoy W. A. Robinson's *Deep Water and Shoal* so much is that he talks of the sky in every chapter. There's a man now who knows how to look; the way he describes a particular sunset off the coast of Peru makes you want to go there.

In the course of this long crossing I saw grey skies, golden skies, skies with clouds like explosions, or cat's whiskers, sometimes one sort tangled up with another (a very bad sign, but that is another point of view), copper skies, skies of an ineffable blue, or of infinite gradations of colour, descending the scale from indigo to livid green, and ranging through golden yellow, cobalt and sea blue, to die away into violet on the horizon.

Understand, it is practically impossible to paint all this: the effect is much too like a picture postcard! Nevertheless, in the real thing there is no vulgarity. I have seen, on the other hand, harmonies of sweetmeaty mauve which, painted, would make one ill; skies which looked as if they had been painted in sepia; clouds the colour of sulphur, and immense haloes joining one horizon to the other, spreading like a great mantle over me. It is thus that I imagine the end of the world; an absolutely opaque halo, advancing and shutting off for ever the sight of the stars. In a few days all life would be extinct on the surface of the planet.

I have seen seas that refused to harmonise with the skies, confounding the accepted formula, 'Water reflects the sky, etc., etc.' Yes, I have seen steely seas, cold grey under a most spectacular fantasy of pink and tender blue; olive seas beneath turquoise skies and turquoise seas under grey. . . . I have seen so many apparent improbabilities of the kind, confounding all logic, that one day I ended by noting at the bottom of a particularly incoherent page, 'All, all is possible.'

It was in Greenland, at Jan Mayen in particular, that I saw the softest colouring, the most impossible to mix on a palette. How many times have I not closed my sketchbook in despair! The effects are so rapid that it is impossible to note them down in colour, which is far the best method. It was heartbreaking to be able to wring so little from the unequalled beauty of those northern skies.

Meanwhile, to return to my narrative. The sky assumed, little by little, its typical appearance; grey, rainy, troubled, the condition one expects to find in the region of the trades. On the 14th June I wrote: 'Too cloudy to get correct latitude.' On the 15th: 'For two days the sea has been wan and the sky overcast like the Channel in January, and we are at 27° lat. Not a wink of sleep.'

I watched clouds travelling in different directions to each other at different altitudes, always rather an uncomfortable sight.

Not being on the wind, the Winnibelle rolled heavily all the time, without exaggerated violence but with a dreadful thoroughness. And there was no respite, not a moment when she was more or less in equilibrium. It was as if the water had been taken from under her on the side she heeled. At these times she fell as though into a hole, only recovering to fall over on the other side; even if a wave came opportunely to oppose the rolling, or at least break the period of her swing, the Winnibelle took no notice of it and just bumped slightly, then fell even further over. There is nothing more maddening than these bumps and the sudden drop that follows them. I became acquainted to my cost with every sharp angle in the cabin. Incessant stumbling. I could not stand up on deck without hanging on, and was nearly overboard several times. I only moved about crouching or even on all fours. Until the novelty wears off there may be an element of romance, for all I know, in this sort of thing, but in the long run it is stupefying.

Two things accounted for this violent rolling: Winnibelle's midship section not being full enough, and the sea of the trades corresponding to her period of swing. Let no one speak to me of 'the long Atlantic swell in which small boats are comfortable!' I do not know who can have invented this balderdash; someone, at any rate, who had never had the experience.

Squalls, of course, began to make their appearance, sometimes with rain, sometimes without. The nearer I approached the Antilles, the more violent, numerous and dense they became. In Douarnenez I had made provision for the case of rain with a following wind, when it is impossible to keep the hatch open without getting a downpour on the cabin floor. I was armed with a thick sheet of celluloid, which I slid into the keyways of the sliding hatch; thus I had light and could look outside without getting soaked. This sort of detail may sound rather finicky, but it is by no means a detail to be soaked every day for a month on end.

Between squalls the wind would die down almost completely, so much so that I had to hoist and hand the spinnaker ten times a day —and night—if not more often.

The job was usually easy enough when I tackled it in time, but once or twice it happened that I had to take in the frail, rain-soaked cloth as it threshed wildly about on the impact of the first blast. Then it was no joke. Several times I thought I had lost my invaluable spinnaker, which was, moreover, the only sail for which I had no spare.

When only four days out I entered in my log: 'The spinnaker unfortunately will be worn out in a few days. It is too light for the trades. (Calico, machine sewn)', and on the same day: '123 miles by the log, getting along faster.' The next day: '117 miles', then: 105, 100, 119. . . . We are making long strides now.'

I then considered it was time, since I need no longer worry about my progress, to amuse myself a little and try a few movie shots.

CHAPTER XVIII

CINEMA

THE vogue today is for small forms of camera, 8, 9, or 16 mm.
In 1925, when I first started to make films, such cameras were
hardly known, and I thought that if it should come my way to
shoot something interesting, the standard size of 35 mm. would
be best, which yields excellent pictures and films ready to
project.

I learned to be a camera man at Vincennes, with the Pathé
people. Dr Charcot realised the documentary value of the cinema,
and before leaving on his first expedition to Greenland, borrowed
a camera and picked me out to look after it.

For a whole week I turned up every morning at the Vincennes
Studios, where, in spite of my seaman's jersey, I went about practically unnoticed. I was probably taken for some player straying
from the 'set'. I went about everywhere vaguely looking for some
good soul obliging enough to explain the secrets of camera set-
up. The camera men, young and old, had little enough to tell me,
when it came to the point. The game is not one that can well be
taught; you have the knack, or you haven't; in other words, you
have to learn by yourself. I soon got the hang of the works of the
machine. It was a clumsy, ponderous old box of a thing, with three
lenses, one of them telescopic. I acquired with a little practice the
necessary 'rhythm' in winding the handle, and when I had also
mastered the correct manipulation of the turn-table, there was not
much else to bother about in the way of mechanics, so my tutors
assured me, and they showed every sign of being much relieved
when I moved off with my old box of tricks, leather satchel, tripod
and all.

I began by making a few 'tests' and shut myself up for hours in
the ship's dark room. Handling porcelain baths while rolling 25° is
quite a lively affair. The advice I had received made me nervous
of over-exposing at sea, and particularly on snow, with the result
that I had a tendency to under-expose badly. Much interesting

material turned out completely blank, due to defective adjustment. Also, like all beginners, I was keen on shooting everything anyhow, without reference to the context, so that that year I produced only about 300 feet of worth-while material.

About this time I began to occupy myself with a problem which does not seem to worry professional camera-men: slinging the apparatus in gimbals. On board a rolling vessel a fixed camera registers falsely; the vessel appears stationary with the sea and horizon heaving about. On the other hand the human eye reduces everything to the horizontal, so that the horizon remains steady. That year a professor of the Ecole Polytechnique, who was with us, had a portable camera, not much of a thing, but mechanically wound, like the machines of the present day, which enabled him to keep to the horizontal.

On the following expedition I used a small portable of the same type, called the 'S.E.P.T.', in addition to my big machine. It was a great improvement on any studio camera, although I had to keep on ceaselessly changing the 15 ft. spools in the dark-room and filling the magazines. More than once I hoisted my enormous old box of a thing to the maintop, together with tripod and all accessories; a truly terrible business.

With the 'S.E.P.T.' I was able to hang under the bowsprit and photograph the bows breaking through the ice. With another of my subjects, a polar bear, I had a somewhat breathless race, which was the more sporting in that Dr Charcot allowed no shooting of any sort. In one way and another I brought back from this second expedition the bones of a good film, which, coupled with the previous year's exposures, were sufficient to make a 'documentary' which the famous explorer used sometimes at his lectures.

While in Scoresby Sound I had met a Norwegian camera-man who was the owner of a machine vastly superior to mine. It was a Kinamo Zeiss, with 150 ft. spools. It ran almost without vibration and was set up much more easily than mine.

Until shortly before my departure in the Winnibelle I had rather lost interest in cine-cameras, being a very ordinary photographer, and consequently no fanatic. Nevertheless it had struck me that there might be interesting things to record, for example, the action of my automatic steering gear, and I realised that later on I should have much less difficulty in explaining such things properly if I brought back some moving pictures.

It so happened that a friend of mine possessed a similar camera to the one which had made me so envious six years before, and he let me have it. Its great advantage over and above its mechanical excellence and good lenses was its delay-action starting gear, which enabled the operator to 'take' himself. I had an iron bracket, which could swivel in all directions, made up to replace the tripod. This could be mounted at various spots on board, bow and stern. I then procured a modest supply of film (2,000 ft.), which forbade any propensity to take pictures merely for the sake of killing time.

Before Madeira I had little opportunity of taking very much, and then only on my departure, when I shot a few feet of my three local handymen and the Consul just as they left me, to keep their memory fresh. Then no more for a fortnight. In mid-Atlantic I began to ask myself whether I was ever going to have any serious occasion to use the apparatus, so I decided to make a record of my ordinary life on board as the vessel rolled her way through the tropics.

Could anything be less tempting to a man alone, 1,000 miles from anywhere, than to play the fool in front of the camera? The constant rolling had worn me out, and I thought only of sleep, without, however, being able to get any worth mentioning. Day after day I came back to this point of view: 'What's the good?' I would say to myself, 'I can do it in the Channel when I get back, with a friend to help me.' But there is something that can't be faked, and that is the vertical lighting which seems to cast no shadow on the deck; then there is the dazzling whiteness of the sails, one's drawn face, and weather-beaten arms and legs. I felt that these things deserved recording, and the opportunity would not recur.

So one afternoon when there was rather less sea and the Winni-belle was not banging about too much, I loaded the Kinamo, fixed up the iron bracket in the stern, and settled down to work out a scenario.

To view someone in the lens is easy. You can make him move about, get your composition, etc. But I, of course, could see nothing but the heaving mast and sails. I had to register on the mast and shrouds, so as to be sure my head and feet would come into the picture. I made chalk marks on both deck and mast, fixed the bracket, and went below to dress. Normally I just wore a bare minimum to avoid discomfort from the sunlight, a hat and unbleached trousers, or shorts. I was still on my guard against burns and sunstroke, for I had had only thirty days to get acclimatised, including my stay at Funchal.

For this occasion, giving way to professional unrealism, I thought fit to 'create atmosphere'. I remembered there was a pith helmet at the bottom of a locker. Now, in all the best films a pith helmet is the emblem of the tropics and nothing could have been more tropical than my present setting. That helmet was a nightmare; it was too big for me, and the slightest puff rushed into it and swept it off my head. I had never worn it before for more than two hours; all the same, I decided to hoist that headgear for the occasion.

Never in my life have I felt such a fool. I was in a vile temper and a dozen times was on the point of packing up, but forced myself to go through with it.

The camera faced forward. I had to crouch down in the cockpit and lie in wait for it, looking through a corner of the hatch cover. The start was indicated by an index arm, under which was jammed a piece of white paper, which would be freed as soon as the arm began to move, a very simple device and visible from some distance away. As soon as I saw the signal I went into action. My idea was to come out of the cockpit from under the cover, with a paint pot in my hand, and move about here and there, without excessive gestures. In a second scene I would come down the ratlines, still with my pot of paint in my hand; scrubbing decks, re-leading and painting are the great daily occupations of a sailor. In a third 'set-up' I thought of sitting on the skylight with a basin between my knees, preparing my meal, by cutting the wings off a few flying fish with a pair of scissors. These were the sort of things I did every day, and the mise-en-scene was perfectly plausible. But I reckoned without my pith helmet.

As I climbed on deck, the rim somehow caught on the hatch cover and jammed it down over my ears. I tried not to look sillier than I could help, and somehow got it straight and carried on through the entire programme. Happily there was no sound-recording apparatus! After a time I moved to a position from which I could see round the side of the camera, in order to make sure if it was turning all right, for the noise of the sea completely drowned the sound of it. It was as still as death and had never even started. I had sweated and gesticulated and made an ass of myself all for nothing!

It needed much patience and frequent loadings and unloadings before my little programme was complete. At last, however, I was able to stow the apparatus back in its locker, with no flowers or regrets of any sort, and only used it on one other occasion—a more interesting one, however—before reaching Martinique.

It was a day of hard wind, not much less than half a gale, with hollow, breaking seas and a superb light. I shut myself up in the cockpit for an hour and a half to load magazines. There in the dark you hear best all the noises of the vessel; you hear her labouring, rushing onwards, breaking her way through the seas. On this occasion I did not stop the camera once it was turning, as the 'set-up' was so abominably uncomfortable that I might not have been able to start it again. I got out to the end of the bowsprit with the camera slung round my neck on a length of marlin and jammed down under my jersey to prevent spray clouding the lens. Unfortunately, the motion was so violent that results were almost negligible. Being well outside the vessel I was sometimes plunged into the water up to my middle. I only managed to get about six feet of usable film. Very few of the people who have seen it appreciate the angle from which it was taken, and anyway it passes in a flash. The rest is much too shaky. I next climbed as high as possible up the ratlines, but did not even attempt a picture; the shrouds were slack and the shaking so excessive that it would have been a mere waste of time.

I then fixed up the camera on the deck, right in the bows, and succeeded in getting two or three short lengths which, if not very wonderful, are at least well worth having, and show the Winnibelle flying before the huge waves, with the rudder working by itself.

CHAPTER XIX
3,000 BY THE LOG

At this season the ecliptic very nearly reaches its maximum north amplitude. It was not long before I crossed the line, where the sun was absolutely vertical at noon; later it began to go into the north. At first it always produces a rather curious impression on an inhabitant of our hemisphere, to find the sun in the north at mid-day. I have also heard the ecliptic called the 'solar equator'. It oscillates with the seasons, whereas the 'terrestrial equator' is a fixed line on the globe. I was disgusted by the climate I found on this so-called equator, as witness my log entry of 15th June:

'Am wearing Chausey clothes, woollen underclothing, sweater and thick trousers. Squally, rain. Put on oilskin; only want sea-boots now.'

On this particular day I decided to make due south, in search of stronger winds. 'It pays every time,' Somerset had written in his letter. And here I was at 24° and dead calm. 'At 22°, still calm, with occasional light airs. Terribly wearing, and I am very tired. The vessel looks after herself as usual in spite of these light variable winds.'

On the 18th: 'The foresails came aback during the night. Calm followed by change of wind. I now really have a reasonable grouse. Gerbault complained of not finding wind at 29° and here am I, on the same longitude, at the same time of year, and only a few puffs at 21°.'

On the 20th, as I had already made a good 1,000 miles since leaving Funchal, I decided to start the diesel up and headed due south for ten hours, or about forty-two miles. At the end of that, victory! From that moment my daily runs were to read: 104, 103, 110, 111, 102, 108, 112, 114, 110, 102, 137, 101, 102, 100, 101, 111 (never less than 100)—and then 'land in sight'.

(Extract from the log): 'The unpleasant thing is that the further south one goes the shorter the days become (in June). At 7.45 p.m. it is night at 22°, and daybreak at about 7 a.m.'

And again: 'I came south so quickly (in a manner of speaking) that I have had no time to get acclimatised as I intended. Here I am already in the parallel of Antigua (only 1° off the island of Guadaloupe) and I still have to be careful of the sun. I wear nothing but a pair of shorts in the mornings, but put on a short-sleeved shirt in the afternoon.'

On all this run the Winnibelle conscientiously followed the arrows on the wind chart, describing a great curve entirely by herself. An amusing demonstration of the accuracy of the information given by the chart. I gave a tracing of her course subsequently to the Washington Weather Bureau.

After 20° flying fish began to fall on deck during the hours of darkness. Five came aboard the first night and thereafter rarely fewer. I have found as many as thirty-seven on deck at once, more than even my appetite could cope with. After ten days or so, I must confess fried fish with potatoes or potatoes with fried fish became rather monotonous. Nevertheless, the flesh of this fish is excellent, quite as delicate as fresh sardines. They are about the same size.

They are strong fliers; their small wings beat the air with incredible rapidity, sometimes enabling them to reach a height of eighteen to twenty feet against the wind. With the wind behind them they make long undulating flights, in the course of which they just graze the crest of a wave here and there with hardly a pause. They see well in daylight and have no trouble in avoiding obstructions, so it is only at night that they fling themselves against a ship's side or sails. Naturally, the lower the vessel is in the water the more chance there is of catching them. In big ships one never finds any, except possibly in waters inhabited by larger varieties.

Now and again, when I was reading or dozing in the cabin, I could hear them falling on deck. They die the moment they open their gills. One evening two of them shot right down the hatch on to the stove while I was reading under the cabin lamp. 'A little patience,' I heard myself saying, as I took them by the tails to throw them on deck.

On every page of my log there is always the same *leit-motiv*— 'Terribly tired, can't manage to get any sleep'. About 11 p.m. one night I turned out of my bunk to stow a pile of plates which were rattling abominably, and to have a drink of water. As I took up one of the two 'unbreakable' tumblers bought by Henri in the bazaar at Boulogne, it exploded in my hand with a sort of muffled bang, for no reason at all. It was completely smashed into little pieces hardly bigger than granules of rock salt. The pieces were everywhere, in the butter, the pans, in my bunk. I was so much on edge from prolonged strain that I had an odd feeling of uneasiness, impossible to define. I collected all the larger pieces I could find, and put them in a cigarette tin. Suppose I was going to have a continued repetition of these bizarre phenomena? But there was nothing extraordinary really, as glasses of this sort, when wet, are subject to this peculiar behaviour.

From the log (three days after): 'Little bits of the famous broken tumbler are still turning up all over the place. I took one out of my mouth this morning (luckily this sort of glass hardly cuts); I wonder where it came from: the gingerbread, the jam or the sugar?'

Sometimes in the night the crest of a wave would foam over the deck with a plop and a swish, followed by the characteristic bubbling of water spilling away. Now and again the waves were very steep, and I marvelled at the way the Winnibelle behaved in the following sea. Driven straight ahead by the wind, she managed as a rule to climb up the steepest wave without shipping a drop of water. It was only when she had the ill-luck to be just on the spot at the very moment one broke that the tip curled on board.

It was equally enthralling to watch her keeping her course dead straight, with no one at the helm, and without yawing either to port or starboard in the great seas which ran on out of sight in the distance, ceaselessly renewing themselves and seeming to get bigger as they went.

When there was less wind, resulting in a hollow sea, I used to amuse myself sometimes by leaning back and pressing with my foot to counteract the tiller's movements, but I could only put her off her course about 10°, when the pull of the brace was too much for me. What man, be his muscles of iron, could hold a boat in this way with a following wind for even as much as four hours on end? And this accurate and silent labour went on for weeks without ceasing.

Naturally one had to watch for corresponding wear. The rudder head was firm now, as a result of the two iron strips which had been well and truly forged for me in Madeira; there was no danger from this quarter. As to the leads of the braces through the return blocks, I had only to tallow them every four or five days to keep everything perfectly fresh and supple. The only things that showed any appreciable wear were the links on the chains and shackles. I have kept a bronze shackle the jaw of which is worn to the thickness of paper. It was a miracle it held until the moment I spotted it.

One day I noticed a hole in the mainsail where it rested on the stern hoop or crutch. This was produced by the chafe of continuous rolling with the sail stowed. It is paradoxical that the only real damage I had to make good should have been in a sail I was not using. I except the spinnaker, which was of such light material that it was really asking for trouble to use it as I did from morning till evening. However, all that happened was that I had to sew a new piece in the foot where it chafed the steel jackstays. Of course, I could not use needle and palm for repairing this sail, and I had all the trouble in the world to find a piece of fine enough material, an ordinary darning needle, and a suitable piece of thread. It was more of a dressmaker's than a sailmaker's job.

I was not keen on lowering the sail for the purpose, so I just carried on while it banged and flapped about as the Winnibelle rolled. It was a job calling for no little patience, particularly as the needle kept slipping through my fingers and getting lost.

The horizon was still bare; never a ship or a bird. It was only on nearing the other side of the Atlantic that I saw phaetons, birds completely ruined, as to their appearance, by a thread-like tail, very badly stuck on, which seems of no help in flight, and some other birds as black as smoke, rather like swallows but which flew more like bats. I detest birds of this kind. Why do the beautiful ones desert the equatorial regions? It seems they must have cold water, which carries marine plankton and, as a consequence, the small fry on which they feed.

No one can account for the number of frigate birds and numerous other Antarctic breeds which are found in the Galapagos (on the Equator), unless the cause is Humboldt's Current, which flows there. The further north you go in the Atlantic, the more birds you find; there are more in Scotland than in the Channel, and in the Faroes the numbers and varieties are bewildering. I love sea birds, and they are one of the reasons I prefer northern waters.

One of the smoke-black birds I have mentioned above, attracted by the poop light, grazed my face one night with his funereal wings whilst I was standing in the stern. He returned once or twice to the attack. It was a nasty sensation, and I finished up by seizing the boathook and striking out blindly like a windmill. After a few shots I got in a good one and never saw him again that night.

I had too little to do, and began to feel, now and again, boredom creeping on. I religiously kept up the marking of my progress on the chart, which finally showed signs of resenting my attentions, so that I had to gum it together in several torn places. The scale was so small that the day's runs were reckoned in millimetres.

I made a note in the log: 'Impossible to stop oneself making forecasts, which is for a sailor the height of childishness. The sort of thing I mean is settling in advance imaginary points, with the dates of reaching them; these sometimes left me a large margin, and at other times were based on the maximum possible speed of the boat, so certain did I feel that they could not be reached so quickly. What did I care, as long as my mind was occupied? No doubt over-stimulation, due to chain smoking, was partly to blame. Once more I would look to see how she was heading, take up my protractor and pencil, and so on, until the moment when, at the end of my patience, and furious with myself, I threw all the charts into a corner and swore I would never look at them again.

Then, on certain days, I deliberately abstained from taking the sun, knowing well that to do so would unleash another fit of cartomania, and preferring to correct my course every other day. That had also an excellent moral effect, by giving me a pleasant surprise, as the log had a tendency to drag and the feeble current (four miles a day) helped my progress S.W.

At one particular time I was surprised to realise that St Vincent, in the Cape Verde Islands, was not far off, only about 480 miles.

Then St Vincent receded and the nearest land was Guiana, nearer than any of the Antilles.

For distraction I tried reading again, but I had great difficulty in concentrating, so much so that I wrote analyses of the books I read as a corrective. When I read them today I am struck by their acid tone and lack of generosity. I seem to have picked on all the incoherencies, improbabilities and prejudices, and to have likened the authors to their least attractive characters. This hard work plus the sea air do not appear to have engendered a benevolent frame of mind.

Slocum, however, always pleased me by his sincere and precise observations. For example, I read:

'Then, losing sight of the Cape Verde Islands astern, I found myself once more sailing with an empty sea on all sides and in unutterable solitude. Even when I slept I dreamt I was alone. This feeling never left me, but waking or sleeping I always had the impression of knowing the boat's position—I saw her weaving across the chart, which had become like a picture before my eyes.'

This bears out what I have just said as to constant preoccupation with the chart, even during sleep. Nothing could be more true.

But it was not always easy to read; at the slightest unusual sound I would jam the book in somewhere, climb on deck, and then it might often be days before I took it up again.

I hardly wrote anything at all, except to keep the log by watch. The 'Remarks column' is rarely filled in. . . . What could I write there? I was much too near my subject.

June 25th. 'Burnt my forearm with the paraffin lamp. Very jumpy, nose started bleeding.'

June 27th. 'Labouring frightfully, intermittent rain showers. Made inventory of medicine chest.'

June 28th. 'My burns do not look too good. Cleaned them with ether inotyl.'

June 29th. 'Seas broke over her stern 7 or 8 times last night. I am outraged and disgusted with the banging about, which is unimagineable. I never remember being so brutally shaken before. There are two cross-seas; the crests of the waves come on board just as they like before the boat knows how to re-act.'

June 30th. 'Weather beastly; yellow overcast sky. Visibility nil. Hell of a joke to make a landfall in these conditions!'

July 1st. 'Continual rain, thunder, lightning; foresee some sweating with the spinnaker tonight. Some shark pilot-fish by the rudder. School of dolphins all day to port playing with an enormous tunny.'

July 2nd. 'Last night while it freshened I put off from minute to minute the inevitable taking in of the spinnaker, which was straining to bursting point. Would have been such a pity to lose speed. Every hour seven more miles showed on the log face. Eventually at 4 a.m. I had to do it. The sail, soaked and heavy with water, banged with an impressive slap several times, and came aback on the boom (where I thought it would tear) before consenting to be transformed into a dirty bundle of wet washing on deck. I'm very keen on my old bundle of washing, all the same. . . . A violent squall came down almost immediately afterwards, preceded by a very nasty wave.'

And again: 'Using automatic steering gear all the time. Have just come through 40 hours of heavy weather with breaking seas. I was worried. But everything worked to perfection. One would have said a very skilful helmsman was on watch. The stern always met the dangerous crests perfectly straight. 200 miles run to W. during this time and nothing at all to do except twiddle one's thumbs!

'The gear has been working now for 23 days, during which time I have never used the mainsail. The vessel has run 1,900 miles. If this continues for another week I shall have crossed the Atlantic without touching the helm. Touch wood (no shortage of that here!).'

The following day the bad weather developed into a real blow. I was on deck from 2 a.m. until late afternoon, uncertain what to do if it got still worse. This is rather unusual in the trades. The barometer only revealed a slight fall, and continued to register the diurnal and nocturnal tides of atmospheric pressure, which are fairly apparent in these regions. So long as this barometric pulse beats perceptibly one can be fairly sure that no cyclones are brewing in their factory, which is situated just abeam.

Nevertheless, the wind velocity of certain squalls was extraordinary. During one of them the appearance of the sea changed completely and became as flat as a table. The wave crests were decapitated, there was just a fuming surface of sea, whipped by horizontal rain. It was impossible to stay upright on deck, but this time it was not because of the rolling. The Winnibelle no longer moved, she shot like an arrow with her forefoot in the air, as though driven by a high-powered motor. This is the only time in my life I have ever seen a sailing vessel lift her bow to such an extent. The impression was the more curious since the stern dropped proportionately, and the wash streamed astern like an eight's. It is a pity I did not think of taking her speed at the time. The squalls usually lasted from a quarter to three-quarters of an hour. Once passed, with a sharp slatting of the sails caused by the sudden reduction of speed, the Winnibelle would resume the normal cadence of her rolling while the grumbling pocket of wind drew off.

I could always, at need, have half lowered the foresails, but would only have done so as a last resort. It is profoundly exciting to fly along at such a speed under sail. Various things might have gone wrong, as could easily be seen. The braces were bar taut and stretched to breaking point, and the foresail booms, which bent in an alarming way, might have snapped. If anything had carried away I should probably have been reduced to running under bare poles for a start. However, everything held until the weather improved again in the evening.

That day the Winnibelle made good 137 miles. This was her best run: an average of six to seven knots in spite of calm periods between squalls.

July 3rd. 'The sea has a very remarkable dark olive green colour. A southern branch of the North Equatorial Stream (Gulf Stream). Fine.'

July 4th. 'A little more wild life around me; some birds. I have scalded my wrist. I certainly have no luck with fires. Fortunately the ambrine was handy.'

July 5th. 'Haven't slept for several nights; pains in the loins and side. Legs weak.'

July 6th. 'Impossible to keep a look-out: tired and nervous.'

July 7th. 'Infernal rolling: demoralising. Not a sign of a ship anywhere: this begins to disgust me. A most baffling sea; comes on board port and starboard. Practically everything that could have been broken is now broken—don't understand it. Nearing medium depths? Bad weather in the offing [it was the day of a cyclone at Trinidad]. No change of colour of the water, no birds. Curious. I no longer make any reckoning and nothing is worth while. To hell with it all . . .'

July 8th. 'LAND! ! !'

CHAPTER XX
LANDFALL

THE ship's log contains little mention of the very dirty night on which I made the land. As it chanced, there was no moon, and rain, as I have stated, is not a scarce commodity in these waters . . .

The day before, I had been not a little disturbed, after rather hurriedly working out my position during the afternoon, to find that I was apparently past the Islands. Had I gone between Dominique and Martinique without seeing them? It was quite possible with the limited visibility I had at the time. I could have banged my head on the deck with annoyance. To turn aside would be difficult on account of currents and headwinds. My course would bring me to Porto Rico, and I had no proper papers for that port, which anyway meant nothing to me. I then took myself in hand, went over my calculations again, and found an error.

The answer now was that I ought to make Dominique that day about 7 p.m. I had selected that island in preference to the others, as there are no outlying dangers. The approach to it is straightforward, whereas that to Martinique to the eastward is the reverse, with coral reefs stretching twenty miles out to sea, which could very easily be hit before the lights of the island became visible, though they carry a long way.

By noon I was already beginning to peer ahead, and to ease the strain of waiting I began to dismantle the famous hatch-slide, which by now jammed worse than ever. This needed patience and was an awkward business with the Winnibelle rolling as she was. At 5 p.m. the work was completed, and the hatch cover at last ran freely; but still there was no sign of land. Night fell, and still nothing. By midnight I began to wonder seriously if I was not in fact passing between the two islands, as I had been afraid of doing earlier in the day. This thought became an obsession, and I nearly reached the point of taking in all sail. Then I said to myself that, after all, my chronometer might be slow.

There was continuous thunder and lightning, which did not add to the charm of the hour. I detest that sort of orchestra. In the flashes, however, I tried to catch a glimpse of land, of some shape darker than the rest of the night. . . . Bah! The sea is large!

As visibility was about four miles during the flashes, and nothing could be seen ahead, I decided to risk half an hour's sleep. I had no alarm clock, but could always wake at will. After exactly half an hour I poked my head through the hatch . . . still raining and as black as ink. I kept watch for a while and then after another flash of lightning, went below and lay down: and so on.

At 4.30 a.m. when, for the fourth time, I came up to have a look ahead, suddenly, like a blow in the face, I saw the land, right over me, quite close, and very high, rising in a sombre wall of rock, unspeakably sinister; it was crowned with grey whirling clouds and the base white with the foam of colossal breakers. Never shall I forget that moment of crisis and relief. In a brace of shakes I was on deck.

'You know,' I wrote later to Rochard, 'after twenty-nine days without exchanging a word with anyone, without seeing a ship, or a flight of birds, or anything else, you begin to doubt everything, your own sanity and the limit of your nerves. At last I saw something: the other side, in fact.'

I had dreamt of land once or twice during the preceding nights, but it had always appeared very different. It now proved to be steep, inhospitable, and covered from top to bottom with dense forest, which I could just make out in the twilight of the new-born day. I had not imagined it so. This, then, was the island Christopher Columbus sighted one fine Sunday, whence the name, Dominica. He must have seen it in a very different light, to have given so enthusiastic an account of it.

I lay to and had breakfast in peace, then headed S. towards Martinique, distant some twenty miles. I soon had the island in view, right ahead, and four hours later I was under the lee of Mont-Pelée in a flat calm. I started up the engine and only found a breeze again on reaching the roadstead of Fort de France, where there is always a breath of wind. The anchorage contained a number of schooners, mostly American, to whom I shouted a greeting as I went by, and a rusty old dredger . . . I beg its pardon. I was told later it was brand new. At the head of the bay, the main part of the town, leprous walls, tile roofs, a church spire made of old iron, no wharves. A black pilot appeared, a husky fellow, who went by the name of Leopold, if I remember rightly. I pointed to my yellow flag, flying at half-mast, indicating that I had come from foreign parts, and must get medical clearance, but he seemed to attach no importance to it. Very well then, if he didn't care, neither did I.

A landing-stage built on piles; a crowd of ragged, toothless, deplorable-looking blacks; all silently smiling. I jumped ashore and had a quick look at my little boat. With some annoyance I found weed had grown all over her black boot-top; there were even teredo worms, by the Lord, and in brushing them off as well as I could, patches of the black paint flaked off. My white paint had turned yellowish in vertical streaks below each scupper, like the marks of shame on a well used wall. A lot of good my painting at Madeira had been! As to the varnish, a bit was left here and there, in pathetic isolation. On the other hand, the copper sheathing was dazzling. I have never seen a boat's bottom gleam so in the water.

The sanitary inspector now put in an appearance: café-au-lait complexion, khaki suit, sunburned, almost brown straw hat, a beautiful dusky colour scheme. An umbrella and a pair of enormous tortoiseshell spectacles completed the picture. It took him a good quarter of an hour to decide to fetch the doctor. I had time to dig out some creased and shapeless flannel garments from the bottom of a locker, put on my new yachting cap, which was now mouldy inside, and do a littly tidying up of the cabin, where the sun shone cheerfully on the varnished woodwork.

In due course the medical officer, a captain, arrived: rather good-looking, with a brown moustache and a strong Breton accent.

I introduced myself: no reply.

'Your papers?'

If he chooses to behave more like a gendarme than a doctor, well and good, thought I. The niggers opened their mouths wider and wider. I invited the doctor to follow me below and take a seat. He preferred not to sit. I offered him a cigarette. No, thanks. A glass of Madeira? It was all that was left; I had kept it specially for whoever should be my first guest on board after touching land.

'No, we don't drink in Martinique.'

Lord bless us!

'Well, here are my papers,' I said. 'Here's the clearance from Madeira.'

'Have you a French health certificate?'

'But why? I've come from Madeira . . .'

'That's nothing to do with me . . . don't know the place.'

'Listen. I left my French clearance in Madeira, with the port medical authorities, who gave me this one.'

'What do I care? We're not in Madeira here, we're in the Colonies.'

This was a bit of a facer to one who, like myself, had supposed Martinique to be a department of France. . . . I timidly suggested that, having been at sea for a month, I could hardly have hatched a malady that would not now be apparent to a doctor. To be precise, I had burnt myself on the arm more than once on the passage. Could he tell me . . .

'No concern of mine.'

He then gave me to understand 'that I could have met contaminated vessels at sea.'

True. I hadn't thought of that. But a port doctor was surely aware that in such a case I was bound, under the gravest penalties, to enter it in the ship's log. Would he like to see it?

'No!'

I wondered at this stage in what manner a French clearance could have put the good man's mind at rest if I had in fact met a contaminated ship. It was not worth while arguing the point. Suddenly an idea struck him.

'Has your boat been de-ratted in the last six months?'

The Winnibelle had been built less than six months ago, and I could have produced her certificate of construction. I knew very well I had no rats on board. I didn't like rats, I assured him, and on a ten-tonner their presence would be impossible to conceal.

This policeman-soldier-doctor was beginning to get on my nerves, which unfortunately were not then in the best possible order, one way and another. The limit was reached when he began to enumerate the perils I was bringing upon the population of Martinique. I had a great desire to tell him that I knew on indisputable authority that the ague, blackwater fever, leprosy, small-pox, typhus, elephantiasis and other lovely bugs ran about open and unafraid in the gutters of Fort de France, and that the mother country doesn't as a rule import them; a last shred of discretion restrained me from expressing myself to this effect, and I have regretted it ever since.

The rest of his discourse he devoted to pointing out that he had absolute control over me; that I could be forced to be de-ratted, fumigated, vaccinated, sterilised, imprisoned. . . . Good Lord above, he thought he was in barracks . . .

'Just a moment,' I interrupted at last. 'In view of the fact that my papers are identical—since tonnage doesn't come into the question—with those of any other French vessel, I have the same rights and powers as the captain of the Ile de France. In virtue whereof I invite you to make yourself scarce. You know the way!'

His jaw dropped, he swept up the forms he had made me sign, climbed up the ladder, and made off.

Once on dry land he shouted orders to me to anchor a mile off the beach, in quarantine, and have no communication with the shore. But now it was my turn to put him in his place. Opening the skylight, I shouted:

'Doubtless your powers are immense, but you have no authority to keep me here for forty days.'

'No? Very well, I shall report you at every port you make for. You'll see.'

He stamped his foot in rage, but I had the laugh, as he had not the slightest idea where I might choose to go. He could send off a hundred cables if he liked, just for the pleasure of paying for them. English Harbour in Antigua floated before my eyes. The remains of Nelson's old arsenal, utter peace, 'not a soul for miles except Dr and Mrs O'Mahoney'. He was not the sort of doctor to put a chap in quarantine, I felt sure.

'But doubtless', Bobbie Somerset had written in his letter, 'you'll prefer a French Colony.' Groans and hollow laughter. . . .

The pilot came on board and asked me to start up the diesel. Still raging inwardly, I told him the ship was a great deal more intelligent than he was, that the wind was fair for the anchorage and that she would get there by herself. A quarter of an hour later I heard him drop anchor, veer the chain, climb into his boat and clear off. Then all was silence.

If I relate this tiresome episode in detail it is because it is typical of the kind of thing that may happen in almost any country in the world to completely harmless people, who have everything in order and are only too anxious to comply with the regulations, but who sail simply to please themselves. The fault lies not entirely with the people who apply the law in an idiotic way, but with the law itself, which dates from another age, that of the filibuster, the slave trade, big epidemics and interminable voyages under sail. 'Papelars, papelars!' as the Customs man said in Madeira.

Villiers, in *The Cruise of the Conrad*, writes that he had to have very nearly a printing works on board. Harry Pidgeon and William Albert Robinson in their accounts of their voyages also complain of red tape; it turns up on every other page, and yet they did all they could to comply with the rules. Once or twice they had to get away by either violence or cunning, even under rifle fire. Local legend relates of Gerbault that, on arriving at Fort de France, he calmly held out his clearance papers at the end of a boat hook and requested the doctor to keep off for fear he might bring germs on board the Firecrest. As the doctor dared not annoy Monsieur Gerbault, who was almost an official personage, the latter was able to indulge in the luxury of a little insolence, and for my part I don't blame him, as these representatives of authority are for the most part only really overbearing with the humble.

The following extract from a letter I wrote shortly afterwards to Rochard will show what I felt like at the time.

'At four in the evening I tied up at Fort de France, only to be greeted by a burst of machine gun fire, or what amounts to it. Jack-in-office gendarmes (black), puffed up with their own importance, suspicious port officials, a ludicrous medico. Ordered out into the anchorage, in quarantine, and on no account to communicate with the shore (how the devil could I, considering I had no dinghy?). Asked permission to send a cable to my wife: refused. Asked for some bread: surely that couldn't be refused? But it was. You will agree this was enough to ruffle one's temper a bit.'

That night, alone, without fresh food, lying off that seedy-looking town, I felt an utter fool. I had pictured all sorts of things,

but never this. By degrees I got really angry, and made up my
mind to slip off during the night. What annoyed me most was that
I could not let anybody know of my arrival and that I had no
bread.

I stood leaning against the mast, with my hands deep in my
pockets, sniffing the strong scent of tropical country and listening
to the fantastic uproar made by the croaking of thousands of little
animals, I did not know what sort. (They were tree frogs.) Suddenly I heard someone hail me by name. It must have been about
midnight. I jumped, for the voice came from just alongside in the
dark. Who on earth could know me here?

'May I come aboard?'

'Not on your life,' I replied, 'I'm in quarantine!'

I heard a chuckle, a boat came alongside, and a man in a wide-
brimmed hat strode nimbly along the narrow deck. I went below to
light the cabin lamp. He followed me. He was about thirty years of
age, with a short beard and confident bearing.

'Pierre Hayot is my name,' he volunteered. Then, looking at me,
he laughed and sat down.

'You and your brother have such a strong family resemblance
that I can't be mistaken,' he continued.

He explained that he had been entertained, a fortnight before, in
the Jeanne d'Arc. It was the second time he had met my brother,
who had been here the year before.

Hayot, as I learnt later, was very popular with the Navy, and
always exerted himself to do the honours of the Island for the
benefit of officers and cadets. He was favourably placed for the
purpose as a member of one of the best known planter families
in the Colony.

'I heard just now in the town that a small boat had arrived with
a chap on board they thought was either a pirate or an escaped
prisoner. As your brother has had often spoken of you, I had a sort
of intuition. So I came to make sure. But, tell me, aren't you here
sooner than you expected?'

An escaped prisoner! Ha, ha! What a nose that doctor-captain
must have! I briefly told Hayot of the incident. He shrugged his
shoulders and said:

'I've got to get back to Saint Esprit, twelve miles from here, where I live, but at about seven tomorrow morning I'll be around again, and you'll have pratique at eight.'

Waiting only to light a cigar and collect his hat, he disappeared into the night, just as he had come.

Left to myself, I proceeded to forage around more philosophically, looked in the salt box for the last of the eggs, sliced an enormous rasher of bacon and cooked supper, whistling the while 'C'est pas pour ça que j't'ai donné ma soeur.'

At 7.30 a.m. I had my papers.

'Your medico wears lovely mauve pyjamas,' Hayot, who had made him turn out, told me.

Once ashore we had breakfast in a café where meat, vegetables, cakes, sweets, eggs and butter were on sale, all at the same time, run by an enormously fat personage with gold earrings and a coloured handkerchief over her head, a genuine coalblack mammy, in fact.

Once again I trod the earth like a drunken man. We went to La Chèvre Bay, on the further slope of the Island, where the eldest Hayot brother was just celebrating his promotion to Captain in the Reserve Artillery.

From the summit of the Island I had looked down on a series of majestic bays, fringed in dazzling foam. Sea water of the deepest blue contrasted vividly with the tropical vegetation, relieved here and there by spots of brilliant colour made by magnificent flamboyant trees with bright red leaves.

A long table was pitched under the foliage almost on the beach. A couple of dozen cars which had come from all over the island were parked in a nearby meadow.

'Now', said Hayot to me, always in the same peremptory manner, 'you will get to know a whole heap of people at the same time.'

The majority were either bathing or roasting themselves on the beach. I joined them without ceremony in bathing kit, and was introduced to a number of people similarly clothed. Amongst them were all the leading lights, such as the manager of the Compagnie Transatlantique of Fort-de-France, the Commander of the Garrison, and the Naval Superintendent, whom I was to meet again four years later in St Servan. A number of people of my own age or younger gathered round and treated me as though they had known me for years, people like the Cottrells, the Dormoys and many others, partly because Hayot had brought me and told them something about me, and partly because they knew my brother. A pirate! The last straw! It was enough to make a cat laugh.

They were busy broiling sucking pigs in hot ashes, and cooking all kinds of vegetables which I could not possibly name. Simon Cottrell warned me that the trees above were manchineal trees, and that if I took off my clothes in their shade I should get badly burnt when I put them on again.

'But if they're as dangerous as all that, why do you put the table here?'

To which he merely remarked that it was protected by the tent. I learned that the legend that the shade of the manchineal is deadly is entirely false: it is the sap that burns, and the effect is as bad as that of sulphuric acid. In rain and wind it is unwise to stand near these trees; the rain melts the sap on the leaves and the broken stalks and twigs become corrosive and burn terribly. I came across a number of children burnt in an atrocious manner on their hands and faces, although they must have been warned of the danger from the time they understood the meaning of words. The sores heal very slowly. The best remedy is to apply olive leaves at once, which luckily almost always grow near manchineals, the good beside the evil.

I leave the reader to imagine the sensation of poor wretches who have the ill-luck to pick on these leaves for . . . hygienic purposes. It appears that this has happened fairly frequently, with deadly results.

The planters are hard put to it to combat the invasion of these trees, as hatchet strokes cannot be made without danger, and naturally wood-felling teams jib at the difficulties.

Thus, in the cheerful atmosphere of a 'fête champêtre', ended my first day in Martinique.

And I very nearly never set foot ashore. . . .

Two Portraits of Winnibelle: (a) At Sea (b) At New York: Gulliver among the Giants

The galley

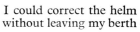

I could correct the helm
without leaving my berth

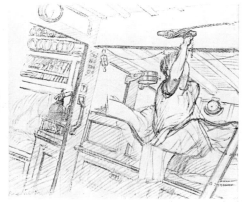

Flying fish and the 'Spy'

CHAPTER XXI

THE ANTILLES

I STAYED three weeks in Martinique. This was far longer than I intended, and is an indication of the deep impression made on me by the place and its inhabitants.

There is a general tendency to liken the island to an earthly paradise. To be perfectly frank, I shall not go as far as that; and I ask the reader to believe that my unfortunate welcome by the 'doctor' counts for nothing in the opinions I set forth here.

Pierre Hayot found me a negro called Massa Houle, as watchman for the Winnibelle. As the local sailors put it, he was not much good for anything except to stay on board all day and doze. But as Hayot said: 'He's the only one I can recommend who won't rob you.' In other words, his qualities were negative. The Winnibelle had been towed round to the Baie des Tourelles, not far from the Transatlantique Wharf, where she was made fast to the buoy which had been used by the Alain Gerbault ten days before. The latter vessel had just gone.

Massa Houle remained on board day and night; as the bay is infested with mosquitoes I took care not to sleep there myself. I used to go on board in the mornings, wind the chronometer, change my clothes, give a few instructions and hasten back to the town, sometimes leaving a pair of shoes with my watchman in the hope that he would clean them. Usually he put the black ones under the pump at the north end of the quay, and as for the white, he never managed to clean more than a single shoe in twenty-four hours.

Whenever I told him to dry the sails I used to unlace the cover myself, strain the sail half up, leaving the halliards turned up on cleats well apart, so that he had everything at hand without groping, and the following day nothing would have been touched, everything being just as I had left it. For this labour (?) I paid the salary of a good technical workman in France; it was the normal rate. In Martinique they don't worry; on our own seaboard I could have had the services of two good sailors at the price.

I gave him my washing, which he took to a laundress, his cousin; they are all cousins on the island. She brought back a formless bundle covered in rust marks. She was a half-bred Chinese, old, toothless and horrible. When I had checked the list and asked the price, I only got an ambiguous smile. Massa Houle was just making off discreetly in the only punt I had at hand. . . . I remembered, just in time, the idyllic propensities of these 'Mamma' laundresses, having experienced their wiles when on board the deep-sea sailing vessels which used to put in at St Pedro or La Pointe. I hailed my nigger who, luckily for me, had had no time to get away, and packed her off with him. As a last resort, I think I would have pushed her over the side, head first; they all swim like fish.

I had practically everything I wanted at hand in the shops which supply the Transatlantique ships at extremely reasonable prices, not to mention a private shower bath belonging to M. Lachenez, manager of the Agency, under the palm trees by the shore. As it was impossible to get my nigger to dry the sails, I unbent and stowed them. The compass, the coverglass of which had cracked again halfway across from Madeira, was put in the hands of a local expert. And finally, I topped up my oil tanks.

The Alabama, Saint Raphael, St André, and Cuba visited the anchorage during my stay. I was given the friendliest welcome on board all of them, and was able to verify my chronometer. If I arrived at lunch time another place was laid for me without a word. In this way I made the acquaintance of several officers whom I met again later. When the Cuba got under way the streets of Fort de France were emptied. Everybody goes, as a matter of course, to the jetty when vessels leave, either to see friends off or just to make a noise. This would be an ideal moment for the local politicians to make a 'coup' in the town.

Fort de France is frankly a sordid place, with its badly painted houses, neglected entrances and deep, inconvenient open gutters, which make it impossible to drive up to the kerb, with the result that until you are used to them, you get out on the near side and sink in filth up to your knees.

There is hardly a public building worthy of the name except the new and impressive Governor's Palace. There are very few

hotels, the Bédia, Gallia, Roma, Excelsior, managed at the time by
the brothers Onorato, one of whom was Italian Consul.

When one thinks of what has been done at Port of Spain, in
Trinidad, and at St Lucia, in practically the same climate, it is
impossible to avoid unfavourable comparison with these miserable
bamboo huts.

Nothing is done to attract tourists. People told me that it was
'impossible' to find a proper hotel here, the 'impossibility', unexpectedly enough, being due to lack of personnel. There are a lot
of these 'impossibilities' in Martinique, where the blacks, as a
natural result of universal native suffrage, have clearly let the
country sink into a lamentable condition. How could it be otherwise, where the negro is master?

I saw the procession from the Cathedral on Ascension Day. A
great show of coloured handkerchiefs and lace; regiments of little
communicants in white dresses, little frizzy-haired niggers, boys
with prayer books, armlets and stiff collars. The black skin of the
little girls showed through their white stockings to such an extent
that at first I wondered why they should be wearing grey ones.
Apart from this, their little black mugs, under the white veils,
could not have looked anything else but terribly funny. I also
noticed a number of men I had seen the day before at a big
funeral, surprisingly resplendent in black ties and bowler hats, in
which they think they are turned out like real Frenchmen. However, it is not for me to laugh at them; such as they are, we have
made them so.

The negroes clamour, among a thousand other things, for
the dismissal of the so-called 'gros baton' gendarmes; in other
words, the white police from home, who are guilty above all of
coming complete with their families, which prevents them marry-
ing half-castes and merging with the populace. No doubt the
Government will give way on this question one day, and then the
white man in Martinique can say goodbye to all feeling of security.

There is a Lycée for secondary instruction, where the natives
take a course of study. From there they go to Paris to complete
their education, and then they return to Fort de France with their
pockets bulging with degrees and diplomas, and no suitable
position awaiting them. Jobs, more or less fantastic, have to be

found for them, and help and pensions provided. They nearly all become active and fanatical electoral agents. Thus you have the entire time of a whole section of the community taken up in electioneering of the most unscrupulous description; you have a town of 20,000 inhabitants boasting fifty doctors, and lawyers by the hundred; you have roads which are a mass of pot holes in spite of the 1,500,000 franc fund, theoretically allocated for their up-keep, but in fact employed otherwise.

Having originally intended to touch at Guadaloupe, I had had my mail sent there. Will it be believed that the Post Office at Fort de France was unable to get it for me in a fortnight, although Pointe à Pitre was only fifty miles away? At the end of that time I sent a telegram, but doubt if it ever got further than the pocket of the Post Office employee. I had the pleasure of listening to her chatting across the counter to a friend for ten minutes or so. (I remember they discussed the merits of a cure for scarlet fever.) When I managed to attract her attention, by timidly holding out my form:

'A moment, Mossier,' she snapped, withering me with a glance of contempt, 'I'm busy.'

My telegram never arrived. A week later I complained, when the Post Office kindly offered to send a radio-telegram, at *my expense*. Of course I refused, nor did my mail ever arrive; I only got it in Europe long afterwards.

Another blessing in this happy land is the impossibility of get-ting money-orders, either French or International, delivered. The post office refuses to transmit them which, for a French Depend-ency, as it calls itself, seems a shade eccentric.

I had innumerable difficulties in getting funds sent out. Every-thing had to come through the Banque de Martinique, which cabled—at my expense—interminable instructions to certain affiliated banks in Paris by most improbable routes. I have no wish to know the reason for this monopoly. It is quite enough to know that a money-order can be sent to Papua or the Cannibal islands of New Guinea, but not to Martinique or Guadaloupe.

One day I met the 'Agent Sanitaire', the man in khaki with the spectacles and umbrella. He greeted me ceremoniously and offered his congratulations that the affair was now regulated. He felt com-

pelled to deplore my thoughtlessness in sailing without papers
which he, in his simian omniscience, judged indispensable! I am
unable to describe what I felt bottled up inside me, but the idea
struck me of taking it out of him in my own way, the old fool!
With the utmost nonchalance I replied that it really didn't matter
at all as very shortly all these formalities would be abolished.

'And why, my deah fellah?' he asked uneasily.

'You know perfectly well, because we're in deep water over the
American debt and France is handing over Martinique to the
U.S.A.'

The hoax went all the better since—although I knew nothing
about it—there is a rumour to this effect which spreads periodically
through the French Antilles.

A thunderbolt falling at his feet could not have produced more
effect. He was appalled, and without another word flew off to
hawk my news around. In no time the town was plunged into despair. I had touched the spot! Once the United States possessed
Martinique, gone would be the beautiful funerals, finished the fine
'drunks', the decorations, the leaves on full pay to France every
three years to 'see' the Motherland again. The fat was in the fire
with a vengeance.

I must have corroborated this news at least twenty times. I
would say without wincing, and with the utmost ingenuousness:

'But don't you see it's quite obvious? The Dependency costs
France much more than it brings in, and this is an easy way to get
rid of it. The Americans are very much worked up against us at the
moment and will only calm down at this price. You won't lose anything by it; they'll build a proper harbour, a town, hotels, clean the
place up a bit, set up a Government that will maintain order and
bring in tourists—much better for everybody. There will be big
trade with Florida, and the coloured people will be given fine
uniforms to wear, as door-keepers, watchmen, liftboys, boot-
blacks. . . .'

Their eyes began popping out of their heads.

At first I had to stop every so often, in order to keep a straight
face. Later I had no chance to finish; with arms raised to heaven,
and stammering with rage, they overwhelmed me with questions,
wanting to know how I got my information. This was easy; all I

had to do was to point out that since they only read the *Courrier des Antilles* and other rags of the kind, they were naturally not in the know about things that mattered; whereas I had just come straight from Paris—a Paris seething with this particular problem. I could have coined money for a time, with my influence!

Bad as the political condition of Martinique may be, I am told things are even worse in Guadaloupe. . . .

I visited the ruins of St Pierre, with Hayot. The town was not yet completely free of the ash under which it was engulfed in the eruption of 1902, when 30,000 people perished in a flash. Ships in the roads burst into flames, and houses on the surrounding slopes ceased to exist; stonework was vitrified, and metalwork simply melted in the terrific heat. Following a series of eruptions lasting eight days, Mont Pelée vomited a blast of incandescent gas which came down with lightning speed, obliquely and unexpectedly, and overwhelmed the whole town. The catastrophe lasted three minutes, and only a few vessels escaped to tell the tale, thanks to not being anchored. The sea literally boiled; officers of the watch and helmsmen shut themselves up in the wheel-houses; everyone on deck was burnt to death. One man only escaped in the town, a negro who had been locked up in some subterranean dungeon for so long that his skin was nearly white when they brought him out. He was pardoned, it seems. 'One man's poison . . .'

Pierre Hayot introduced me to an old American seismologist who founded, at his own expense and with the help of a few special endowments, the museum and volcanological laboratory, which the Government of the Island had been incapable of conceiving or building themselves. This man, to whom the authorities had naturally taken a dislike, spent his time listening and figuratively pressing an ear to the mountain against which his own house leans.

It was a perfect arsenal of apparatus, mostly of his own invention. He listens to the mountain with a kind of love; he has also 'examined' Etna, Vesuvius and Krakatoa.

'Mont Pelée is the one that interests me most,' he said to us, giving his goatee beard a twist. 'In six months the crater completely changes its shape. It is altogether a most intriguing volcano, and a vicious brute into the bargain, more dangerous on the whole than any other.'

The populace considered him a safeguard. At times of threatened activity they obeyed him blindly. They had helped him to build an observatory on the nearest bluff, from which it was easy for him to scrutinise the summit through his telescope. He dreamed of having a ferro-concrete casemate, thick enough to stand a temperature of 10,000° F., in which he could be closeted during an actual eruption.

On the other hand, the blacks do not bear Mont Pelée any grudge. Since it did not take their own lives, and has brought them so much in the way of indemnities, assistance, pity and benevolent interest, they speak of it affectionately as 'Daddy Volcano'.

Following the coast, I made a tour of the fishing villages. The boats are hollowed out of gum-tree trunks, and sail well enough, though their idea of a sail plan is somewhat rudimentary. The Carib fisher folk form the only hard-working section of the community, and are estimable people and comparatively pure-blooded. I say comparatively, for there are hardly any pure Caribs nowadays. Their reserve is in St Dominique, not far off, on British territory, where they are very wisely forbidden strong drink; which is why the King of the Caribs throws sensational 'drunks' from time to time in Fort de France.

My departure drew near. A few days before it was due, Hayot had a severe attack of ague. The poor chap was unrecognisable. As always when sick, he retired to what he called his 'Chateau', built of concrete to his own design, fifty yards from his galvanised iron, venetian-blinded Colonial house. This 'chateau' looked exotic enough, tucked away in the tropical vegetation; inside, it was charmingly furnished. On the walls were a number of pictures of Martinique by visiting painters, including several from the brush of Marilhac, a most agreeable American who had settled there for fifteen or twenty years, and who came with us everywhere.

In spite of his concrete 'chateau', wood and iron represented for Pierre Hayot the true formula for a colonial house.

'Don't let anyone tell you', he said to me, 'that the Europeans have forced unhealthy dwellings on the natives, or that the prevalence of galvanised iron has made the black tuberculous or rachitic, or again, that shirts and trousers have weakened their physique. The truth is that galvanised iron has been a blessing for everyone, it is clean, it cools rapidly, and above all it harbours neither vermin nor snakes, both of which swarm in the dirt and heat of palm leaf roofs. The negroes imitate us of their own free will, mark that well.'

I shall never forget the Hayot house at St Esprit, the black and yellow bird there which could whistle like a man, and keep the tune so well that you could not distinguish it from its master (I was often mistaken), the sound of the morning rain on the vast fields of sugar cane, Mont Carbet capped in clouds (a sign of continued rain during the day), the lassitude, the desire of doing nothing, peculiar to the climate. . . .

But I had to go. Hayot showed signs of getting on his feet again. I set out in quest of meteorological information, for there is a 'service météo' there. The officer on duty was 'on his rounds', his typist could tell me nothing.

'But what's your glass doing?'

'We haven't got one.'

No barometer at a meteorological station. . . . It is true that I was once told the same thing at Fishguard by the signalman on duty.

I went to the Harbour Office to get the ship's papers back, and to the Military Hospital for a new clearance. There I came across the same captain-doctor, who now absolutely insisted on knowing the exact time of my departure, as if that could have the slightest bearing on my health. I did not even know myself; getting under way in a small boat being always subject to all sorts of things. However, in order to keep him happy I named a time, which seemed to be all he needed.

Shortly afterwards, when I was on the point of letting go my warps, someone from the meteorological station ran up to tell me a cyclone had been reported, so I doubled and quadrupled them instead, only letting the stern ones go; took some additional turns of the anchor chain through the ring on the barrel of the buoy, got ready another anchor and waited. . . . Nothing happened.

The next day I said goodbye to M. Didier, the Harbour Master, and Commandant Prunes (S.N.O. Antilles) who, it happened, was a friend of Da Cunha. We had a look at his reading and barometer, which showed nothing very alarming.

M. Cloche, First Officer of the St André, was leaning over her rail. He was a man of herculean strength, having exactly the same chest, arm and leg measurements as Rigoulet, the champion dumb-bell artist and weight lifter. I knew this for a fact, as all the officers of the St André and myself were measured one day after lunch. Although M. Cloche was by nature one of the gentlest and most patient of men, he was also a sailor of the old school, inclined as a matter of course to take a strong line in an emergency, a thing which it seems has slightly hampered his career. Like all old sailors, he prided himself on his skill in weather forecasting, so seeing my blue-peter he shouted across:

'We've just come in! There's a fairly heavy sea outside at the moment, but you needn't worry about cyclones for ten days at least, for there's no moon.'

Comforted by these words, I liquidated my famous Massa Houle, who wanted another 'cent sous' to 'light a candle' on my behalf, and put a slipping hitch on the buoy preparatory to getting under way. Ten minutes afterwards the Winnibelle was on a broad reach for the open sea.

Roland de Malglaive had told me he would give a blast on the Alabama's whistle when I left the anchorage. The Alabama was a Transatlantique freighter which happened to be in the roads. She remained dumb; probably the steam had been shut off in the engine room.

A very small tug, the Gilbert, let off a short, falsetto wheeze, and after a couple more attempts thought better of it and gave up.

The intention was there.

Hayot came along as he had promised, still rather pale, in a large twin-engined launch with the Dormoys, Richards, and other friends. He had brought his camera, and we duly exchanged politenesses while we 'shot' each other. Thereupon an icy squall from the N.E. came down on us to cool our enthusiasm and remind me that I was again 'dans le bain'.

I set a course along the coast, and before long my view of the bay of Fort de France was drowned in cataracts of rain.

I learnt later that Pierre Hayot was put to bed again when he got home, soaked and shivering with cold.

What a climate!

F 2

CHAPTER XXII

TOWARDS NEW YORK

It turned out to be blowing pretty hard at sea. I kept inshore, and was under the lee of Mont Pelée the whole length of the island. As the Winnibelle emerged the wind hit her like a slap in the face. She heeled obediently and gathered speed. I was anxious to know if I could lay a course to clear Dominique without making a board. This would depend on the exact bearing of the trade wind. At the moment it was heading me with the tide under it.

Opinion had been very divided over the route I ought to take on leaving Martinique. The majority of the officers of the St André and Alabama were in favour of passing to leeward of the islands (less sea). The second officer of the Karimare even went so far as to tell me I ought to go by way of the Florida channel, so as to benefit by the four-knot current up the coast. That was a valuable tip, but on the other hand, 'a man is not a horse, he must lie down sometimes', as the saying goes, and I had no one to relieve me on watch, which would mean eight or ten days without rest, in those intricate waters.

My intention, on the contrary, was to pass to windward of everything: Dominica, Désirade, Antigua and the Barbados,

(i) because I should get quickly away from the track of the cyclones. (Reply: Cyclones my foot!);

(ii) because in the lee of the Islands I should have frequent calms and squalls, and should be unable to sleep until I had cleared Sombrero, i.e. not before the fourth night;

(iii) whereas, to windward, once clear of Désirade after the second night, I should be able to let the vessel sail herself close hauled. Obviously this would mean a slightly longer course, but in the event of bad weather, 'plenty of sea room'. While via Sombrero (even assuming that the weather held till then) the Bahamas would be no distance away, reaching out in a labyrinth of banks and shoals.

So my mind was made up. But I had not marked my course in

advance on the chart, and I had not imagined the winds would be so inconstant.

As night fell, the dark mass of Dominica loomed much larger than I could have wished. That I was closing the land was all too evident, and it was impossible to point higher into the wind. I was beginning to hesitate: it was hardly wise to risk sailing a few cable-lengths to windward of an unlighted shore in the dark. . . . At that moment, fortunately, the wind suddenly piped up. The Winnibelle gave a snort and went ahead like a train, not without wetting her sails halfway up the mast. Little by little, I managed to edge nearer the wind's eye.

Night closed down. I steered with the utmost caution till morning to avoid drift. The shore was hidden in the darkness, but I should have seen breakers in time to go about if necessary. Dawn brought a pleasant surprise. The craggy silhouette of Dominica had become a mere blur astern, and Marie Galante was visible abeam, sheer and flat-topped, like a Camembert cheese. I was quite close to Petite Terre, and ought to have sighted it, for the island was nearer than Désirade, which was already visible right ahead. A prolonged search revealed a few coconut palms apparently sticking up out of the water, and the white tower of a light-house. I had the feeling that the first big wave would submerge the lot.

I then noticed that a big bubble of air had formed in my large compass, and on examining the cover, found to my surprise that the Transat workshops, through using a piece of glass that was not thick enough, had been unable to screw home the collar and washer. The workmen had simply puttied it over and the alcohol had, of course, dissolved it: a nice piece of work by the local 'experts'.

It was written that I should have trouble with this compass from beginning to end of the trip, for lack of a workman capable of fitting a mere piece of glass properly.

At midday exactly I cleared Désirade to a nicety, within gun-shot. A hundred miles in twenty-four hours close-hauled; it was very satisfactory progress, allowing for the steep sea. In fact, this point of sailing suited my vessel much better than a following wind: her deep, heavy hull worked admirably through the seas

without losing headway. As soon as I was well clear I eased a foot
of main sheet, lashed the helm and let her sail herself. Heading
thus, I was very nearly on a course for New York. I had no idea
how long the N.E. trades would remain with me now. They vary
considerably year by year.

When I arrived in New York they told me a cyclone had been
felt at Fort de France on this very day. In St Lucia, over which the
centre passed, not a roof remained, and the whirlwind moved
thence back towards Haiti. If I had gone inside the islands I
should inevitably have felt the effects of it.

I now had the most difficult stage before me, and I knew it.
About halfway across I should find uncertain winds, the gales
which are characteristic of Bermudian waters, and prolonged
calms. With these latter in view, I carried a reserve of five tins of
oil—twenty-five litres in all—little enough, but representing nevertheless a ten-hour spell under power. I should also find, on
approaching New York, fog, unfavourable W. and N.W. winds,
and a contrary set of the Gulf Stream. It was within a day or two of
the beginning of August, when the dirty-weather season begins.
The wind chart was hardly reassuring, as two-thirds of the
cyclones followed exactly the course I was making; the others
crossed it, to lose themselves in Florida or the Gulf of Mexico. I
should be right in their path for three weeks at least.

The following day, the 29th July, the log totalled 102 miles.
During the night I ought to have seen, but did not see, the lights
of Barbadoes. By a series of coincidences, I never once saw a single
light during the whole of my passage through the Antilles. That
same day I burnt myself badly with boiling oil frying some flying-
fish: I was on the point of transferring them to a dish when the
boat gave a lurch and the burning oil slopped all over my hand. I
wiped my fingers, which at once began to peel, and I immediately
proceeded to coat them with ambrine, which is pretty painful stuff
to apply. It is made up in the form of a candle; you light the wick
to melt the special wax of which it is composed and run it hot
over the burn. Unpleasant though the process is, it is by far the
most effective treatment known to me, and I am told it was invented during the war by Dr Rothschild. This mishap was a serious
matter, and I hardly cared to think what my situation would be

if it came on to blow while I was still deprived of the use of one hand. To make matters worse my ankles were more or less raw from mosquito bites, and I had on one of my legs a nasty little round sore, the size of a halfpenny, the cause of which was obscure.

On July 30th, the following day, from dawn onwards, calms alternated with storms. Caution prompted me to change the jib, for the squalls were very violent and between whiles the boat hardly moved. The Trades were leaving me already. No luck!

I pricked the secondary blisters on my burns and made numerous applications of ambrine, which cracked and came off as soon as I made the slightest movement. In the late afternoon, exasperated by a long, calm spell, I fished out of the sail locker a large jib which I had not used so far, a very light sail, bought second-hand from the sailmaker and cut down for the Winnibelle. It was hardly stretched before a white squall appeared to windward. I took little notice at first, but when it was within five or six hundred yards I saw the sea boiling and fuming violently in front of it. I made a dash to shut the cockpit cover, which as a rule I kept closed but which I had opened when getting the new jib on deck, slammed-to the cabin skylight and from there reached the tiller in a bound. The squall had already reached the Winnibelle, hitting her full on the beam. Caught thus without any headway, she lay over on her side, taking more and more of a list, and shuddering from truck to keel; green water reached the skylight. At last she gathered way and began to come up into the wind. This was just what I did not want. In stays, in a wind like this, the jib would have slatted once or twice and torn itself to shreds. I pushed the helm up into the wind with my back and let the mainsheet run at the same time, to get her to pay off.

All this had not taken more than half a minute, and just as she was beginning to bear away, I heard a report like a field-gun going off: my jib had literally exploded under the pressure of the wind and the cataracts of water. All that was left of it were the seams and bolt-ropes. 'It won't be difficult to stow you now,' I said to myself. Its career had been of the briefest, a matter of five minutes or so, and there was no question of repairing it. The Winnibelle was now hopelessly out of balance, and I had to get the mainsail off her with the squall at the very top of its form. Somehow or other this was managed.

What pleased me least was that in the course of smothering the mainsail the ambrine came off my fingers again, and the effect of salt water on raw flesh is the reverse of soothing.

That day I crossed the ecliptic for the second time, but it was much warmer than on the previous occasion, on account of the Gulf Stream. My cabin began to be uninhabitable by night, owing to the heat collected by the deck during the daytime. I slapped on a bit of whitewash and brought my bedding on deck. This worked fairly satisfactorily, until the heat of the deck began to penetrate the bedding. (Extract from log):

'Much warmer in making up towards Bermuda than in approaching the Antilles from the E. Sweating under the chin. Sunstroke. Slept on deck. Sun vertical at 18°. (Declination 18). Rarely want to drink anything cold. Fierce squalls. Sky cloudy and peculiar. Rain every ten minutes (!)

'I am convinced that the climate is unhealthy at sea towards 25° lat. The wind may be fresh, yet it is still hot in the cabin. You come on deck bathed in sweat and catch cold. The draughts below deck are also bad. Have never been so bronchial for a week on end in my life.'

31st July. 'Forgot to mention that I have let her steer herself since leaving Désirade. When once you have developed bad habits . . . ! Tried to find out how I got a new cut on the knee; it seems I must have knocked it on the oil pressure gauge, which is placed in the cockpit, for the glass is broken. Streaks of sargasso weed plainly show the direction of the stream as marked on the chart. The log gets constantly caught up in it, and it is no longer reliable. Hardly any flying fish now.

'You would think that the sargasso had claws. Trail your log through the middle of a patch of ordinary floating seaweed and it will clear easily enough; but with two or three straggly bits of sargasso about you may be certain that at the end of five minutes the fins will be clogged up with a lovely great bunch of the stuff.'

1st August. 'The Winnibelle does not keep her course well with the wind abeam. I have to keep an eye on her all the time. Have set up the spinnaker as a balloon-jib. It is really too much for this hard-

tried sail; one strong puff of wind and it will be goodbye. 3 p.m.,
dead calm, but the engine can wait; there's worse to come, and
besides I haven't the heart to stay at the helm for ten hours for the
sake of 20 miles or so gained. 5 p.m., balloon-jib came unhooked.
Lost one of my linen hats in securing it. Only two more left, so be
careful! 10 p.m. No great fun handing the spinnaker in a fresh
wind and pitch darkness.'

2nd August. 'My averages have dropped seriously; 77, 65, 100,
75, 70, 60, 50. Progress is royal rather than meteoric, about 2½ kn.

'The mainsail, of heavy, rather stiff cloth, no longer draws and I
am trying a new combination with the spinnaker as a sort of triangular mainsail; the balance is better so, and if a squall comes, it
is less risky than using it as a balloon jib. Fine weather so far, but
"poco wind", the thing sailors can tolerate least.'

The days were in fact finer, between squalls, than at any other
stage of my voyage. I was even able to take a sight without holding
on, which was quite an event on board the Winnibelle and never
happened again.

So far I had hardly bothered about fishing. I had ineffectually
trailed a tunny line on leaving Madeira, and after that flying fish
had been sufficient for my well-being. I tried once or twice for
sharks, but without result; they are very wary in these waters. The
trace of my line was steel chain made fast to a swivel ring, with a
hook of special steel, the line itself being strong wire. If I had
caught one my plan was to heave in on a winch and then hoist my
capture up by one of the halliards; the rest would be hatchet work,
not for the sake of the flesh, which is poor stuff, but to get the tail,
and nail it to the bowsprit end for good luck. In the old days every
sea-going ship had a shark's tail at the bowsprit end, fixed there by
a steel peg.

As there were no more flying fish now, I turned my attention to
bonito. This fish has an enquiring turn of mind, and usually makes
a careful reconnaissance of any object that interests it. It does not
surprise me in the least that Gerbault made them come near
enough to be harpooned simply by dipping his toes in the water,
as he states in one of his books. The story sounded a tall one when
I first read it, but experience has taught me to believe it.

Quite often I used to see bonitos almost on the surface. Little would be visible except their bright blue fins, making the whole fish appear blue. In reality their bodies are entirely silver, so sleek and shiny that the newest chrome steel would look dull in comparison, that is, when they jump clear of the water; a moment after death, this brilliant lustre disappears and they become normal silvery fish, with lines of red spots down each side of their bodies.

My first attempts met with no success. I tried a little of everything on the hook, silver paper, anchovy, a bit of biscuit, a piece of ham: they showed not the slightest interest. Finally I tried a piece of red rubber and the effect was instantaneous; they fought to get at the hook. I could have caught a hundred. I was satisfied with half a dozen or so; they all leaped prodigiously before letting themselves be pulled aboard. I cut fillets off them and potted them in salt. Then I stopped fishing. I had enough to last me a fortnight, and what was the good of taking life without rhyme or reason?

So with shooting. I could often have shot birds or porpoises, but refrained, as it would have served no useful purpose. Porpoises would come and gambol on calm days quite close to the boat. They played with the log, so that I had to bring it in, as they might easily have cut the line in their games. They quite clearly delight in a sailing boat, for they show absolutely no fear and rush straight at it, cutting a thousand capers; then just when you think they are going to crash into the hull, they dive vertically, to pass under the keel and emerge on the far side, puffing and blowing noisily. The propeller of a power vessel, on the other hand, worries them, so they only play around the bows, and even then with a certain amount of distrust.

I succeeded in getting a few amusing photographs of them, though they somehow or other always seemed to stop playing, as luck would have it, just when I was ready to press the button. They were companionable beasts, and I much appreciated their company.

By the 4th August I was nearer to Bermuda than to the Bahamas, and was in the direct route from the South American ports to New York. I began to see smoke by day and lights by night. After dark I shone my headlight on to the sails, and was 'challenged' several times by Scott signal flashes, but as I was not keen on replying I simply switched off.

This kind of sailing was hardly in my line. I detest waters where the weather changes every two hours and you have to be moving about on deck doing things the whole time, with all the risk this entails, particularly at night. It is impossible to sleep in peace, for you never know if a squall is going to be violent or not. Most have a real devil in them, and it would be folly to carry all your canvas. But then you make little headway. There are moments when you feel like sticking to a much reduced sail plan for good and just taking things philosophically, but the mood inevitably passes and you begin messing about again with balloon jibs and what not.

However, the worst was yet to come.

CHAPTER XXIII

SOLITUDE AT SEA

I BEGAN to feel the loneliness less acutely as my goal approached, though at the same time I hated the thought of arriving. I thumbed the chart more and more frequently, peered more often at the sky and the horizon, and had a look at the glass about twenty times a day. I found it impossible to lie in my bunk for more than an hour on end. I tried sleeping on deck, but then it rained—an irritating warm rain. I had not a stitch of dry clothing left, nor any means of drying anything, even in the fiercest sunlight. When I spread my bedding on deck, in a matter of five minutes it was burning hot, but it stayed damp, as the evaporation from the sea made the air like a Turkish bath. The sore on my leg got larger every day, keeping perfectly circular the whole time. As no ointment seemed to do any good, I resolved to scour it with a couch-grass brush and black soap and then pour on a bottle of iodine. It will astonish no one to know that this did the trick.

The nails of my burnt left hand began to slough, which did nothing to alleviate my anxiety about what would happen if it came on to blow, as I felt sure it would before long.

I have often been asked (I am sure at least ten people at Funchal alone asked me the question), why I did not take a dog or a cat with me for company. That I should prefer to be absolutely alone was incomprehensible to these good people.

But a cat! No, thank you! There is nothing more awkward than a cat in a boat. I had no desire to jump overboard in the middle of the night, as Carl Weagant did to rescue his. As to dogs, they drink as much water as a man, so that I should have had to double my water tanks; moreover, they are seasick all the time, and I am not sure that in a small boat as lively as the Winnibelle in her motion, a dog would not have died or gone mad. It was the risk of hydrophobia that chiefly prevented Slocum from having a dog in the Spray. Only once did he take an animal on board, his famous goat, which proceeded to make his life a misery by eating his charts, his straw hat, and anything else within reach, until he was only too glad to put it ashore when he reached St Helena, and give it away to the first comer.

No, the only possible companion is another human being, provided he has the same staying power as yourself. There is nothing very pleasant in the prospect of having to look after someone ill or prostrate with exhaustion; as against that it is a hundred times better to be single-handed. Being myself blessed with a constitution above the average, I often reflected in moments of depression that I was lucky not to have brought a companion who would probably have been more 'down' than I was myself.

Moreover, I have always maintained that two is a bad number in a boat. It is not merely a question of the sound having to minister to the sick, besides looking after the vessel; there is very little real companionship possible.

With two people you only meet at relief times, one going on watch and the other going below to sleep, so that actually you hardly see each other. But there are more serious consequences. The man resting below is never quite happy about the man on deck. If he hears the other walking about and doing things by himself, he wonders what it is all about; if he hears nothing, he imagines the other has fallen overboard. If it begins to blow the man below comes up to the cockpit immediately to help.

When I am sailing with Henri and he is at the helm I always ask him to whistle a bit, shuffle his feet or make some sort of a noise so that I know he is still there.

And suppose an accident happens to your friend and you do not know what to do? Or he falls overboard and you do not manage to fish him out? Can't you see yourself coming into port after leaving him in the 'soup'?

This is not all. There are almost bound to be differences of opinion about the best course or a hundred other things; hence arguments. One of the two perhaps considers the other too careful, and the other may, therefore, tend to take risks if he is easily influenced. Whereas a man by himself chews things over thoroughly and follows his own line of thought.

Two men do not necessarily have the same tastes or like the same times when it comes to cooking and meals, or rest. Thus they impose on each other a restraint which can only be painful for both. Nervous tension increases with fatigue.

Everyone who has had experience of it knows how difficult it is to keep even three or four people in perfect harmony when there is no diversion or outlet, as is the case in the confined space of a small boat at sea for days or weeks on end.

You can read this between the lines in most accounts of cruises. No! I would never risk taking another person on a long voyage. The truth is you must either be alone or with a minimum of three, when the whole problem is changed, necessitating a vessel of larger size than mine and considerably more expense.

Single-handed, you have at least the advantage of being entirely your own master, getting up when you like and leaving the helm or not, just as you feel inclined. With two or three it is not at all the same thing. In this respect, to be alone is ideal. I prefer sailing alone, even with its bad moments, to being a hand, as I was formerly, and having to go on watch whether I liked it or not.

It is not to be denied that you get hideously bored sometimes. The boredom is of a peculiar brand and is not, I think, attributable to mere inaction. It appears at the start of a trip; towards the end you feel perhaps more nervous, and also more depressed.

It was back in the Bay of Biscay that I felt my isolation most acutely; right at the start, when I counted on my fingers the weeks and weeks I should have to remain tete-à-tete with myself. Slocum, on leaving Cape Sable in the Azores the first time, felt the same way.

'After the second day', he wrote, 'an unspeakable sense of solitude came over me, which from then on never left me.' Nevertheless, I have noticed that one somehow becomes hardened to this feeling, which scarcely affects me now.

At these times everything serves as a pretext to make you feel lonely. Good and bad weather, the pleasant and the unpleasant; pleasant things because you would like to share them, such as the serene beauty of a lovely night, a smart bit of work in handling the vessel, or simply poached eggs perfectly turned out according to the rules of the art; unpleasant things, because you feel weak and lost, without help or advice, without refuge of any kind; there are moments when you could do with a little co-operation, a gesture of approval.

You have to think quickly sometimes, and then, with hands clamped to your head, you realise that it is a question of getting out of it quite alone.

I have been scared sometimes, on the occasion, for instance, when on going below I felt water up to my ankles. I lit the cabin lamp. The water was four inches above the floor. The ship was sinking! I caught sight of my face in the small mirror under the ladder; it was perfectly normal. I breathed more easily, saying to myself: 'Pooh, what's all this?' But at the same time I felt my heart contract and my hand sought automatically in my pocket for a cigarette, a confession of nervousness. Actually the trouble was that the stopcock on the lavatory waste-pipe was clogged by sargasso weed. It took me some time to find that out, and having to do so involved working out in my mind all the possible ways in which a leak might occur on board, without haste and bringing my brain to bear on the problem in a thoroughly methodical manner; in a word, there was no time for panic.

Another time, I thought I had got into the clutches of an un-accountable wind. In a most sinister fashion, airs seemed to blow from all directions, completely boxing the compass. I reduced canvas, spread my charts on the table and, pencil in hand, read and re-read the sailing instructions, made plans and determined on a line of action. Eventually I managed to pull myself together, came to the conclusion that there was nothing really in it after all, that I was imagining things and that I could safely hoist my sails again. Keep cool, my friend, keep cool. Not as easy as it sounds, though, when you have no one to talk things over with.

One night, during a storm, I had to go to the masthead to adjust the lightning conductor. The thunder and lightning were so close, the flashes so continuous, that I hesitated for quite ten minutes before starting; it really was a storm and a half. I can see myself peeling off my jacket, as I always did before going out in heavy rain, so as not to get it soaked. Before climbing into the ratlines I glanced round the cabin: either I should be back there in three minutes, or else. . . . When I got down from aloft, having adjusted the wire and regained the shelter of the empty cabin, with the lamp swaying wildly from side to side, I felt how small a thing I was in all the pandemonium.

You get into the way of never changing your expression. You make some little unexpected discovery, you cook and eat your meals, you see the dawn of a new day, and your face remains exactly the same. For whose benefit should it change? You think 'Good!' or 'Damnation!' with exactly the same expression. Fortunately I have the habit of talking aloud to myself. When I drank out of my big enamel mug I would see a pair of round, fixed, expressionless eyes reflected there, and I used to wink, not for any particular reason but simply by way of starting a chat.

I remember that one day, the engine room door being open, I shut it to with a kick, saying to the engine: 'Blast you, I don't want to see your dirty —— at meal-times!'

Another time, when I had made a mess of getting the mainsail down, so that the peak fell into the water, I shook an admonitory finger at it as a schoolmaster might do to a refractory pupil, and said: 'As to you, my boy, there'll be trouble coming to you if you go on like this.'

When you sight a ship, you say out loud: 'Hullo, look at that chap!'[1] If it turns out to be a big boat with white upper works, you add: 'Got his best collar on, too.' Even when you only see the smoke, it's interesting; if it disappears you watch for it to show up again. There it is; you look at the clock; one minute, forty seconds. 'Ah,' you say, 'on that ship they stoke methodically, every so often.' You take pleasure in counting the seconds, and you rap out 'Time!' at the precise moment. Away on the horizon another puff of smoke appears. Down in the stokehold of the ship the men wait for the bell and, as it rings, open the furnace doors and throw in their four or five shovelfuls of coal. You would never take the trouble to notice such things in ordinary circumstances. And there are innumerable others which normally you would be unaware of: the smell of moist earth in the rain of the Trades, the marine life, minute but discernible, in every piece of floating seaweed, the small fish which follow in the shadow of your hull. After trying in vain to tempt them with a baited hook, you spend an entire afternoon straightening a big double tunny-hook and making it into a miniature harpoon, sharpening the end with a file and using a saw to give it a barb; then you spend hours lying flat on your stomach,

[1] Note: Ships are masculine in French.

with your home-made weapon stuck into the end of a broom handle, trying to harpoon elusive shadows. (They are mostly pilot-fish.)

I had thought the gramophone would be a most valuable resource in moments of depression. It was just possible, despite the ship's motion, to get the poor devil of an instrument to play without the needle slipping, by jamming it into a particular position against the raised edge of the table with the help of a tin of petit beurre biscuits and either another tin of a different shape or the old Verdun's signal code-book, which was just the right size. Then I used to sit and listen. Every tune I put on, without exception, evoked some disturbing memory, whether of a place or a person, and it was far from being an undiluted pleasure. I even began to feel a nostalgia for things which in reality need not have stirred me so deeply. It might be a record from Paris, bringing back my studio; then would come one I had scrounged in Martinique from Simon Cottrell's house, and I would hear again the sound of the warm rain coming down outside his window. I have kept most of these records, but I never play them now; they would too vividly bring back days and hours which can never be lived again and which, whether they entered my being through eyes, ears, nostrils or however it may have been, remain deeply engraved there.

Sometimes I could stand it no longer, and climbed on deck to escape from myself. Strains of music were still wafted up to me from the entrails of the boat, soon to die away in a deplorable whine. Despite frequent dismantling and applications of the special oil belonging to my Excelsior Log, the gramophone motor never managed to keep going long enough for a whole record. This maddening state of affairs generally resulted in my cutting the concert short, whereupon silence reigned once more, a thousand times more heavily than before.

I recall once when I had put on the celebrated love-song 'Dein ist mein ganzes herz', and it petered out when the impassioned tenor was in the very middle of his super top note. At the moment I scarcely noticed it, having just heard what sounded like the noise of an approaching squall outside. But the effect of the interrupted spasm was so ludicrous that I seem to hear it still.

People have often asked me why I did not take a wireless set with me, but they do not realise how extraordinarily tactless a wireless can be at times. In September 1928 the Pourquoi Pas? passed through the centre of a cyclone. When the gale was at its height she laboured very heavily, rolling thirty-five degrees and more (measured) and dipping her lower yards into the tops of the waves. The passengers had been barricaded into their cabins for two days. The officers' wardroom was inches deep in water which washed from side to side without anyone taking any notice of it; the galley was stove in, the fire put out and the crew had had nothing to eat or drink for a day and a half. Such was the state of affairs one morning when it fell to me to make my way into the wardroom to rouse one of the officers. I noticed that the wireless loud speaker had fallen from its bracket and was sliding about on the floor among the mass of débris, with its connecting wire still plugged in. I picked it up in order to stow it somewhere, and in the midst of all the hubbub, I suddenly heard a comic song being sung out of some operetta or other, and realised the thing was still working. At that particular moment I was not in the mood to appreciate the contrast. Keeping my feet as best I could, propping myself up by one means or another—anyone who has actually experienced a thirty-five degree roll will know what I mean—tired out, dirty, with three days' growth of beard on my chin, a feeling of absolute rage took hold of me and I tore the plug out. What a game! What a world we live in! Good God, the next thing is they'll be blaring out their tripe to condemned men in the electric chair, men dying of thirst in the desert or shipwrecked sailors freezing to death on an iceberg (I am not so far from the truth). Do you see me on board the Winnibelle listening to a political speech or an advertisement for pills?

It must be added that in 1933 it would have been difficult to get a set capable of receiving the stations which then existed at a range of 2,000 miles, unless by paying a great deal of money. Seventy-five francs for my famous gramophone represented my total budget as far as music went, and I consider that was just about right.

Taking it all round I would say that solitude at sea is not so dreadful or intolerable as might be thought.

People who shake their heads when they read these lines might be greatly surprised if I were to suggest that they very likely live more lonely lives themselves than they realise. The worst I have known myself was in Paris, compared with which my loneliness in mid-Atlantic was as nothing. To be alone in the midst of a crowd is much harder to bear than to be a thousand miles from the nearest human being. It has sometimes happened to me to come away from a lecture, to find myself back in the street, hardly knowing where I was, and to walk blindly off into the night, with the sudden realisation that I knew not one person in the now darkened lecture hall, not a single one who would think of coming with me even for a few steps.

For weeks on end, in my time, I have only left my studio to go to the restaurant, and the restaurant to go back to my studio. I much prefer being at sea to that sort of thing.

Far worse is the case of those who carry solitude in their hearts. For them there is no harbour to look forward to at their journey's end, no inhabited land on the surface of the globe. There are many more such people than is commonly supposed, I am convinced.

CHAPTER XXIV

MIDNIGHT TO MIDNIGHT

It is important not to confuse this particular kind of 'cafard', which comes purely from solitude, with the boredom of the man who has nothing to do from morning till night; the single-handed sailor has no lack of occupations. At the same time, the sense of isolation is present even while you work, and somehow takes the edge off your enthusiasm.

Thus, I had on board a 'zombi', to use an expression of Massa Houle's, that is to say an influence, a ghost. The Winnibelle was haunted. The zombi made its presence known by certain shocks or bumps, sometimes violent, sometimes less so, which occurred at intervals not attributable to the regular rolling and pitching of the ship. I tried to localise this banging, which at first disturbed my sleep, but it eluded me, and after a while I became more or less indifferent to it.

I 'laid' the zombi quite by chance at the end of my voyage. A heavy tool had dropped into the oil tank; whenever the vessel rolled, this tool, after a pause until the angle was steep enough to set it in motion, began to slide across and, gathering momentum as it slid, knocked against the side of the tank with enough force to shake the whole boat.

I had to discipline myself in various ways. For instance, I made it a rule to have at least one hot meal a day. Once, in heavy weather, I decided to make some white sauce, which involves stirring over a slow fire with a wooden spoon. This occupation had the advantage of taking my mind off the unpleasant prospect outside, where something really dirty seemed to be brewing. I wanted a dish of asparagus with white sauce; the sauce was on the table, done to a turn, and I was giving it a last stir, when it overturned and made a lovely mess all over the floor. I patiently swabbed the floor and the table clean, got some more milk and flour, and began all over again. The point was, never to give in.

Another time I made over fifty pancakes (having prepared rather

176

a lot of batter). To toss a pancake in a rolling boat is quite a test, and I am ready to take on all comers. Making coffee, too, was a problem in itself. I noted at the time: 'Coffee a failure: ground too small apparently, the filtre gets clogged. In despair, decided to treat it as Turkish coffee, and put the water and grounds to boil in a saucepan. Then poured the lot into two bottles; result, marvellous. At the end of twenty-four hours the grounds had settled so thoroughly and firmly that the bottle could be shaken without disturbing the coffee, which is clear, very strong and quite excellent.'

The daily programme was roughly as follows. Assuming I had gone to lie down at about two in the morning with a reasonably clear horizon and passable weather conditions, I could, in the most favourable circumstances, and always allowing for frequent verifications of my course by means of the tell-tale compass hanging upside down above my bunk, sleep more or less through one watch, that is until six o'clock. Then I would get up, put out my side lights, the cabin lamp, searchlight and stern light, and set the daytime canvas, such as the spinnaker, which I never cared to keep on her while I slept. Next I made a cup of tea, took the reading of the log, marked my night's progress on the chart, and entered my position, the state of the sea and certain observations in the log book.

I had had my log book printed to my own specification, with eight columns and a space for observations or remarks. In the first I set down the time, and in the others the log reading, compass course, direction and force of the wind, state of the sea, estimated drift, and finally sailspread. This done I wound the chronometer— at exactly eight o'clock—and also my watch and the binnacle clock, after which I gave the deck a rough swab down. On Sundays only, I polished up the metalwork of the skylight and big compass, and gave it a light coating of oil to prevent it becoming oxydised. Cleaning done, I went below to shave; a ceremony which I never allowed the state of the sea to interfere with.

W. A. Robinson, in his *Voyage to the Galapagos*, says that he could never stand a three or four days' growth of beard, which he found both irritating and demoralising. Those are my sentiments also. There is no virtue in this; it is a question of morale.

At this moment along comes a squall. It is nine o'clock, and the first squall of the day; we are comparatively lucky. This necessitates handing the spinnaker, sending up another sail in its place and at ten o'clock or so reversing the operation. Between times I may have decided to inspect the food department. This has to be done every day; you have to look out for mouldy lemons, fillets of cod which have begun to go bad, and in general anything which may turn poisonous or spread decay. It is absolutely necessary to be thorough and relentless over this task, as a mere matter of prudence. From time to time it will be necessary to rebake bread or biscuits which show signs of mouldiness.

The evening before one of the electric lamps had gone out: fuses must be looked to, or perhaps the accumulators are found to want topping up or recharging, or a dynamo brush needs adjusting. Another time it may be the sail locker, situated in the fo'c'sle, which claims my attention; it must be given an airing whenever the weather permits. But here comes rain; I shut the skylight, put on an oily and take a look at the weather.

As likely as not I shall stay on deck till two o'clock. There are plenty of odd jobs, more or less essential to the well-being and efficiency of the boat, to keep one occupied: a rope to be spliced here, a piece of whipping to be renewed there, and so on. On some days, when I had to stay for long periods at the tiller, and was thus prevented from doing any other manual work, I took a volume of the Sailing Instructions and studied the general conditions of the waters through which I was passing, though the motion was apt to make continuous reading impossible. One day I took a packet of sugar, the kind of sugar which is made up in small cubes, each wrapped separately in paper and which ranks, with liquid soap that tips up into your hands, bits of cheese in silver paper, and mustard pots like pumps, among the most glorious achievements of modern man. . . .

From my journal: 'I am beginning to hate with a mighty hatred this wrapping up of bits of sugar in bits of paper. It takes about a quarter of an hour, with both hands free, to sweeten a cup of tea. Not only that, but you have to mess about so much with each wretched little lump before you can get it out of the wrapping, that the sugar is not nearly so clean by the time it gets into your cup as it would have been if packed loose in the usual way. I have misspent hours on end at the tiller undoing a fair supply of the wretched things (after taking care to wash my hands first). The little white bits of paper trailed off astern at regular intervals in the Winnibelle's wake and made an effect like a paper-chase. . . .' Being very absent minded, I more than once threw the sugar overboard and gravely put the paper into the sugar jar.

My next job would be the meridian observation. First, take the sextant very carefully out of its box, then crawl on deck, watching all your movements. There is nothing trickier than taking a sight practically at sea level on a deck which makes a habit of dropping away from under your feet and which tops the crests of the waves at one moment and sinks into the trough the next. Every sailor knows how hard it is to get a creditable result in such conditions, and yet strange as it may seem, you do get it in the end. Personally, I hardly ever managed without holding on to something with one hand and manipulating my sextant with the other. I tried every possible method, kneeling, crouching, straddling, leaning up against mast or shrouds, even lashing myself to them, but in that way a certain amount of shaking is inevitable, and what with one thing and another it is much more satisfactory in the end to 'tickle' the micrometer screw through a series of approximate adjustments and to stand up to it, balancing to the best of your ability and holding the instrument with one hand. The sun, it is true, careers about your horizon like a meteor, too high at one moment, and too low the next. Or another time your horizon may be faulty; a little judicious guesswork has to come into the performance. . . . Eventually, pop! you have got your sight as near as makes no matter. But be content with that; you'll be less successful if you try again, most likely. . . .

The sails often got in the way and it was necessary to shift them and alter course while taking the altitude, which hardly made things simpler. As a general rule I confined my efforts to the sun, choosing either noon or whatever time of day it condescended to show itself, as opposed to a star. For it was sheer hard labour, even in good weather, to spot a star and then get an accurate sight of it, having regard to the incessant motion of the boat.

Between two and three in the afternoon I prepared a hot meal, such as eggs and bacon, grilled ham, or some fried fish, with potatoes and a little coffee; after which the plates had to be washed up.

If there seemed to be a prospect of two hours' sleep in the course of the afternoon, bringing the total to six for the day, I then 'described a longitude' on my bunk. But it was a toss-up; more often than not the variable weather, or a change in the direction of the wind, or some unforeseen occurrence kept me awake. All the same it is important to accumulate sleep, as a provision against bad nights.

The close of day is always depressing and the hateful task of lighting up makes it more so. Washing up plates and dishes and knives and forks is bad enough; the thought of the water (sea) warming up for the purpose while I eat always spoils my appetite. But lamplighting. . . . At nightfall, however vile the weather, you must crawl forward, and bring back, one after the other, the two sidelights, which are as big as canary cages and as heavy as trunks, taking care all the time not to knock them against anything. In semi-darkness you have to open them up, wipe the lenses and reflectors, and pour in paraffin, half of which drips on to your knees or makes a mess of the floor; then comes the lighting, after which you stagger forward again with the heavy brutes, rig them in position, and as often as not have to do it all over again on account of a flaring wick. There remains the white stern light; a repetition of the same entertaining performance. And the cabin lamp, and the paraffin stove, and the compass lamp and God knows what else besides . . . the number of things that have to be filled with paraffin is inconceivable. There is paraffin everywhere; the galley reeks of it. . . . While the stove is being filled the drawer containing the knives and forks opens, and the 'silver' gets a nice dose of the stuff. When the rolling is bad it becomes a problem to know where to put things, and every so often my bunk gives hospitality to a lamp, or a filler, or a lamp-glass; a resting-place has to be found for them somewhere. . . . And when I next lie down the mattress gives off a delicate aroma of paraffin.

Next comes the job of changing sails for the night, always necessary unless the weather is absolutely settled. Thereafter follows a spell of three or four hours on watch, during which I can at last give rein to my thoughts, scribble a few pages, etc., not without periodical interruptions in the form of some unaccustomed noise, an adjustment of sails, or the preparation of dinner, if tea and biscuits can be called dinner. At midnight I change the page of my ship's log, which is pinned to a board with drawing-pins, and begin a new one.

Such, in brief outline, was an average day on board; but there were, of course, occasions when by reason of heavy weather, I had to be at the helm for twelve hours, and the reader will readily appreciate how quick off the mark you have to be in order to get through the bare minimum of routine jobs when it is impossible to leave your post for more than five or six minutes at a time. In one way or another, a man alone at sea in a ten ton boat has plenty to occupy his days.

CHAPTER XXV

IN THE TRACK OF THE CYCLONES

On the afternoon of the 7th August I had a little excitement. It was almost calm, with an occasional anaemic breath from the N.E. Suddenly to starboard, a little abaft the beam, I saw a sail, or rather what I took to be the upper canvas of a three-masted barque. With one bound I got my cinema out. In such light airs it would be an easy matter for me to sail round the almost motionless barque, and perhaps, who knows, she might be able to throw me some bread and even butter. The butter I had bought at St Servan was more or less rancid, and I was using lard to cook with, for the tinned stuff I had laid in at Fort de France was worse than the other, and I had chucked it overboard.

I opened the engine-room door and set about starting up the motor, so as to close with my new-found companion as quickly as possible. Needless to say I was in a state of great excitement: result, a backfire and violent contact between the tool case on the back of the door and my right shoulder, which received a nasty cut. . . . As soon as the motor got going I staunched the blood as best I could, threw in the clutch and jumped to the tiller. A painful surprise awaited me! My three-masted barque was simply a big motor-ship steering straight towards me; her two-tiered bridge, with its varnished woodwork, had looked, with the help of a little mirage, exactly like the brownish square sails of an ocean-going windjammer. I contented myself with hoisting my burgee at the masthead and the national flag at the peak. By then the liner, which was moving at fifteen or sixteen knots, had closed with me and was quite near. She was a Furness Prince boat, flying the British flag. I waved my white cap to her and watched her go by, privately consigning her to all the devils in the world. In her arrogance she had sent me a huge bow wave or wash, which reached me just as I was beginning to turn the handle of my cinema, and caused me to lose my balance, thus spoiling the shot. Thereafter I attended to

Staysails properly trimmed

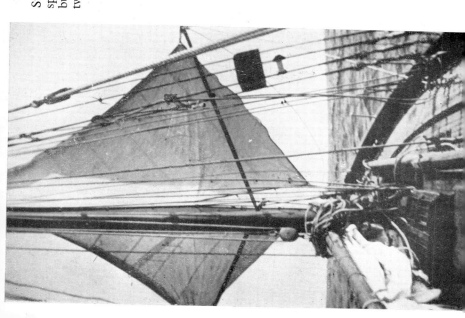

Staysails spread, but stays twisted

Pilot, from a painting by the Author

my shoulder, which was bleeding copiously, and gave vent to my feelings with considerable eloquence.

During the evening the weather took a turn for the worse. An ominous-looking cloud had been following in my wake since the evening before. Every night a new storm developed astern of me, accompanied by blinding lightning-flashes, and each day came squalls which, in point of fact, moved at no great speed, hardly more than that of the surface wind, so that I was able to have races with them.

They extended all round me as far as the eye could see, thick and vertical like the columns of an immense cathedral. It was a strange, disturbing spectacle. I found after a time that I could calculate their speed and direction, and was thus able on numerous occasions to pass astern or ahead of them. At home a small white cumulus is a delightful affair, a pleasantly decorative touch in the general scheme. But in these waters it is a signal to batten down the hatches and make sure that everything is ready. I have seen the first flash come out of one of those little white clouds at three in the afternoon, followed by a clap of thunder. Fifty minutes later the sky is black all over and the wind rising, and in ten minutes more the full force of it is on you with a roar. The entire sky is filled with thick cloud, heavily charged with electricity, completely masking the sun. Squall follows squall in rapid succession, blinding, horizontal; the sea flattens, swept by the terrific wind. By now you will just about have finished stowing all the canvas you had on her; never mind how you do it, it must be done, though it will only be possible if you get the mainsail and jib down on deck before the impact of the first blast, which is heralded by a fringe of smoking wavelets two or three hundred yards off, and a distant murmur, a sort of hissing sound made by the rain slashing down into the sea.

The vessel heels to the blast under bare poles, or possibly a storm jib, and then off she goes, bound for glory, like a torpedo-boat. . . . You hunch up your shoulders and squeeze yourself into as small a space as possible, lashed by the fury of the wind, your shirt flapping against your back in little clammy flaps, your linen hat plastered over your ears. Every moment or so you squeeze the water out of it, with a mechanical gesture. Ugh. . . . You squeeze

G

the water out of your hair too; it streams down your face and into your eyes.

On the day of which I am writing, one of these squalls suddenly turned as black as ink and showed every sign of making straight for me. Its aspect was far from engaging; I let my big jib go by the run, got the mainsail off her and cleared the decks for action. Nothing whatever came of it (this being typical of what one had to put up with) and at nine o'clock I got on my course again under reduced canvas; there was a nasty coppery look about the sky still. Late in the evening an enormous waterspout formed to the eastward, and once again I prepared to lower all sail. It was the biggest water-spout I have ever seen, and at its base the sea boiled in a most significant manner. This sort of weather was not at all to my taste; I prefer the ways of the North Sea; when the North Sea goes in for being unpleasant, it does so in a straightforward, honest fashion; it never frightens me.

During the night corposants, or St Elmo's fire, played in the rigging.

> 'Corposant at the masthead
> Brings the seaman luck, 'tis said.'

When the bluish gleam of the corposant, which arises from strong electric tension in the atmosphere, is seen at sea level, it is a bad omen, apparently, but less so when it appears aloft. All the same, it is not an agreeable sight; it looks as though the rigging was on fire. Meanwhile I could hear a continuous roll of thunder from the direction of Bermuda.

And there is another rhyme, by the way, which hardly squares with the one just quoted:

> 'When corposant aloft you see,
> Blowing hard 'twill shortly be.'

The poor sailor has to draw what comfort he may from these conflicting masterpieces of observation. . . .

Extract from my log: 'We are crossing a region of very heavy condensation. Let's hope it will get cooler soon—the extreme heat of the last few days is barely tolerable. My burns practically cured, by a miracle. The sore in my leg is clearing up; I was afraid it might turn into a carbuncle. Glass low, bad weather, forbidding skies; but so far none of the characteristic signs indicating a cyclone. I am all the time running away from a storm which never succeeds in catching up with me.'

Next day: 'Rumblings to the E. still. Went through a thunderstorm between six and eight a.m., when it blew very hard.'

The ball eventually opened with a bang: 'The change forecast by the low glass has come. Wind jumped suddenly round to S.S.W., had to run before it under storm jib and No. 2 staysail, well hardened in. All one to me, am on my proper course. At 11.30 p.m. took in the jib, and at 11.45 had to get the staysail off her. Midnight, hove to under bare poles, wind on the beam. This has ceased to be a joke.'

At this time my position was exactly equidistant from Cape Hatteras and the Bermudas. The spot has a bad reputation with the Americans.

> 'If Bermudas let you pass,
> You must beware of Hatteras.'

In consequence I was not greatly surprised. The seas had suddenly become enormous. The crests of the waves came halfway up the mast, and it would have been dangerous to carry the smallest shred of canvas. This punishment lasted for forty hours.

It was for me an excellent chance to see how much a small boat can stand. Practically she will survive anything, even though she goes clean under, which happened more than once to the Winnibelle. My log for that day contains but a single sentence, for the simple reason that I was incapable of anything but a kind of scrawl. Nothing very clever about it, but it came from the heart . . .

'Vile weather, got the sea-anchor ready, everything battened down, impossible to stay on deck.'

Why bother with the sea-anchor, in any case? If necessary in the last extremity, it would have been easy enough to put it over the side. For the moment there was no point in doing so; the Winnibelle, lying at right angles to the sea, was a great deal easier in her motion than she had been running before the Trades, when she had given me such hell, the bitch!

I had spread my mattress on the cabin floor again, and slept for half-an-hour now and then, in the deafening uproar. I was unable to resist sticking my nose out through the hatch from time to time. The pressure of the wind was suffocating. The spectacle was stupendous.

Whenever I saw a breaking sea bearing down on me I shut the hatch without a second's delay. Then followed a dull, heavy thud, water spurted through the chinks in the hatch and even in the skylight, then the boat gave a kind of snort, dropped down like a stone into the abyss, paused at the bottom and began the upward climb, preparatory to repeating the entire process. Seen from some distance off the Winnibelle, with her bare mast, must have looked like a fisherman's float when the fish bites and it goes down with a plop. I cannot sincerely recommend this kind of sport to those whose nerves are at all delicate. It is rather as though you were thrown out of a first floor window every thirty seconds or so.

The main thing in such conditions is, of course, to have plenty of sea-room all round you. In the Channel I should have thought it was all up with me, and it probably would have been, for the drift is considerable, one and a half to two knots at least. . . . This means that in forty-eight hours you cover something like a hundred miles, and if the coast is anywhere close by, that's that.

It must be understood that, when I say a small boat can stand anything in the way of weather, I do not intend to imply that she is completely under control. Failure to appreciate this distinction is responsible for the confusion in the minds of the many old sailors who refuse to admit that a ten ton coastal craft will 'take it' as well as an ocean-going three-master. It is, however, literally true that she will not sink; but neither will she be, to any serious extent, under control. Whenever I have emphasised this point in conversation, I have found that men who had not before looked at the matter in this light were prepared to agree with me. Apart from this, those who mention that a 10 or 12 metre boat is a mere nutshell forget that lifeboats are rarely any bigger. The most modern lifeboats, with the most reliable engines, are not in the least afraid of the open sea, but only of rocks and shoals, as is well known.

I can quote more eloquent examples: ordinary undecked ships' boats, heavily loaded with survivors, have often weathered the storm in which their parent ship has foundered.

A short time before leaving St Malo I happened to meet one of the crew of the three-masted schooner Rouzic, which had recently gone down on her way to the Banks. This man had come home by way of Portugal, which he had reached in an ordinary dory after coming through four hundred miles of an Atlantic gale. The Rouzic had had her bowsprit torn out and the whole of her forward part holed by a huge sea. The captain, who was quite a young man, put her before the wind in the hope of reaching the Azores, but the vessel was sinking by slow degrees under his feet despite all the efforts of the crew at the pumps. At the end of two or three days, as the gale showed no sign of abating, he got the men together and told them off in pairs, each pair consisting of one qualified seaman and one man with less experience in the handling of boats. Each pair was allotted one of the ship's dories. The dories each contained two coils of warp, a mattress to serve as a sea-anchor, a compass, water and food. Then they abandoned ship, and by the morning after the following night, had all lost touch with one another. Only a single one of the ten dories went down; the rest were either found and picked up at sea or reached the land, some in Portugal, others in the Azores.

With regard to heaving to and sea anchors, I will not here re-capitulate the various theories with which those interested in the subject have been made familiar by the many experienced sailors who have dealt with it. I will, however, say that I share the opinion of most writers on one particular aspect, namely, that a small boat should not lie anywhere near head to wind when hove to; at right angles to the wind, or nearly so, is better. What I call a small boat is too small not to be in danger of capsizing head over heels when she points in the same direction as the run of the huge waves, as has more than once happened to lifeboats. It is better to take the avalanche on the beam, i.e. at the angle in relation to which her stability was designed, and she will not roll over if it is sufficient, which it will be in the case of a deep draught boat. I will add that I do not favour attempting to maintain any headway; on the con-trary, the ideal is to have a boat which will lie with the wind roughly on the quarter, the helm being lashed down (as elastically as possible, for which purpose the long cotton halyards I had fitted were admirable).

As regards sea anchors I have a theory of my own which differs slightly from the prevailing notions; though I do not wish to be dogmatic about it. It refers, not to the dimensions or method of using them, but to their value as between different kinds of craft. It is beyond question, in my view, that any open boat, such as a ship's lifeboat, or a whaleboat, or a motor launch, or for the matter of that any craft, big or small, which has little or no keel and is not designed to operate under sail, should ride to a sea anchor as soon as the seas begin to get too big. But I am by no means convinced that the same is true of deep draught vessels such as the Winnibelle.

Such vessels, even under bare poles, have a tendency to make a certain amount of headway; with a sea anchor out they behave rather like a circus horse at the end of its leading rein; a stage comes when the lead is at a dangerous angle, when the sea anchor becomes more of a hindrance than anything else, the strain being so great that as likely as not it will part.

In a word, the use of a sea anchor presupposes a vessel which makes sternway, and this the majority of sailing boats do not naturally do. Hence the small riding sail aft which is recommended on these occasions, and which is theoretically supposed to make her luff (though in practice it fails to do so for three-quarters of the time); this puts an additional strain on the boat which, with her after part hard pressed by the wind and her bows pinned by the anchorwarp, and all the time lying nearly broadside on to the seas, ends by being far worse off than if she were left free to shift for herself. Luard, who has written on this subject, takes the same point of view: let us leave the deep draught vessel to her own devices, and if her mast is not too far forward, she will find the position, relative to wind and sea, which best suits her. It is scarcely desirable to force her, against her natural tendency, to look up into the wind. And what is gained by doing so? With shallow draught vessels, and particularly motor boats, the case is altogether different; no motor boat ought ever to undertake an ocean passage without a good sea anchor, preferably two, forming part of her equipment.

It can be roundly stated that if definite errors of judgment are avoided, such as running too long before it or getting too close to a lee shore, a 10 metre boat, well ballasted and soundly built, will weather gales which the great transatlantic liners find troublesome. It may be argued against me that more than fifteen tunnymen, extremely solid vessels, much more powerful than the average yacht of similar dimensions, went down together in the same notorious gale only a few years ago. But the exact circumstances in which these boats foundered are now pretty well understood, thanks to the detailed reports of survivors; in some the ballast had come adrift, being too loosely stowed in the rather flat holds characteristic of a tunnyman, while others capsized stern over bows, thanks to running too long with the wind and sea dead aft.

For the rest it must be admitted that bad weather in a small boat is an experience most people would willingly forgo; the violent motion makes all sleep impossible, and the minutes pass like hours. A night, a day, another night . . . it seems to blow harder and harder. Another day . . . and there is no possible relief or diversion. I ended by putting on oilskins, tying a souwester over my linen hat and wedging myself firmly in the companionway with only my head and shoulders above deck level; there I stayed, with my chin on my arms, stupid with lack of sleep, incapable of thought, simply waiting for things to get better. That is the nearest I can get to describing the scene.

Before throwing my hand in and being blown out of my course I had tried every conceivable combination of sails: No. 2 jib, double-reefed mainsail, reefed staysail, storm jib, third reef in the mainsail, mainsail down (it was virtually down with three reefs in it); storm jib down, staysail down, staysail unbent, mainsail unbent, gaff lashed on deck. Nothing was left but the mast and rigging; and if the gale had developed into a true cyclone I should have unrove the halliards and taken in the running rigging so as to offer less resistance to the wind, except those whose standing parts were made fast aloft, as I had no desire at the moment to shin up the mast. The whole lot would have had to be rerove afterwards, and that would have been no great fun either.

On deck I was reduced to crawling on my hands and knees, a posture which is not calculated to improve one's morale. Several times I got such a slap in the face from one or another of the slatting ropes that the blood rose to my head.

At one particular moment, when I saw an exceptionally monstrous wave coming and had to drop everything and hold on by my eyebrows—it was the third time running that a big sea had prevented me from finishing the job I was engaged on—I remember banging on the deck with my fists in inarticulate fury. On such occasions things have a way of taking such an apparently fiendish delight in putting you out that it is quite impossible not to lose your temper, which is childish no doubt, but perhaps salutary too, by reason of the additional energy it gives you.

Another time the tattered end of one of my shirt sleeves, wringing wet, of course, flapped in my face in such a maddening way that I seized hold of the shirt between my shoulder blades and tore it off over my head, to get rid of the nuisance. As I did so I saw the name 'Madelios' on the inside of the neckband, which made me laugh out loud. That's the way to treat a Madelios shirt!

As soon as it was possible to get on my course again I got up my sails one by one, all soaking wet and stiff as boards, beginning with the staysail. But I felt less and less easy in my mind the nearer I approached soundings eighty miles east of Delaware Bay. Progress was very slow: a bare forty-nine miles on August 15th. Now and again I sighted steamships either crossing my course en route to some neighbouring port or following a course parallel to mine. Visibility was marvellously, I would even say excessively good. For instance, the tops of masts could be seen perfectly clearly emerging above the horizon at a distance of at least twenty miles. The glass was extraordinarily high. I wrote in my log:

'Tonight excessively high barometer readings give food for thought, though admittedly the weather is the best so far. Only hope it lasts! Got my lead and line ready; also the foghorn.'

I looked with disfavour on the mackerel sky. This same 15th August I passed abruptly from the waters of the Gulf Stream into the adverse coastal current. During the night the sea had changed colour, and I woke up to find myself surrounded by an expanse of pale green. How much I preferred it to the deep blue of the Gulf Stream! At the same time a narrow, compact cloud joined North to South across the sky, seeming to mark the extremity of the great warm current. The Wise Men of the East can have had nothing clearer to guide them in their navigation.

The practical result of these changes was that I hastened to put out a bottle of Tuborg beer on the end of a line to cool. Hitherto it had all been undrinkably warm.

On the 16th I reached soundings. I was now in the midst of a heterogeneous mass of flotsam of all sorts; something bobbed up every few yards, a lemon, an electric bulb, a roll of bread, candles, bottles of all sorts and sizes, a camembert cheese, a tin of boot-blacking, a hatbox, flowers, halves of grapefruit, a cabbage, all the contents of a liner's dustbins.

At noon I took a cast of the lead. According to my calculations, I should find twenty-eight fathoms, sand and broken shells, and that was precisely what I did find. At seven I sounded again; fifteen fathoms, sand, said the book, and fifteen fathoms, sand, it was. It was a strange sensation to touch bottom so close with the land out of sight. An hour later, pricking my position on the chart below, I realised that Atlantic City was only some thirty miles distant on the port beam.

'It's getting dark, it should be possible to see the glow,' I suddenly thought. 'Atlantic City is a big place, and no doubt brilliantly lit.'

I put my head out, and there, exactly abeam, a vast halo lit up the sky. Thus it was that I first had touch with the land this time.

All would have been well but for certain signs and portents which had appeared just before nightfall. The 'cats' beards' had become 'mares' tails', then thick cirrus. Astern the horizon stood out more and more clearly. I hardly dared consult the oracle—the glass—so well I knew what it would tell me. The dangerous proximity of the coast was a strong argument in favour of getting to shelter at all costs. The night had brought with it a dead calm. I reckoned up the distance I still had to cover, sounded the fuel tank, topped up the oil, cleared the injector, and away we went! I started the engine at five in the morning and wrote in my log:

'I fancy there's a cyclone on the way: horizon too clear, characteristic sky, ominous calm. Instead of dispersing at sundown the cirrus has thickened, a thoroughly bad sign.'

When at last I ventured to tap the glass, very gently, with the point of a pencil, it shot up in the most impressive fashion; an hour later it fell as precipitately. I set a course for the Barnegat lightship, which I ought to have reached at about 11 p.m., but doubtless owing to an adverse current I was an hour and a half behind time. The light from it was minute, indistinguishable from those of neighbouring vessels but for its occultations. By now the sky had completely clouded over, and was as black as ink to the south. I listened anxiously to the note of my little Diesel, which had never worked so hard in its life. Every four or five hours I had to stop it in order to clean the injector, without which the smoke from the exhaust became black and sickening and the engine began to lose a lot of power, a thing which had never happened before.

I stayed all night long at the tiller, half asphyxiated by the cloud of gas which enveloped the entire boat and travelled along with her. I put a piece of canvas over the exhaust, in the hope that it would deflect the fumes, but it was labour lost. I had to go forward at frequent intervals for a breath of fresh air, and felt anything but brisk. Ships by the score seemed to be closing in on me, not singly but in a regular line of battle extending far to the south. They were of all shapes and sizes, from great clumsy freighters high in the water, poorly lit, their engines making a noise like a steam hammer, to rakish little turbine-driven craft, speedy and brilliantly illuminated, which I presume were coastal passenger vessels. I did not keep my searchlight on, because it dazzled me, but at a given moment when I had to pass dangerously close between the red and green lights of two converging vessels, I switched on the current. The effect was instantaneous; I saw the white masthead lights of the two ships first unmask and then slowly pivot round. My object having been achieved I switched off.

I was now practically in New York waters. About 2.30 a.m. a breeze came out of the E.N.E. and rapidly freshened. I stopped the engine and got sail on her. It looked like being a head wind as far as Sandy Hook, but what matter? A boat can sail on either tack.

When the dawn came I saw the flat, low-lying coast of New Jersey and kept close inshore in case the sea should get up. The wind continued to freshen and I had to double-reef the mainsail. I passed several fishing boats making for shelter, the crews all in oilskins, lashed by the frequent rain squalls.

The wind suddenly jumped round and blew from the west. This

put me much too close for my liking to a lee shore; I could count the panes in the windows of the houses. Then, once more without warning, it fell calm again. What next? A dip in the fuel tank showed that I had not enough left to get me as far as New York. Then I remembered the five spare tins stowed in the locker aft; it was a case of giving a passable imitation of a snake before I was able to dislodge them with the help of a boat hook. At last it was done, and I emptied them into the tank, filled up with oil and once more cleaned the injector. There was no time to lose; fortunately the tide was in my favour. The sea was a most peculiar colour, quite red, as if clouded with cayenne pepper.

I passed a number of motor-launches and steam yachts, chartered by agencies which for a few dollars offer a day's fishing to enthusiasts of the sport. It was amusing to watch them, all lined up along the rail, rod in hand, as expressionless as hard-boiled eggs. I took pictures of them as I went by. One of them asked where I had come from. 'English Channel,' I shouted back. There was a pause, and then the whole row of fishermen burst into one tremendous laugh, which went on and on, while their rods bobbed up and down like the feet of a demented centipede. Evidently I had made a good American joke.

At 10.50 a.m. passed the Scotland lightship, and at 11.10 rounded Sandy Hook, and thence followed the well-marked channel, though I found it advisable to give the buoys a wide berth, on account of the traffic, which was dense. There was a slight haze, out of which there loomed every now and then the huge mass of a transatlantic liner; they came along at fifteen knots or more, leaning over perceptibly as they rounded the successive bends of the channel. Their wash, of which I was nervous at first at such close quarters, proved to be harmless. The Manhattan came by, and I made several attempts to take a picture of her, but to my great disappointment the camera jammed. It needed great self-restraint on my part not to chuck the whole box of tricks overboard.

In the haze I suddenly found myself almost colliding with a small islet surmounted by a turret. During the night I had seen another of the same sort which was not marked on the chart. And I had been much exercised by a flashing light between Atlantic City and the Barnegat, of which no mention was made in the book.

What with one thing and another I thought it advisable to circle slowly round the next lighted buoy I came to, in order to read its number (for all the numbers are marked on the chart). To my relief it was the number I wanted it to be. There were two men fishing from a small boat moored to the buoy. They seemed to come out of their piscatorial torpor for a moment while they eyed me curiously, wondering what I was at.

When finally I entered the Narrows I had been thirty-seven hours at the tiller. I lay to within the limits of quarantine, and kept my eyes skinned for the harbour authorities.

As to the cyclone, I could laugh at it now. It was the sort of cyclone that refuses to be hurried and takes its time. No doubt it liked to do its job thoroughly. It was, in fact, forty-eight hours late, but off the New Jersey coast along which I had just come it sank four vessels and drowned a hundred and twenty souls.

CHAPTER XXVI
NEW YORK

THE health and Customs formalities proved to be a very simple business. I had my bill of health, and also an American safe-conduct which Mr Robertson, United States Consul at Fort de France, had provided me with on his own initiative. By rights I should have anchored in the Hudson, but I dared not do so, having regard to the difficulty of handling the cable and the anchor itself on my own in the midst of all the traffic and in the main stream of the river, which is very deep at that particular spot. Before long a launch belonging to the authorities came up and directed me to a little harbour for pilot boats, the entrance to which was close by. As the entrance was extremely narrow, with a strong cross current, I had to take it with a good deal of headway on, only to discover when I got in that the interior was hardly bigger than a box of dominoes. Luckily I just managed to turn the boat on her heel and let go the big anchor in the nick of time, and as the cable tautened the Winnibelle came quietly to rest alongside a little steamboat. It was early in the afternoon of Sunday, August 17th.

Like a good skipper I inspected ship. My voyage was over not a day too soon. Not more than a dozen potatoes were left; the box of petit beurre biscuits was nearly empty and the few remaining ones had begun to go mouldy; white wine all finished, ditto butter, and the last roll of toilet paper was drawing to a close.

Above deck, all trace of varnish had disappeared from the woodwork, skylights, bowsprit, etc.; the wood was white and getting ready to go black, as is the way of wood. The bobstay and the shrouds as far as halfway up the mast were a superb rusty red, just to prove that they were made of the finest quality galvanised iron.

There was a crowd of spectators in summer clothes on the quayside, and when I set foot on dry land, still wearing my canvas jumper and sea boots, after the violent squalls of a few hours back, I felt I must look like a penguin. Greatly to my surprise the medical,

Customs and immigration officials were all there waiting to greet me. They at once conducted me on board the medical boat, which was moored on the far side of the landing stage. Without raising his eyes from his documents the doctor said: 'You look in pretty good form, eh? Fit as a fiddle, I imagine? That's that, then . . .'

His cross-examination bore little resemblance to that of the Sergeant-Major-Medico of Fort de France; but I was at a loss to understand how he came to be aware where I hailed from. It transpired that the coastguard station at the Narrows, seeing my tricolor ensign and yellow burgee, had telephoned the French Line, who had been warned to expect me by M. Lachenez, of Fort de France.

The Customs officer sealed up all the beer I had not succeeded in drinking since leaving the Gulf Stream—though I must do myself the justice to say I had done my best—and also my small remaining stock of wine, which I relinquished without a pang as it had turned sour. But I put in an impassioned plea to be allowed to keep three bottles of 'mineral water', which my Paris doctor had declared to be 'indispensable to my good health.'

'Where is this mineral water of yours?'

'It's down there by the stove, in the bottle locker.'

'I see what it is all right,' he said with a grin. 'Every liner that docks here brings thousands of cases, all medicinal, of course, so you needn't be afraid of your three bottles troubling my conscience.'

Naturally, what was in those bottles was white rum.

There was an old man on the quayside who was evidently much interested in the Winnibelle and myself, and who now came up and asked me where I was from. He was half paralysed and spoke with difficulty. I was astonished to find that he had known Slocum well. He had frequently met him at the house of President Theodore Roosevelt, their common friend. He described him to me as a 'dry little man, who took an incredible amount of salt with his food, evidently through his long connection with salt water.' This story had a doubtful ring to me, and I did not conceal my scepticism from the old man.

He also talked about Slocum's disappearance: Slocum, it would seem, ran into harbour for shelter in consequence of a hard blow which subsided, then put out to sea again just in time to meet the full force of a cyclone of which no warning had been received, and which was probably the cause of his loss.

After a short interval I got under way for Pier 57, North River, ten miles higher up, where at that time ships of the Compagnie Transatlantique berthed, between the Cunard Line at Pier 56, and the United States Line at Pier 58. I had great difficulty in getting in my anchor, which was hooked up in some débris or other at the bottom of the little harbour, and naturally had to put up with shouts of advice and encouragement from the crowd of spectators.

Once under way, I soon made out the Statue of Liberty. Then, emerging out of the haze, appeared the imposing mass of Manhattan buildings. It was my first sight of the famous 'sky line', and corresponded exactly with what I had imagined. The moment was an exciting one for me, and I kept running forward to put things shipshape on deck and then jumping aft again to take the tiller.

In preparation for my entry into New York I had brought with me and now wore a magnificent false beard and an old opera hat, in order that I might approximate to the film producer's and caricaturist's idea of the typical Frenchman. I sang everything that came into my head, and ceremoniously greeted each passing tug and lighter, Miss Liberty and the world at large. As she scraped past the sterns of barges and ferryboats and described graceful curves round landing stages and pontoons the Winnibelle caused general astonishment if not alarm. The Sunday promenaders who crowded the river banks cheered loudly without the least idea of what it was they were applauding. In fact, a good time was had by all.

About 7 p.m. I saw the Leviathan's three tall funnels, and a little beyond them the funnels of the Ile de France emerged above the sheds on one of the piers. Fifty of the crew of the latter stood motionless and in silence on the landing stage. The comedy was over. I discarded whiskers and crush hat. My sails slid down as it were of their own accord. Slowly Winnibelle came alongside the pontoon and lost headway; I passed a warp forward and another aft; not a word, not a sound was uttered. The end had come.

By chance, it was the hundredth day since I took my departure from France: sixty-five had been spent at sea.

An officer of the Ile de France exchanged a few words with me. I thanked him for being there to meet me and jumped on to the pontoon, intending to shake him by the hand. It was one of those immense pontoons used for keeping huge liners at a distance from the wharf, and I had failed to observe that it was covered with slime and very slippery. I described a magnificent somersault before finally landing on my back, and that was how I first established contact with the soil of New York City.

The newspapers next morning credited me, after their imaginative fashion, with having made a speech on landing, and for once their guess was not at fault. I did indeed make a speech, but it was not one of those which could be printed in the columns of a respectable journal. It was received with loud laughter, and I was there and then adopted by the entire Compagnie Transatlantique, from cabin-boy to managing director.

Reporters and cameramen were now unleashed and came at me in full force. I made haste to remove my sweater, which I had just realised was full of moth-holes, and put on a collar and tie, flannel suit and shoes. Then I was ready to face them.

Such was the origin of the drama which once and for all put an end to my career as a hero. I had committed a grave error in putting on clean clothes. By now, too, my boat was another mistake in herself, for she looked as though she was just back from a week-end cruise. They would have preferred to see me arrive clinging to a cask or astride of a spar. I scandalised my audience by assuring them that I had nothing to relate; that really and truly I had had no adventures; no, I had seen no whales; no, I had not been wrecked; no, I had not been attacked by sharks; yes, of course I believed in the sea serpent, but somehow or other it seemed to have given me the cold shoulder so far. Yes, I ate like anyone else, with a knife and fork; not at all, adventures are things that happen to those who make mistakes; I had no wish to boast and nothing to boast about, but my story was an interesting one after all, and would be, in a word, an account of how to set about things in such a way as to avoid having anything interesting to say. . . .

This was the last straw, that a man should have the effrontery, after bringing them out on a fool's errand, to disguise himself in plain clothes and declare he had nothing sensational to tell them!

They made off at full speed with long faces and I saw no more of them from that moment.

I know people who say they are incapable of shaking off reporters. To listen to them you would think it was a martyrdom: do what you will, lock the door, threaten them, put on black spectacles, dodge round corners, get police protection, back they come with a patience and bloodthirstiness nothing will stand up against. This is all very odd; for my part I like them, I welcome them with enthusiasm, I am only too anxious to interest them, I tell them everything, and from that moment they are the ones that take to their heels. The case is that of Montmorency, the fox-terrier, in *Three Men in a Boat*, who ran after cats because all the cats fled from before him. Then one day a tomcat stopped short and asked him what he wanted:

'Nothing whatever, begging your pardon.'

'Because,' went on the tom, 'if there's anything you would like, I am only too anxious to oblige.'

And Montmorency turned round and went off in disgust.

What with one thing and another it was now nine o'clock and I had had nothing to eat since morning. They carried me off to dine in the wardroom of the Ile de France. As soon as I set out for the liner, which was alongside the far side of the pier, I found myself running the gauntlet of the ship's company, who were present in such crowds to greet me that I could scarcely tell at what moment I left the jetty and stepped on board. They gave me an ovation which took me completely by surprise and covered me with confusion; altogether a most embarrassing moment.

I was asked whether it was my intention to sleep on board the Winnibelle.

'By no means,' I answered, 'I'm far more comfortable here, if it's all the same to you.'

Whereupon they gave me a cabin, with a real bunk and sheets. I found it quite difficult, as was but natural, to get to sleep. Towards morning, being in a sort of doze, I heard a strong puff of wind and thought I was still at sea.

'Here it comes ... more trouble!'

I got ready to jump up and go on deck. Then I opened my eyes

. . . and stayed for several seconds in a state of bewilderment. The noise of the wind came from a buzzing air inlet in the ceiling.

My first visit after breakfast was to the barber. Then I called on the ship's doctor and showed him the sore on my leg. He attributed it to a small scab or pimple which had somehow become infected and had spread outwards from the centre sporadically; this accounted for its circular shape.

The secretary-general of the Company, M. Jean Artur, turned out to have been at school with me, he having been near the top when I was a junior. It was a pleasant surprise to meet again thus unexpectedly. The following day he gave me the use of a little room at the extreme end of the pier. The window looked out over the Hudson, and it made a unique observation post, though terribly infested with mosquitoes. By day as well as by night the view was entrancing; hundreds of ships going up and down the river, the great Cunarders berthing close by, the little tugboats passing along here, there, and everywhere.

These tugs, with their bright colours, reminded me of elaborate pieces of confectionery, made of icing sugar and nougat, or of the crude old-fashioned wooden toy boats you sometimes still see, much knocked about, in junkshop windows. They are festooned with logs and pitprops to deaden shocks, and are painted in the loudest colours conceivable. There are the Beseck boats, with green hulls and yellow smokestacks; the Baltimore and Ohio with B and O on the funnels and carmine bridges; the Moran tugs with a white M on their black funnels, red bridges and white lifebelts, and so on. They have no condensers, as they work exclusively on fresh water, and consequently their steam escapes by way of the funnel, as in the case of locomotives, and they make the same sort of noise, choo, choo, choo as they bustle along.

By night they communicate with each other by means of their syrens from one end of New York to the other; they have regular conversations together, and I assure you they excel in repartee! When one of them came alongside the pier and bumped against it rather roughly, the wardrobe shook and the bed moved an inch or two across the floor; all the New York piers are built on sixty-foot piles, and in consequence are more or less elastically constructed.

The first morning I woke up in my new room I saw from the window the two Italian training-ships, Colombo and Vespucci, coming up the Hudson. They are fine-looking, square-rigged, three-masted vessels, painted black and white like the ships of a hundred years ago.

Strange as it may seem, I had no desire to go into the city. This was partly due to nervousness regarding the streets and crowds, such as is always experienced by those who have lost the habit of them for any long period; in addition, when you come from the sea you are not as suitably rigged as all that, and consequently people turn round and stare at you, which is not calculated to diminish your already only too obvious awkwardness.

Next morning I received a packet of letters which had been awaiting my arrival. Having had none in the Antilles, I now learned of things which had happened three and a half months back.

Not many cables, five or six at most; the first I opened, which was the most recent, ran as follows (I have it before me now):

'Regret inform you death Pierre Hayot from drowning. (Signed) Cottrell.'

I was stupefied. I had naturally cabled Pierre the day before, and was expecting a reply from him. Alas! I walked up and down my room with the pink cablegram form in my hand, unable to believe the tragic news it contained. How could the fates be so unjust? I vainly wondered in what circumstances the calamity could have happened. It was not until three weeks later that I learned the full facts, in a long letter from Simon Cottrell. A sudden flooding of the river at Cassis de Grand Rivière had endangered the lives of five children who were playing in the almost dry river bed. Pierre had rushed into the raging torrent to save them; had rescued three, and had then fallen back into the water, exhausted, and been carried over a fall, receiving fatal injuries from which he died almost immediately. His death had thus been a splendid one, and in that fact I sought what consolation I could for the loss of a dear friend.

'Death, you find it everywhere.' I remembered those words of Massa Houle, from whom, over the more impressive signature of Denis Céricla, which was doubtless his official name, I received two missives by the same fatal mail:

'MY DEAR CAPTAIN,

'Knowing the esteem and affection you always showed me, per-
mit me to address these lines to you, in order that, if possible, you
may come to my assistance. The little money you gave me was
soon spent, and mother and father, who also pray God for you,
have spent theirs too.

'I hope your voyage was successful. Awaiting your reply, I still
live in the Route des Religieuses, in the state I have mentioned,
and of all that you will do to help me, God alone is master. Papa,
mama, the children and I send you by these lines our best wishes,
begging you to believe me your faithful and devoted

'DENIS CÉRICLA.'

'P.S.—When writing to me do not forget to give me news of the
fruit trees and anything else of interest.

Always your

DENIS CÉRICLA.'

'P.P.S.—Let me know also if you have had a fine reception in
New York; the people here admire what you have done despite the
ill-will of those who worked for you. So much the worse for them,
and so for the last time, your

DENIS CÉRICLA.'

'P.P.P.S.—I am sending you by the same mail a packet of newspapers. Please say if you wish me to continue sending them. And
so I will say goodnight and goodbye.

DENIS CL.'

The other cablegrams were from my wife, da Cunhas in
Madeira, the Jeanne d'Arc, the Boulogne shipyard and others.
A second message from my wife was as follows:

'Insurers refuse continue policy boat. Love from Rochard.
When do you return?'

Evidently Lloyds were affected by the idiosyncracy common to
all Insurance Companies, of always wanting to pocket the premiums
(which were far from insignificant in my case) but never accepting
risks. As on my side I hate shelling out for nothing, I now insure
as little as I possibly can, which is far more economical in the long
run.

Among the letters which reached me by the first mail I received from France, a few days later, were several from people I had not seen for ages, such as Collins, my one-time passenger from Liverpool to the Isle of Man, and Captain Thomas, of the Trinity boat *Mermaid*, whom I had met at Penzance in 1927, and who had made me a present of my old flag-signal code-book, salved from the wreck of the Verdun.

My colleague Bernard Lachèvre, painter to the Ministry of Marine, wrote as follows:

'Someone having declared in my presence that you only escaped making a hole in the water by pure luck, I couldn't resist answering that plenty of other people had been a good deal unluckier, such as those who sailed in the Titanic. Another fool asserted at a dinner party I was at the other day, there being fourteen or fifteen people present, including several political big noises, that your time from shore to shore was 'impossible', and that he knew for a fact you had never left the coast of France. After dinner Léon Chiris wanted to knock him down, but it wasn't worth it.'

I also heard from Captain Rallier du Baty, of *Six Thousand Miles in a Ketch*, and from Commandant Charcot who, having scarcely come ashore from his regular summer trip, was kind enough, with his usual good nature, to address me in the following terms:

'I have just come back from Greenland, to find your card from Fort de France waiting for me and simultaneously to hear the news of your magnificent achievement. I congratulate you with all my heart and most sincerely. You chose your boat like a true sailor, and the course you followed was that of a true navigator. . . . I am immensely proud of my ex-A.B. Yours most affectionately.'

Necessity compelled me to brave the streets of the City. It so happened that it was on a Sunday. Robert Estachy, of the Company, came with me, and by a miracle we discovered a shop open where it was possible to buy a hat, shoes and some clothes. The shop assistants had a fit when they saw me. I was sorry I had not come in my Douarnenez wooden sabots and with my beard still growing. Incidentally I gave my sabots to one of the Company dockyard hands, a Norwegian, who had never seen such things before, and who I believe re-varnished them, and transformed them into hanging flower-pots.

I had my films developed, though it was not till long afterwards that I joined them together and made them into a continuous reel with the addition of some animated drawings. As I had foreseen, no cinema would show the film when it was complete, for they made it a condition that I should also provide a running commentary on the sound-track, and that was something I had no desire to let myself in for. I contented myself with putting it on the screen for a few friends, notably the Association of Ocean-going Skippers, who were the sort of audience I wanted. I still recall the somewhat laughable objection raised by one cinema proprietor: 'I like the film well enough,' he said, 'although the sequences are rather too short and there are too many cuts. But unfortunately the thing's so fantastic that it would be impossible to make the public believe that it was true.' I took it as a compliment, but all the same I think a business man should have been able to turn the surprising and occasionally even improbable elements in these pictures to profit, precisely because of this quality. Rarely, I imagine, has a single-handed cruiser taken pictures of himself on 35 mm. film.

Meanwhile the Winnibelle was urgently wanted in Paris for the Salon Nautique. This was particularly tiresome, as the yachting season was in full swing round New York, and I had intended to visit the various sailing clubs in Long Island Sound. It was necessary to make a quick decision, for the only vessel capable of shipping her, namely the De Grasse, had just come in. I can still see Captain Estachy, the freight manager, coming into my room and exhorting me to make up my mind one way or the other. I paced back and forth across the room for minutes on end like a caged lion, before finally telephoning the order to unstep her mast and put her on board. Then for a time I stood by the instrument, my senses numbed. When I had the curiosity at last to lean out of the window, the Winnibelle was already as shorn as a raft—and how insignificant and shabby she seemed, dirtied as she had already become by contact with the oily water and black quays. She might have been any grubby old ditchcrawler.

Then I suddenly remembered that except for a comb and toothbrush I had left all my things on board of her, books, clothes, provisions, instruments, etc. . . . When she had been chocked up and lashed down on the deck of the De Grasse, I went along with a suitcase into which I hurriedly crammed the most indispensable things, and I just had the sense to take my chronometer along to the liner's watch-room. I had completely lost my bearings.

I stayed on the De Grasse until she cast off, only an hour; the time went by all too fast. There were already crowds of passengers elbowing and jostling one another all over the vessel. Round the Winnibelle stood a circle whose remarks for the most part were worthy of a lunatic asylum. I caught sight of a man in a navy blue suit, wearing a pilot-cap, as they call them in St Malo, whose face seemed familiar to me. The recognition was mutual, and he came up and introduced himself.

'Do you remember the three-master Theresa, which got crushed in the lock-gates, and Captain Amicel?'

Of course; I now perfectly recalled Amicel, and how he had declared that this year he would see the strawberries ripen, but what was he doing on the De Grasse, here in New York?

'It's quite simple; I got command of another vessel, and I have just lost her off the coast of Greenland. We were picked up, and now they're sending us back to St Malo. That's all there is to it!'

The poor fellow had lost two boats in one season, and after all had not managed to see the strawberries ripen. . . .

The syren blew, the bell rang for those who were not sailing to go ashore. I walked slowly to the gangway where, as ill luck would have it, I met some Paris acquaintances. I had no idea what to say to them, there was such a lump in my throat that I was quite incapable of uttering a word; I don't know what they can have thought of me. Once on shore, I went straight to my room and locked myself in. I was almost as wretched as if the Winnibelle had just gone down before my very eyes.

About the rest of my stay in New York there is little of interest to record. I busied myself about my exhibition and unpacked my crates of pictures. Naturally, the K . . . . Gallery had not been advised of my arrival and no arrangements had been made. Their Paris representative, despite having given me a formal undertaking, had not even troubled to write. I had not been mistaken in feeling that he had never taken my voyage seriously; yet I had been introduced to him by M. Alexandre Bordes, a man who is not in the habit of saying what he does not mean.

With the ground thus slipping from under my feet, I had to begin again from the beginning. I set off with a portfolio of drawings under my arm in quest of a gallery, just as I had done fifteen years before in Paris, when I began my professional career. A kind providence guided my footsteps to one of the most delightful and appreciative galleries in New York, and one which specialises in marine subjects. Marvellously situated on Fifth Avenue, it undertook to run a one-man show for me, though it had to be in the autumn, after my departure.

It was a pleasure to be rescued from these worries and depressions by Mr Singer, the well-known American yachtsman, who was good enough to seek me out on Pier 57. He took me to dine with some friends of his, this being the first dinner invitation I accepted in the city.

Through the good offices of Captain Rogers, a member of the New York Yacht Club, I was made a temporary member, and dined several times at the club, which is too well known the world over for any description by me to be necessary. I cannot adequately express my gratitude and indebtedness to Captain Rogers, who directs a Tug-boat Company and made me free of all the boats belonging to it, authorising me to go on board them for the purpose of drawing subjects in New York Harbour whenever I wished. I have not so far been able to profit by this most friendly gesture, but a time will come.

I went as a guest to a dinner of the Cruising Club of America, which had just decided to award its 'Blue Water Medal' to Roderick Stephens for his triple victory in the Atlantic, Fastnet and Bermuda ocean races, on the magnificent little boat Dorade which he and his brother Olin designed. Rod was called upon for a speech about his performance; he spoke very simply, and was clearly more embarrassed than at the tiller of his boat. I was called on in my turn, and contented myself with answering to the best of my ability any questions my fellow-diners liked to ask me. These chiefly concerned the automatic steering of the Winnibelle in the Trades, and the rate of sailing I had been able to maintain by this means, which was quickly calculated to be the best recorded up till then, though only by a narrow margin. It amounted as near as makes no difference to four knots and a little above that figure for the crossing of the ocean proper; much the same as Slocum's in the Spray, though of course in the opposite direction.

By way of returning all this hospitality I invited a number of yachtsmen and editors of yachting periodicals aboard the Ile de France, including among others Herbert L. Stone, of *Yachting*, and John G. Alden, the naval architect. The duties of host and hostess at this luncheon were undertaken by my friend Jean Artur, Secretary-General of the Agency, and my wife, on whose right sat the French Consul-General, who had been good enough to accept our invitation. On this occasion I found myself sitting next to M. Burosse, Captain of the Ile de France. With my customary bluntness, I expressed surprise that he should not be wearing the ribbon of the Legion of Honour. It must be borne in mind that the Ile de France was at that time the largest French Transatlantique liner and the biggest ship flying the flag of our country; even now there is only one bigger. The men who rise to command such boats can be regarded as among the country's most distinguished servants. Captain Burosse smiled a little sadly and made no reply. Two years later he retired and, after a brief sojourn on dry land, died.

I see that I have mentioned the presence of my wife at this luncheon. She had arrived almost unbeknown to me (I say almost, because she had intended to spring a surprise on me, and it was only by chance that I happened to see her name in a passenger list forwarded by wireless). She was accompanied by Master Yves, who was sadly disappointed not to find his papa's boat at New York; he had never seen it, and that was what he had come all this way for. . . . But no, the Winnibelle had already departed without waiting for him, and in fact he had passed her in mid-Atlantic. This was an entirely incomprehensible affair.

One day I surprised him deep in consultation with Olsen, a rather deaf sailor who worked in the freight unloading department and who had served as a hand on the Westward. Master Yves was pointing to a tug, and describing his papa's boat as being far, far bigger than that. Olsen laughed; he was one of the men who had unstepped the Winnibelle's mast. Master Yves was full of wisdom, and manifested but a single desire, namely to possess a pair of roller-skates, so that he could skate in the street, like all the little boys in New York. I took him to a huge toyshop with innumerable floors, and there he selected a fine pair of skates. On the way out, when I asked him if there was anything else he would like, he simply answered that you couldn't buy just anything:

'Pooh, you can't buy just anything, papa!'

The first day he had more than a hundred and fifty falls, on his hands or his back. As he was dressed in white, the hall porter nearly had a fit when he saw him come in from this day's work. He was somewhat damaged in both body and soul by the experience, but I reassured him by declaring that his apprenticeship was now over, and that he would fall no more. Miraculously, it was so; neither on the second nor any of the following days did he have a single fall. He followed us everywhere, along uneven footways, and over street crossings, jumping tramlines, going with us into restaurants and lifts, climbing up stairs; he put on his skates in the morning and only took them off when he went to bed at night.

There is no reason that I can see why a Frenchman should feel particularly lost when he lands in New York. The traffic keeps to the right, the coinage is on the decimal system, there is an antediluvian metro and earsplitting tramways. It is true that the barbers' shops refuse to sell you soap or razor blades, both of which you have to get at a drugstore; it is true that the drugstores sell you books and cigars and pairs of shoes and ices and spectacles and milk and cameras and fried eggs, but once you know that your worries are at an end.

As for me, I was too much taken up with my own affairs to have much time for exploring New York, and besides I am extremely lacking in curiosity where towns are concerned, too much so, perhaps. It was only on my last day there, a couple of hours before the boat sailed, that I took a taxi to Brooklyn and made one or two drawings of the city as seen from the celebrated bridge. Nor am I ashamed to confess that this was the extent of my virtues as a tourist.

I let myself be taken to several speakeasies, merely in order to find out what a speakeasy was. Prohibition was past its zenith; through the open windows (the heat was stifling) the passing policemen could easily see row upon row of bottles in the so-called 'clandestine' bars. At any rate I could see them myself. People told me it was of no importance. The wine and spirits drunk in these places were terrible, as everyone knows. It was on all counts preferable to confine one's attention to the bars of the berthed liners, where the drinks were served in an equally clandestine fashion, but were at least genuine. Each preserved its national characteristics. On the Mauretania you found real Bass, and on the Champlain real Noilly-Prat vermouth.

And yet even to me, seeking adventures as little as I did, one befel which more than satisfied my appetite for such things, the very day after my wife arrived. A passing taxi-driver, seeing me come out of the Waldorf-Astoria, and no doubt taking me for a millionaire, volunteered to introduce me to a restaurant famous for its shellfish and drove me to the 41° West, next door to the Stork Club. The place was in a basement; two enormous individuals were waiting for me behind the door; they politely took my hat and invited me to drink a gin cocktail in the depths of a kind of cellar, whither they began to propel me gently but firmly by the elbows. I thought as fast and as hard as I could without hitting on a satisfactory way out of my predicament. Eventually I succeeded, thanks to the fact that I was wearing a particularly shabby old flannel suit, in making them believe I was a steward off a French Line boat, whereupon they ran me out of the place as quickly as they had helped me in, giving my chauffeur to understand that their opinion of his intelligence was negligible, while he in his turn described their characters in the raciest phraseology.

Next day I learned that it was a very rare thing to escape so lightly, and that by rights I ought to have been found in the small hours lying in the gutter, with no shoes on my feet and no purse in my pocket, that being the usual end to such a story. The police never bother their heads over such goings on. My usual taxi-driver, to whom I related my story, told me what he thought of the affair:

'Say, I know that joint. They're just robbers, and I wouldn't work for those boys, not for anything in the world. Figure it out for yourself: thirty per cent., with all the trouble it is! At that price they can't get any but ignorant half-wits to round the people up for them. One of these days we'll give 'em something to think about. Me, I only work for serious houses. . . . For night work, I've got a dandy little Chrysler roadster. I'll run you around some time.'

I was sufficiently enlightened, however, in these deep matters, and declined his offer with thanks. Four years later, only the other day, in fact, I re-met this same good chap as I stepped ashore from the boat at New York. He greeted me like a long lost brother, practically ordered me into his waiting taxi, took me all the way to Manhattan and would not hear of it when I tried to pay the fare.

I left New York with the feeling that I was only beginning to understand how to set about getting to know the country. It was with the sincerest regret that I had of necessity to leave so soon.

The Compagnie Transatlantique, who had generously undertaken the transport of the Winnibelle, free of charge, added to their kindness by making me a present of my ticket home, officially on the grounds that I had designed one of their posters, but really as a friendly gesture.

Since that time I have placed myself in their debt in a thousand other ways, as I shall doubtless record at some future date.

CHAPTER XXVII

RETURN

I COULD have completed the circuit by returning in my own one-man liner. It was not too late in the year. Winds favourable, a shade boisterous at times, but September weather keeps within reasonable bounds: at most I should have had the equinoctial gales to deal with, and that would not have worried me overmuch. Once the Newfoundland Banks were astern of me there would have been very little likelihood of encountering a cyclone, which is always the principal worry. I should have had a chance of getting across in under thirty-five days, which would have given a total of one hundred days for the round trip across the North Atlantic and back. I had hesitated a good deal, and in the end decided against it for three reasons. First, my exhibition which, owing to my having been so badly let down, involved me in a considerable amount of labour; secondly, the Salon Nautique in Paris, at which the builders of the Winnibelle had begged me to let her be shown; and finally, the exhortations of certain friends, Captain Estachy in particular, who were of the opinion that I was behaving a little too much as though I were a bachelor without ties, and indeed they were perfectly right.

As it was, this was my first experience of being a passenger on a liner, and I found it full of surprises. I did not want to make myself a nuisance to the ship's officers, and saw but little of them. On the other hand I had to listen at meal-times to a woman journalist who knew all there was to know about America as a result of a three days' visit, and to signify breathless admiration when impressive personages majestically counted the number of their Atlantic crossings on their fingers. The day came, as I knew it would, when one of them remarked with infinite sublety that he understood I was some sort of Christopher Columbus. After a day or two I took to having my meals in my cabin, and only emerging at night for the sake of a little fresh air.

There came a day when, as we drew nearer to the French coast,

I looked out of my cabin port-hole and saw, a few cables' lengths off, a Breton tunnyman with her patched, faded, pale pink sails: a wonderful vision. I followed her for a long time with envious eyes. She was already far from her home port, more than three hundred miles.

Master Yves, meanwhile, found the palatial existence entirely to his taste. He had a nurse all to himself, to whom his lightest word was law. He ordered his own meals, which invariably consisted of sole, followed by an ice. The only fly in the ointment, from his point of view, was the rule against roller-skating on the sun-deck. The consequence of his ocean-going diet was that when we got back to Paris he still expected sole and ices for every meal, and was furious when he found his orders no longer obeyed. I had to intervene personally in order to make him understand that he was not Mr Vanderbilt junior but plain Master Yves, aged five.

At night the lights from the French coast shone out, one after another, and I stood on the upper deck, with my elbows on the rail, to starboard, my head full of memories. How quickly the great vessel drove ahead! There were the Casquets already, and then Alderney. . . . I had a friend there who had built himself a house close to the lighthouse. A tiresome individual who was standing near me would insist on telling me the name of it. 'That's the La Hague light,' he assured me. For once I was forced out of my usual role of resignation. 'You're wrong,' I answered. 'La Hague is the next bus stop: I'll ring you in time.'

A similar incident awaited me in Paris. I went straight from the station to the Cours-la-Reine where the Winnibelle was exposed to the wondering gaze of the crowd. She had been entirely repainted, far too much so for my taste; all the copper and brass on deck, the skylight rods, belaying pins, etc., had been treated with aluminium paint. No doubt it was impossible, in Paris and under the roof of an exhibition hall, to polish the metalwork which I had kept bright in the driving rain of the Antilles and the haze and spindrift of the Gulf. Her waterline presented a strangely undulating appearance, presumably symbolic of the ocean swell. A commissionaire sought to prevent my climbing on board, and for one hideous moment I thought they had ignored my categorical instructions to the contrary, and were charging an entrance fee. But no, it was not that, only one had to show a card. A card from whom? The builders. How about a card from the owner? That was impossible, the owner was in America. Oh no, he wasn't! And I climbed up.

What was my surprise when I found the saloon packed with people of every sort and description, testing my bunks, pulling open my drawers, looking among my papers and sticking their noses into everything they could get at.

A fat man with a rosette in his buttonhole was in the middle of an eloquent speech. He was explaining the working of the automatic steering-device. His vocabulary was technical to a degree, so much so that he made use of words I was quite unable to understand myself. On my entry he favoured me with a hostile glare, in deference to which I refrained from making my presence known and stayed discreetly in the background, leaning up against the companion ladder.

The disquisition went on and on until eventually, just to annoy him, I ventured to express a difference of opinion on a point he seemed not to have properly understood. The audience was scandalised and the orator, by no means pleased at my interruption, asked me what I knew about it, anyway.

'I would have you know, young man,' he declared, annihilating me with a look, 'that I had all the details explained to me by M. Marin-Marie himself.'

It was my turn to get caustic:

'So you know him personally, do you?' I asked.

'Yes, monsieur, I do know him personally, monsieur.'

'Wow! A lucky devil you seem to be!'

I could think of nothing else to say, and I clambered up the ladder again as fast as I could go. The manager of the shipyard had just come on board, having learned of my arrival. I begged him to get rid with all dispatch of the intolerable gang of intruders on my private property. 'And take particular care to lock all the cupboards and my chronometer box,' I added. 'They're quite capable of winding it up and putting it right, the brutes!'

I imagine he put the fat know-all wise as to my identity, but to tell the truth I never heard, for that very evening I boarded the train for Granville, and so home to Chausey, and since then I have not seen the good shipyard manager again.

When I stepped ashore on the island next morning, I saw a huge tricolour flag flying from the semaphore-mast and asked Charles, the master-pilot, who had brought me across in his boat, what it was there for?

'It's for you,' he said. 'It's flying in your honour.'

No doubt it was highly irregular for the local coastguard to make so free with the national emblem; but it counted for as much with me as if he had been at the top instead of the bottom of the naval hierarchy.

My father made no comment on my voyage beyond observing that I had put in my appearance very late in the season; but a few days later he organised a monster punch-party, the main ingredient being at hand in the form of a mighty joram of rum, brought back by my brother from Martinique. Every man on the island was invited, and every man, without a single exception, came.

Then indeed I felt rewarded far beyond my deserts.